D1567162

BEBES AND THE BEAR

SWAIM-PAUP SPORTS SERIES

Sponsored by James C. '74 & Debra Parchman Swaim
and T. Edgar '74 & Nancy Paup

BEBES AND THE BEAR

Gene Stallings, Coach Bryant, and Their 1968 Cotton Bowl Showdown

RON J. JACKSON JR.

Texas A&M University Press • College Station

This paper meets the requirements of ANSI/NISO Z39.48-1992
(Permanence of Paper).
Binding materials have been chosen for durability.
Manufactured in the United States of America
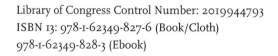

Library of Congress Control Number: 2019944793
ISBN 13: 978-1-62349-827-6 (Book/Cloth)
978-1-62349-828-3 (Ebook)

Contents

Preface

Dare to dream. Dare to live.

For as long as I can remember, this has been the mantra I have tried to live by in my life. The men depicted in this book did the same, whether they realized it or not. They boldly stepped into the arena (as President Theodore Roosevelt so eloquently described in his famous "Citizenship in a Republic" speech long ago) and dared to fulfill their dreams.

Roosevelt—one of the most prolific dreamers in American history—left us words from that 1910 speech that still echo through time:

> It is not the critic who counts; not the man who points out how the strong man stumbles, or where the doer of deeds could have done better. The credit belongs to the man who is actually in the arena, whose face is marred by dust and sweat and blood; who strives valiantly; who errs, who comes short again and again, because there is no effort without error and shortcoming; but who does actually strive to do the deeds; who knows great enthusiasms, the great devotions; who spends himself in a worthy cause; who at the best knows in the end the triumph of high achievement, and who at the worst, if he fails, at least fails while daring greatly, so that his place shall never be with those cold and timid souls who neither know victory nor defeat.

No one chronicled within these pages fits the definition of Roosevelt's man in the arena more than Paul W. "Bear" Bryant, who arose from the poverty and obscurity of Moro Bottom, Arkansas, to become one the greatest college football coaches of all time. In his relentless pursuit of greatness, he inspired—and often willed—others around him to also achieve greatness.

Others like Gene "Bebes" Stallings of Paris, Texas.

Fate ushered Bryant into the native Texan's life in the summer of 1954, when Texas A&M University hired Bear as its new head coach. Stallings was then a gangly 6-foot-1, 165-pound sophomore end who already knew how to dream. Bryant taught him to dare to live by first showing him and his Aggie teammates how to survive.

Bryant did so at the drought-plagued outpost of Junction, Texas, where he pushed players to their physical limits during 10 hellish days of camp at the Adjunct on the South Llano River. Stallings became one of the fabled "Junction Boys" who survived that camp, as well as a loyal disciple of the Bryant way of coaching.

In April of 2017, I stood on the rugged, sticker-infested field where Bryant and Stallings first became acquainted 65 years ago. I stood on the very ground where Stallings and his teammates bled, vomited, and in some cases, passed out from the sweltering heat.

I walked in the footsteps of legends.

A year earlier I had done the same, when my research carried me to Bryant's Arkansas birthplace of Moro Bottom and the nearby town of Fordyce, where he achieved local notoriety as a high school football player on a state championship team. I even walked in the Main Street building that once housed the Lyric Theatre, where Bryant famously wrestled a circus bear for money.

Bryant received a legendary nickname. I received a sense of the legend.

At every opportunity, I tried to retrace the footsteps of those written about here in a quest to tell as truthful and as accurate a story as possible. In some instances, I relied on dogged research from various primary sources in university collections, old newspapers, game programs, and autobiographies. I was also able to mine the greatest resources of all—the colorful participants who lived and witnessed the historic events of this narrative.

Readers will learn about not only the intertwining lives of Bryant and Stallings but also the many behind-the-scene moves that led to their memorable showdown at the 1968 Cotton Bowl Classic in Dallas. This book will also introduce readers to many of the football heroes who played for both coaches, such as the 1967 Texas A&M Aggies whose season teetered on the brink of disaster.

Bebes and the Bear will bring readers inside the huddles for all the big moments and take them inside the locker rooms and offices where fateful decisions were made with high stakes on the line. Readers will experience history in all its unvarnished glory, from barking coaches to the violent shaking of a player's facemask to the deafening roar of the crowd. Ultimately, this adventure will shadow the lives of men who once dared to dream and live—and became legends.

BEBES AND THE BEAR

CHAPTER 1

The Legend

Coach Bryant always seemed to be indestructible. He was a monumental figure in intercollegiate athletics, a man who set standards not easily attainable by men. He was a giant in our profession and a giant among men.

—Joe Paterno, Penn State University head coach

Folk heroes color the pages of American history. They are larger-than-life characters like John Henry, a Herculean former slave and railroad worker who wielded a sledgehammer like no other against the machinery of progress (Henry, as the legend goes, died with a hammer in his hand in a man-versus-machine showdown.) Or nurseryman Johnny Appleseed, who devoted his life to agriculture and love, spreading goodwill and a pocket full of apple seeds wherever he traveled. Reams of literature have also been written about the tall tales of frontiersman David Crockett, whose wit and courage carried him from the Tennessee backwoods to the halls of Congress, and finally, to a hero's death at the Alamo.

And although these flesh-and-blood men came from all walks of life, they shared one common thread: their lives and deeds inspired the kind of collective memory that placed them in a shadowy borderland between reality and myth. As a result, each achieved a certain kind of immortality.

Paul William "Bear" Bryant attained this eternal status in his lifetime. He did so on a football field. At the time of his death, in 1983, sports fans had already hailed the 69-year-old Bryant as football royalty—then the winningest coach in college football history, with 323 victories. His illustrious coaching career spanned 38 years between the University of Maryland, University of Kentucky, Texas A&M University, and finally the University of Alabama, where he reigned as king during a 25-year run with six national titles.[1]

Today, photographs and paintings of the 6-foot-4 Bryant leaning against a goal post, peering intensely from underneath his trademark houndstooth hat, speak to the power of his enduring legacy. The famous image presents an instant symbol of strength and leadership from a bygone era, dating back to a time when sports legends could still emerge from obscurity to become celebrated pioneers in their chosen sport.

Bryant earned his reputation with a relentless drive to succeed. He roamed the sports landscape like a giant, a blunt-spoken, chain-smoking, no-nonsense coach who carefully cultivated his rough-and-tumble persona for one purpose—winning. Mal Moore, a former Alabama player and assistant coach, once marveled of Bryant, "You never saw defeat in him"[2]

Bryant never would have allowed such weak behavior. He was too damn stubborn.

"Coach Bryant always seemed to be indestructible," said Joe Paterno, the late Penn State University coach who later broke Bryant's record with 409 wins over 45 seasons. "He was a monumental figure in intercollegiate athletics, a man who set standards not easily attainable by men. He was a giant in our profession and a giant among men."[3]

President Ronald Reagan eloquently echoed those sentiments upon hearing the news of Bryant's death just 37 days after his retirement from coaching. Reagan's words were a fitting tribute to the football icon who rose to fame from an impoverished childhood:

> Americans have lost a hero who always seemed larger than life, a coach who made legends out of ordinary people. He was a hard, but loved, taskmaster. He was patriotic to the core, devoted to his players, and he was inspired by a winning spirit that would not quit. Bear Bryant gave his country the gift of life unsurpassed. In making the impossible seem easy, he lived what we strive to be.[4]

Bryant passed into the realm of a bona fide American folk hero long before the president's tribute. His journey—mirroring the path of other folk heroes—began in a humble place, where the legend was borne from the shadows of obscurity by a memorable deed and a courageous heart. For Bryant, that place can be traced to the muddy lowlands of Moro Bottom, Arkansas, and the deed to an ornery circus bear.

Back then, Paul William Bryant was simply a flesh-and-blood boy with a dream.

. . .

On a clear July morning in 1979, Bryant peered out of his University of Alabama plane en route to his home state of Arkansas. His plastic-rimmed glasses were perched characteristically on the end of his nose. Al Browning, then a sports editor for the *Tuscaloosa News*, sat in the seat next to him, reading a book.[5]

Bryant planned to attend a business meeting with old friends in Little Rock, but other thoughts clearly crowded his mind.

"Alfred," Bryant barked in a deep Southern drawl, "there's home."[6]

Startled, Browning snapped to attention and looked out the window. He noticed vast stretches of trees broken by patches of pasture and only a few buildings. Browning stumbled in his mind for an appropriate response before finally saying, "I guess coming back to Arkansas brings back a lot of memories."[7]

The veteran Alabama coach nodded and replied, "Yeah, a ton of 'em."[8]

Suddenly, as if traveling back in time, Bryant sentimentally spoke of his late mother and her strength in the face of countless hardships. He recalled hitching the family mules to the wagon every morning and peddling vegetables in the nearby town of Fordyce to "the city slickers."[9]

"There were eleven of us in a little ol' house in the woods, nine kids," he openly reminisced. "When Papa got sick, it was up to Mama to make us work and to teach us the difference between right and wrong.

"Damn, we didn't have anything back then . . ."[10]

Tears welled in Bryant's eyes. Browning respectfully pretended not to notice, turning a page or two in his book. The reporter realized he was witnessing something rare—an unfiltered glimpse of the heart of a living legend who had built a career on dogged determination and toughness.[11]

A silence finally prevailed as the old warrior sat alone with his past. His earliest memories sprang from the family's old farmhouse in Moro Bottom, where he entered the world on September 11, 1913, as the 11th of 12 children to Wilson Monroe and Ida Kilgore Bryant. Ida gave birth to Paul in the Bryants' four-room, wood-plank home without the assistance of a doctor. The Bryants didn't believe in doctors; only faith in the Lord. The home offered no electricity or running water, and wind, rain, and snow often seeped through the cracks in the walls. The "big room," as they called it, featured a large fireplace and ran down the middle of the home—the only room where Paul remembered one could stay warm. Often times the children slept on pallets in that room, located next to a large kitchen that served as the central gathering place for checkers, storytelling, and readings from the family Bible.[12]

Ida and Monroe occupied one of the rooms, while the other was shared by the children, with the girls sleeping in one bed and the boys in another. During the winter, the children always huddled together for warmth. At one point, 11 souls were crammed into the home, including Ida and Monroe. Three of their children died in infancy. The surviving children, from the eldest to youngest, were Barney, Orie, Harlie, Jack, Ouida, Kathryn, Louise, Paul, and Frances. "It was comfortable enough," Louise once recalled of the old family homestead, "yet hot as blazes during the summer and cold as ice during the winter."[13]

Poverty gripped the Bryants in Moro Bottom. So did love. Together, they tackled life's many hardships in their tiny section of the country. Ida always led the way. She gave birth to all her children at home and was generally back in the fields after only a few days of rest. Monroe, a large, big-boned man, was a semi-invalid by the time Paul was old enough to chip in with chores. He likely suffered from high blood pressure and other ailments that went undiagnosed because of his refusal to accept any formal medical treatment. Some nights the elder Bryant would simply disappear. The family often found him the next morning wandering aimlessly in the woods or sitting in the middle of the dirt-and-gravel road that ran in front of the family's homestead. Some suspected a mental illness, but he may have suffered from a series of strokes or maybe even Alzheimer's.[14]

Ida, therefore, commanded all authority within the home. A tall, handsome woman whose haired grayed prematurely, she proved exceptionally tough under circumstances that required nothing less for survival. She oversaw the work on the family's 260-acre farm, carved from the thick timberland that dominated their property. The rich, black soil provided ideal conditions for growing vegetables and patches of cotton. Ida maintained a large garden, where she raised potatoes, watermelons, and a variety of other vegetables that, along with the cotton, served as the family's sole income.[15]

No one went hungry in Ida Bryant's home. Aside from the family garden, they were well stocked with plenty of milk and butter from the cows, eggs from the chickens, and pork from the hogs. In addition, the elder Bryant boys—and later Paul—hunted wild hogs, squirrels, and opossums along Moro Creek, which snaked through their tiny community of a half-dozen families scattered over 3 square miles. Paul remembered hunting rabbits and hanging them above the fireplace in the "big room" to roast. Decades later, Paul fondly recalled in his 1974 autobiography, *Bear: The Hard Life and Good Times of Alabama's Coach Bryant,* "You never tasted anything so good."[16]

Dean Kilgore, Ida's nephew, remembered one night he slept at his aunt's house on "a pallet." He awoke the next morning to the delightful smell of a country ham, biscuits, and red-eye gravy. Nearly 75 years later, Kilgore told a Dallas County Historical Society interviewer, "Man, oh man, that was some good eatin'."[17]

Laughter also echoed frequently from their rustic home. One of Paul's favorite memories involved his elder brother Jack and Mr. Dukes, a middle-aged man whom Monroe hired to help on the farm. Paul never called Mr. Dukes by his first name, nor apparently bothered to learn it throughout his childhood. Regardless, Paul grew quite fond of Mr. Dukes. He cherished his presence and especially his shenanigans.

One day a wagon rolled past the Bryant homestead with a casket in tow. Mr. Dukes, who taught Paul the art of cussing, used the occasion to tell the impressionable youngster stories of "hants"—ghosts of deceased people who failed to reach the afterworld. As Paul would later tell the story, he was deathly afraid of hants long before that day. Yet thanks to the imaginative Mr. Dukes, Paul found himself suddenly thrust into a fearful state of mind.

Jack later joined the fun that evening, at dusk. Jack noted the grave on the family's property behind the smokehouse. There, near the cotton patch, stood a tombstone surrounded by weeds. Jack dared his youngest brother to go to the grave alone to see if there were any hants present. If successful, Jack promised he would give him 35 cents. Paul later recalled how he swallowed his fear and "took off running, up the trail through the weeds."[18] He quickly pushed through the weeds and stood before the lone grave. At that moment, a ghost rose up from behind the tombstone. A wide-eyed Paul instantly bolted, fell down halfway to the house, and in a panic, crawled the rest of the way—much to the amusement of Mr. Dukes and Jack.[19]

Mr. Dukes had played the role of the ghost under a white sheet.[20]

Jack and Paul's other elder brothers also earned reputations as hustlers. During periods of rain and snow, the dirt-and-gravel road in front of their home often proved impassable for automobiles. The road turned easily to mud, so the brothers were always on standby with the mules and wagon, ready to pull a stranded driver out of the mire for a "buck or two."[21] Inevitably, another vehicle always came along to rescue. Paul later mused, "They would be listening all the time and as soon as they could hear the grinding they'd hitch up."[22]

Money didn't come easy in Moro Bottom. Work began before dawn at the Bryant homestead when Ida first arose. She roamed the home with an oil lantern to wake her children, and each undertook their assigned chores. By the time Paul was seven or eight, he was the only male child left in the house. His elder brothers had already departed to start their own families. Paul therefore inherited the task each morning of hitching the mules—a black one named Pete and white one named Joe—to the old family wagon. Other chores included slopping the hogs, fetching buckets of water from the well, and chopping wood. Of course, Ida relied upon her youngest son to also plow the fields and chop cotton alongside his sisters. He did it all almost exclusively in worn overalls and bare feet. In fact, he was 13 before he owned his first pair of shoes.[23]

Ida leaned heavily on her youngest son, who was the sole person in charge of hitching and caring for the mules. Paul didn't mind the responsibility. In fact, he was probably more comfortable with animals than people in those days, although he freely admitted to being a "mama's boy."[24] Those who knew Paul best back then generally described him as a socially awkward and sensitive country boy. "He was so damn country it was unbelievable," recalled Ike Murry, a friendly rival of Paul's in high school who later became the Arkansas attorney general. "He had never been around anybody except mules and chickens."[25]

Paul soon became acquainted with the world beyond Moro Bottom, which was really nothing more than a wide spot on a nondescript, backcountry road. Moro Bottom didn't even appear on any state maps, and the area was easily isolated whenever Moro Creek flooded after heavy rains. Once, in April 1927, the rampaging flood waters of Moro Creek wiped out crops and livestock and left some residents homeless. Rescue workers could only reach the destitute by boat. But the land of Moro Bottom was cheap and plentiful, and that provided enough reason to settle there for some. Geographically, the two rural burghs of Kingsland and Fordyce sandwiched Moro Bottom; Kingsland could be reached 5 miles to the west, while Fordyce was a 6.7-mile trek to the north. Fordyce—located 70 miles from Little Rock—is where Paul later attended high school and starred in football. Locals considered Fordyce the area's "big city," with a population of nearly 3,000 residents in 1920 and 3,206 by 1930.[26]

Mickey Herskowitz, a *Houston Post* columnist, once famously asked Bryant if he was born in Fordyce. The question made sense, since Fordyce officials had long proudly proclaimed their hamlet Bryant's hometown. Bryant attempted to correct the record by mumbling a few words Herskowitz didn't quite understand.

"Moro what?" Herskowitz pressed for clarification.

"Bottom," Bryant loudly replied. "Like your ass. Moro Bottom."[27]

Not everyone was fond of the name. Louise, Paul's elder sister, declared she "hated the name," suggesting it made the family and other residents sound "like a bunch of morons."[28] If Paul didn't have an inferiority complex about his Moro Bottom roots in his earliest years, he did once he and his sisters began attending elementary school in nearby Kingsland. Shoeless and dressed in his usual overalls, Paul faithfully drove his siblings into Kingsland each morning aboard the family wagon. In order to arrive on time at Stonewall School, Paul had to have the mules hitched and ready by 4 a.m. The laborious task usually meant his body was covered in sweat by the time he entered the schoolhouse. And during recess, when other children played, Paul used the time to feed oats and chops to his mules.

Still, his hard work and dedication only resulted in ridicule. He remembered how his teacher often preached to the class about hygiene. Paul failed to understand her intent until one day, after a long lecture on the subject, she asked him to trade seats with a boy at the front of the classroom. Paul obliged, only to hear the girls break out in giggles as he walked by. Paul felt embarrassed and ashamed. Decades later, the shame lived in his mind as he admitted, "I haven't forgotten their names, either."[29]

Paul encountered similar class snobbery in the "big city" of Fordyce, where he and his mother ventured regularly to peddle milk, butter, eggs, turnip greens, black-eyed peas, and watermelons. They sold their produce mainly in the black sections of Fordyce—then a thriving outpost for the cotton and lumber trades.[30]

Fordyce initially grew out of a patchwork of scattered farms after the Civil War. Prior to the war, the town mainly revolved around a general store and sawmill owned by the local physician, Dr. A. S. Holderness. Then at the outset of the 1880s, Fordyce's fortunes changed dramatically. The owners of the St. Louis Southwestern Railroad sought to penetrate the agricultural areas of eastern and southern Arkansas, connecting those regions with the port city of St. Louis on the Mississippi River. Fordyce was on the proposed route. By 1882, workers completed the railroad line, known as the "Cotton Belt." Fordyce suddenly became the major trading center not only for Dallas County but four other nearby counties as well.[31]

Railroad cars filled with cotton and lumber were soon departing Fordyce at an increased rate. By 1920, when Paul and his mother were making their rounds, Fordyce featured paved streets, a sewer system, electricity, a large mercantile store and hotel, and two banks. The modern amenities were of little interest for Paul, who dreaded those trips into Fordyce. In fact, he *hated* those trips. Everything about those excursions was painful, from the predawn hitching of the mules to the wagon and creek crossing to the tedious door-to-door knocking and long ride home.

During the winter, Paul and his mother endured the harshest conditions. Monroe would bake bricks and place them in a burlap sack for his wife and son to sit on to prevent them from freezing. Still, there were countless days when Paul had to be carried from the wagon and into the house after a trip because he was so frozen.[32]

Heavy rains presented an entirely different challenge for Paul and his mother—crossing Moro Creek. Staying home wasn't an option. They had to get their produce to market. So Ida and Paul would raise the sideboards of the wagon and drape a tarp over the top. They would then carefully place their hard-earned produce on top of the tarp, so it would remain dry during the crossing. Or at least that was the plan. "Sometimes the wagon would actually float," Paul marveled. "I was always amazed how those old mules . . . could swim the Moro Creek as they pulled that wagon."[33]

The hardships encountered on those trips into Fordyce ultimately brought Paul much closer to his mother. He would lovingly refer to her as his "favorite person in the world."[34] Together, they shared adventures no one else in the family could speak about firsthand. Paul cherished that aspect of those memories, and throughout his life, he would draw on his mother's toughness and love for inspiration.[35]

Peddling produce in Fordyce also brought the wounds of ridicule for the country lad from Moro Bottom. Neatly dressed town children always teased Paul for being a "hick" aboard his creaking wagon and laughed at his scraggly mules whenever they chugged past the school yard. Paul seethed with humiliation. The mocking words and laughter cut Paul deeply, so much so he never forgot them. Even more than 70 years later, he bitterly remarked, "I can pass that school now and hear those voices."[36]

Nearly 80 years later, Kelsey Kaplinger admitted to being one of those obnoxious school children who laughed at Paul in an interview with the Dallas County Historical Society. "Paul got so mad he started throwing turnips at us and fell off the wagon," he recalled.[37] Kaplinger, however, received his payback a few years later when he lined up opposite Paul during a Fordyce High School football practice. Paul punished Kaplinger mercilessly for his insensitive derisions. "He whupped me all over the field," Kaplinger confessed. "I couldn't hardly walk after that practice."[38]

The humiliation of those experiences in Kingsland and Fordyce caused Paul to become more reclusive. He was now painfully aware of his family's poverty, and he began to feel increasingly inferior beyond Moro Bottom. Paul became somewhat of a loner. Nothing exemplified his mind-set at this time more than his solitary habits when visiting his uncle Ransom Dean Kilgore's general store in Fordyce. Ida always stopped at her brother's store—Kilgore Brothers—at the end of the day to sell their remaining produce. Ransom, who also owned a hotel, always invited his sister and nephew to an afternoon dinner in the hotel's dining room. Collins Kilgore, Paul's cousin, remembered, "Paul was always welcomed, but he never ate with us, not once."[39]

Paul instead purchased a hunk of cheese and a stack of crackers for a dime. He would then purchase a quarter's worth of oats and chops for his mules and go to the livery stable across the road from the Cotton Belt Railroad Depot. Invariably, he would sit atop or under a boxcar as his mood dictated and eat his cheese and crackers. He washed his food down with water from a nearby pump. Sometimes Dean Kilgore, another of Ransom's sons and Paul's cousin, would pay him a visit and try to coax him into coming into the restaurant for a hearty meal. Paul always declined the invitation. He claimed he would rather watch the trains.[40]

A deeper reason existed for his reclusive habits. Decades later Paul confessed to having "such an inferiority complex [he] was too ashamed to go with [his mother]. [He] didn't know whether to use the knife or the spoon or what."[41] So he remained alone with his cheese and crackers, those trains, and his thoughts, waiting for the clock on the courthouse to strike 4:00 p.m.—the signal to pick up his mother at the hotel and load up for the return trip home.[42]

Over time those trains became an intense fascination for Paul. He watched them for hours as they pulled out the train station, bound for destinations beyond his imagination. There, atop a boxcar, Paul first encountered his fears and pondered his future. He dreamed of something bigger than Moro Bottom and Fordyce; something beyond his immediate reach. He dreamed of riding one of those fancy trains out of town and toward a better life.[43]

Paul William Bryant realized he just needed to find his ticket.

NOTES

1. *New York Times*, January 27, 1983. Bryant's Alabama squads were ranked number one by wire service polls in 1961, 1964, 1965, 1973, 1978, and 1979.

2. Al Browning, *I Remember Paul "Bear" Bryant: Personal Memoirs of College Football's Most Legendary Coach, as Told by the People Who Knew Him* (Nashville, TN: Cumberland House, 2001), 144.

3. Ibid., 140.

4. Ibid., xvi

5. Browning died April 25, 2002, at the age of 52. He served as sports editor of the *Tuscaloosa (AL) News* from 1977 to 1982 and covered two of Alabama's national championships under Bryant (*Tuscaloosa [AL] News*, April 26, 2002).

6. Browning, *I Remember*, xiv.

7. Ibid.

8. Ibid.

9. Ibid.

10. Ibid., xv.

11. Ibid.

12. Paul W. Bryant and John Underwood, *Bear: The Hard Life and Good Times of Alabama's Coach Bryant* (New York: Little, Brown, 1974), 22; Browning, *I Remember*, 282; Allen Barra, *The Last Coach: A Life of Paul "Bear" Bryant* (New York: W. W. Norton, 2005), 9.

13. Browning, *I Remember*, 282.

14. Keith Dunnavant, *Coach: The Life of Paul "Bear" Bryant* (New York: St. Martin's, 2005), 18; Browning, *I Remember*, 281.

15. A Dallas County map in the Arkansas Historic Commission shows the Bryants owning 160 acres, circa 1920.

16. Bryant and Underwood, *Bear*, 22.

17. Barra, *Last Coach*, 9; Allen Barra, interview with Dean Kilgore, video recording, Dallas County Museum, Fordyce, Arkansas. At the time of research for this work, the museum's videotape collection on Bryant had been either lost or misplaced.

18. Bryant and Underwood, *Bear*, 22.

19. Ibid.

20. Ibid.

21. Ibid., 19.

22. Ibid.

23. Mickey Herskowitz, *The Legend of Bear Bryant* (New York: McGraw-Hill, 1987), 39.

24. Bryant and Underwood, *Bear*, 20.

25. Browning, *I Remember*, 6.

26. *Dallas County News*, April 21, 1927, and April 28, 1927; Bryant and Underwood, *Bear*, 18; *United States Census, Dallas County, Arkansas*, 1920 and 1930.

27. Herskowitz, *Legend*, 39. Today, a large wooden sign reads "Paul Bear Bryant Birthplace" outside the property where the Bryant homestead once stood. Tourists stream through Moro Bottom on an almost daily basis, stopping at the site to take photographs. The sign was erected by Ray Bryant, Paul's great-nephew.

28. Barra, *Last Coach*, 7.

29. Bryant and Underwood, *Bear*, 21.

30. Ibid., 18.

31. Carl H. Moneyhon, *Arkansas and the New South, 1874–1929* (Fayetteville, AR: University of Arkansas Press, 1997), 27; George Walter Balogh, "Entrepreneurs, City Builders, and Pine Forest Industries in South Arkansas, 1881–1963" (PhD diss., University of Oklahoma, 1992), 12–23.

32. Browning, *I Remember*, 280.

33. Bryant and Underwood, *Bear*, 20.

34. Ibid.

35. Browning, *I Remember*, 280.

36. Bryant and Underwood, *Bear*, 21.

37. Barra, *Last Coach*, 14.

38. Ibid.

39. Browning, *I Remember*, 7.

40. Bryant and Underwood, *Bear*, 20; Barra, *Last Coach*, 14–15; Browning, *I Remember*, 7.

41. Bryant and Underwood, *Bear*, 20.

42. Ibid.

43. *Houston Post*, October 20, 1967.

CHAPTER 2

Becoming Bear

There is a touch of Shakespearean actor in his soul.
—Mickey Herskowitz, *Houston Post* sportswriter, on Paul W. Bryant

No single moment in the illustrious life and career of Paul William Bryant defined him more than the time he climbed onto a theater stage as a teenager to wrestle a circus bear. For in that moment, the stunt gave birth to a living legend, and the reclusive country boy from "the Bottom" faded into yesteryear.

The mere act of tangling with a live bear showed courage, more than a touch of recklessness, and in Bryant's case, an emerging gift for showmanship. He would draw on all these qualities throughout his storied career to become the winningest coach in college football history. "Like other men of charm and persuasion, and great drive, Bryant has an instinct for the right moment, the right word, the right gesture," Herskowitz would write nearly four decades after Bryant's bear-wrestling encounter. "There is a touch of Shakespearean actor in his soul."[1]

Bryant arguably delivered his first great performance at the old Lyric Theatre in Fordyce—site of the legendary showdown. Whether he planned to wrestle a bear that day is still a matter of conjecture. Chester Darling, one of Bryant's former high school football teammates, witnessed the match as a theater employee selling popcorn and peanuts. Bryant, he has long been convinced, "knew all along he was going to wrestle that day."[2]

Bryant, however, claimed his decision to grapple with the bear was strictly impromptu. In Bryant's version, he wandered into downtown Fordyce one afternoon with his pals—Jordan twins Clark and George and Ike Murry. The boys strolled along the town's new cement sidewalk until they stopped outside the Lyric Theatre, fronted by three rounded archways and a brick façade connected to C. B. Hickey and Company's clothing and shoe store next door. A poster advertising the appearance of a wrestling bear caught their eyes, as did the presence of Drucilla Smith, a stunningly beautiful older girl with "reddish-blonde hair."[3]

Mayor George Smith, the theater's owner, paced nervously outside. The man who had promised to wrestle the bear that night couldn't be found, and customers had already purchased tickets to see the show. Smith and the bear's owner needed a replacement—quickly. So the traveling showman offered a dollar a minute to anyone brave enough to wrestle his bear.[4]

The boys bantered back and forth until someone said to the 6-foot-1, 180-pound Bryant, "Why don't you go in there?"

A dollar a minute was a lot of money not only to Bryant but to most people in Dallas County. At the time, Bryant earned 50 cents a day for long hours chopping cotton for his brother, Jack. How hard could it be to earn a dollar a minute to hold onto a bear? The boys prodded Bryant to accept the challenge. The money sounded good. And frankly, so did the thought of impressing Drucilla. Bryant glanced at the girl and, in a fateful moment fueled by testosterone, boasted, "For a dollar a minute I'd do anything."[5]

Bryant told Smith he would wrestle the bear with one caveat: he and his friends could watch the movie that followed the bear-wrestling match for free. Smith eagerly agreed to waive the 10-cent movie admission, and the showdown was set—young Bryant would wrestle a "wild" bear. Throughout the day, Smith and the showman promoted the event to the growing crowds, who were likely in town to see another circus. Traveling circus troops were extremely common and popular throughout the United States in the 1920s. By the time Bryant climbed onto the wooden stage to meet the beast, spectators had packed the tiny theatre.[6]

"I don't remember who won," Murry later said. "Paul or the bear. But I do remember that half the crowd was pulling for Paul, half for the bear."[7] Collins Kilgore, Bryant's cousin, also purchased a ticket that evening. Echoing Murry, Kilgore remembered, "To tell the truth, I'm not sure who had fan support during the match. I think the real bear had more people pulling for him than Paul did."[8] Clark Jordan described the mood of the crowd in more blunt language: "Half the people in there probably wanted to see him get torn up by that bear."[9]

To this day, no one can determine with any certainty when the match took place, thus leaving Bryant's age unknown. Bryant stated in his autobiography—penned with sportswriter John Underwood—that the "bear-wrestling episode" occurred around the time his mother rented an apartment in Kingsland. He remembered that this, in turn, took place around January 30, 1925, when Kentucky spelunker Floyd Collins became trapped while searching for a new opening in the Mammoth Cave system. Initially, rescuers were able to deliver food and water to Collins until a rock collapsed, sealing off the lone passageway to the entrapped explorer. For two weeks, rescuers made voice contact with Collins. The dramatic episode became a national sensation, finding coverage in newspapers and on the radio. During this period, Bryant walked to the railroad station every day to see the latest newspapers delivered by train. "We didn't buy the paper," Bryant recalled. "We just looked at the headlines to see how old Floyd was making out."[10]

Collins met a tragic end. After two weeks of communication, rescuers determined Collins had died on or around February 13, 1925, when they heard no response.

Bryant's recollection of the Collins episode is too specific to have been misremembered. However, he was probably relating the cave tragedy with his mother's move to Kingsland, and not his encounter with the bear, since he was only 11 years old when Collins became entombed alive in Mammoth Cave. There's no way Bryant (or any other 11-year-old) could have wrestled a bear at that age.

Most Bryant biographers place the famed bear-wrestling episode in 1927, either before or after his 14th birthday on September 11. Some suggest it was even later, but that isn't possible—Smith had already closed the Lyric Theatre by December 1927. Moviegoers were still watching flicks at the theater as late as May 1927, showing up for a benefit to help local flood victims.[11]

Bryant was surely living in Fordyce at the time he wrestled the bear, since he was already hanging out with future Fordyce High School teammates like Murry and the Jordan twins. By Bryant's own estimation, after living in Kingsland, his mother rented a "big house" in Fordyce and began taking in boarders. Odds are the legendary event occurred in 1927, and a review of the *Dallas County News* suggests two possible times—April and October. In April, the Christy Brothers Big Five-Ring Circus rolled into Fordyce, boasting "500 horses," "50 Caged Animals," "30 Lions," and two "Cars of Elephants and Camels." Then in October, the Robbins Brothers Four-Ring Circus came to town with three herds of elephants and 200 "wild animals." Both circus troops undoubtedly featured "wild" bears in their shows.[12]

Regardless of the finer details surrounding the event, the Lyric Theatre's closure in 1927 meant Bryant was no older than 14 when he tussled with a live bear. That fact alone is hard to comprehend, and it is certainly worthy of remembrance. Simply by accepting the match, Bryant displayed a special type of courage that comes with those who stand alone in a crowd at the risk of ridicule and humiliation. Most people avoid the spotlight. Bryant seemed drawn by its heat.

The harsh voices of his childhood left Bryant with something to prove, and by his own dark admission, he often sought this proof through violence. "I am embarrassed to say it, but I lived with a chip on my shoulders in those days," Bryant said. "I enjoyed fighting. I suppose it was a way of expressing myself, and I never missed a chance."[13]

Bryant desperately wanted revenge for all those times children mocked his country ways and impoverished pedigree. He also wanted to be noticed and respected—by force, if necessary. Murry addressed Bryant's temper years later with his own harsh assessment. "Even when he was young, Bear had the ability to attract attention and lead," Murry said. "But certainly when he came out of Moro Bottom, you never would have thought he would become famous. In fact, you would have wondered if he would end up in the pen."[14]

Collins Kilgore certainly understood the demons that haunted his cousin.

"Paul had a lot of Barnum and Bailey in him before he wrestled the bear at the Lyric Theatre," Kilgore recalled. "He was a showman. He wanted to prove his worth and he enjoyed the spotlight. He got ridiculed a lot. He fought that with his fists. He got challenged a lot. Normally, he'd answer every one of them."[15]

Bryant never shied away from a challenge. Shortly after his move to Fordyce, Bryant boasted he could run barefoot from the railroad depot beyond Moro Bottom to Smith Chapel in a half hour. The Fordyce railroad station stood slightly more than 7 miles from Moro Bottom, and Smith Chapel—the Bryants' church—was another quarter mile past the Bottom. So in all likelihood, Bryant bragged he could cover the roughly 8-mile distance in under an hour. As the story goes, word "spread like wildfire," along with the "snickering."[16] A large crowd gathered to watch Bryant race against the clock. A few boys even pooled money to bet Bryant he would fail in his endeavor.

The weather certainly wasn't in Bryant's favor that day. Temperatures exceeded 100 degrees. Naturally, Bryant remained steadfast in his claim. He welcomed the challenge, and at the signal to start the race, he shot down the gravel road toward Moro Bottom with a fierce determination. Cheers and jeers reverberated in his wake.

Then, with time running out, Bryant appeared in the distance from beyond Smith Chapel. The drama mounted as he desperately raced toward the finish line, pounding the gravel and black soil with his large, calloused feet. Bryant crossed the finish line with "a minute or two to spare."[17]

"The big rascal collapsed as he reached the finish line," recalled W. R. Benton, one of Bryant's friends and another high school teammate. "Had it not been for one of the guys knowing first aid, Bear might have died. As fate would have it, Bear didn't have many doubters from that day forward."[18]

Those who dared to doubt Bryant were usually proven wrong. His bluster and flair for the dramatic were matched by his inner strength and physical toughness. In short, Bryant usually backed up his mouth. His toughness can be traced back to his earliest days on the family farm and those grinding excursions with his mother to peddle their produce. Chopping cotton in the blistering sun, driving a team of mules in the freezing rain across Moro Creek, enduring the mockery of snobbish peers—all prepared Bryant for the hard road ahead.

In retrospect, his success seemed obvious to those who knew him best. Childhood friend Joe Runnel, who lived down the road from the Bryants, remembered Paul's harsh demeanor and unique toughness. He witnessed both traits firsthand on a number of occasions during his youth, although one episode is branded in his memory more vividly than all others.

"He was meaner than hell growing up," Runnel recalled. "He was tough, too. One day we were going to Fordyce in a wagon. We hit a chuckhole [pothole] and the wheel ran over his [Bryant's] head and pushed him down in the mud. Mashed his head to where it looked like a butter bean. We thought it had killed him."[19]

Instead, the fallen Bryant lifted himself off the ground and continued walking.

Bryant's toughness sprang from a time and place few outside of his family will ever remember. When Paul was about four years old—long before the circus bear—his elder brother, Harley, periodically called upon him for a dangerous task. Harley hunted wild hogs along Moro Creek and would call them into a pen, where Paul fought them off until Harley could mark them. Hogs are notoriously vicious, and the job always terrified the then-diminutive Paul.

"I can still see that little boy in there battling those hogs," recalled Senora Bryant, Harley's wife. "He was so small then. He could've been killed. He was scared to death, too, but he stayed in that pen and tried."[20]

So when Bryant agreed to wrestle a bear in public, the decision made more sense than simply that of a reckless lad acting on a whim. Bryant's willingness had purpose, girl or no girl. The insecure country boy in him—the one who wrestled wild hogs or endured the harassment of other children—still had something to prove to the world.

The Lyric Theatre would provide the arena. Today, a dusty film covers the front windows of the old theater building on Main Street, where his legions of fans still pay homage to the legend. Buster Garlington first worked in the building in 1959 after it was converted to a hardware store, and since its recent closure, the old theater has become a bit of a time capsule. Old rifles and leather harnesses are mounted on lofty shelves that line the brick walls. Throughout the old store, one can still find boxes of nails, wooden ax handles, plumbing parts, and a variety of tools.

"This is where Bear wrestled the bear," Garlington said proudly. "This is where history was made, although it really wasn't much of a theater back then. But it was all we had."[21]

At the time of the famous match, the Lyric Theatre was little more than a narrow shotgun building—typical of many downtown stores of that period. The seats sloped downhill to a raised wooden stage, which partially blocked patrons from the movie screen if they sat in the first two or three rows. Thus those seats always remained empty. The theater seated 200 people, yet by the time Bryant stepped onto the stage, the entire town seemed to be in attendance. The place buzzed with anticipation.[22]

Bryant remembered how the bear's owner tried to heighten the excitement with a hyperbolic, man-versus-beast speech. Amid the noise, Bryant formulated his plan. He realized he knew virtually nothing about wrestling, but by his own estimation, he had to prevent the bear from rolling him over. He concluded he had to maintain distance between his body and the bear's by holding on and not letting go. Bryant planned to play prevent defense.

Handlers finally brought the brown bear onto the stage. The bear, almost certainly declawed, wore a muzzle. Murry later described the bear as "one of the scrawniest he had ever seen," but then again, he could afford to be critical: he wasn't on stage. "To me it looked thirty feet tall," Bryant later quipped. "I must have wanted that money real bad."[23] Bryant would famously tell *People* magazine nearly 50 years later, "I felt I would wrestle King Kong for a dollar a minute."[24]

By all accounts, the match ended within minutes. As soon as the bear reared up on its hind legs, Bryant charged the animal and tackled it to the floor. He then held on tight, momentarily preventing the bear from moving. His adrenaline pumped wildly. A few seconds passed, and the bear's owner started poking Bryant with a stick. "Let him up!" the man whispered in Bryant's ear. "Let him up!"[25] He wanted action. But Bryant had other plans, admitting, "For a dollar a minute I wanted to hold 'em til he died."[26]

The bear finally broke loose. Young Bryant charged a second time only to have the bear again break free. The bear acted ornery at this point, and when Bryant once again attempted to topple the bear, the animal's muzzle slipped off. Suddenly, Bryant felt a "burning" sensation on the back of his ear. The bear had drawn blood.[27]

Seated in the front of the theater, Bryant's sisters watched in dismay. "The bear is gonna kill him!" someone heard one of them scream. "The bear is gonna kill him!"[28] Other women started screaming as well. Louise recalled how the men "first thought it was part of the show and laughed." Then Bryant jumped from the stage, nearly breaking his leg as he crashed against the anchored seats. Darling said his friend jumped "like a man who had seen a ghost."[29]

"I was being eaten alive," Bryant said. "I jumped off that stage and nearly killed myself hitting the empty front seats with my shins."[30]

The laughter stopped. Patrons bolted for the exit in a panic.

"They were getting out of that door as they hollered, flying like birds," Darling recalled. "It was worse than a fire."[31]

Once calm prevailed, Bryant sought out the bear's owner to collect his money. His search proved fruitless. The man had skipped town. "I never got my money," Bryant would often moan in his molasses-slow drawl. "All I got were some scars and a name."[32]

Over the years, Bryant's feat became mythological. Embellished stories began to circulate and increase in number. Garlington said his former bookkeeper, Irene Ramsey, witnessed the event and always claimed Bryant and the bear continued their match in the alley behind the theater. Murry further added to the legend, once claiming the bear's owner offered Bryant a rematch "as long as 'Bear' would agree to wear the muzzle."[33]

Then in a September 1977 issue of *Esquire*, writer and humorist Roy Blount Jr. topped all Bear Bryant storytellers. Blount penned, "I have spent only ten or twelve days in Arkansas in my life, but I've already met two different people who claimed they witnessed that event. One of them said that he, in a suit, was the bear; but he was drinking and I believe he would have said anything. In Arkansas. I don't think he would have said that around folks in Alabama."[34]

One footnote to the bear-wrestling episode is true. Years later, Bryant and his former college teammate Don Hutson saw that same bear and his wily owner while bird hunting in Fayette, Alabama. The man and his bear were performing a bear-wrestling act with a carnival sideshow. Bryant was an assistant coach at the University of Alabama at the time and felt he had "achieved a certain amount of dignity" by then. Otherwise, he confessed, he might have choked the money out of the old carny.

Bryant, however, also possessed a heart. He never confronted the carny, concluding the old man probably needed the money worse than he did.[35] Such a concession was probably hard for Bryant. He never wanted to feel content and secure. Nobody ever won anything by feeling content. And Bryant won a lot. So he always sought to stay hungry and often made a point to wear undershirts with holes. Once, someone asked him why he didn't just buy new shirts—after all, he was rich. Bryant replied without hesitation, "I never want to forget where I came from."

Bryant possessed this desperate hunger the first time he walked past the Fordyce High School football field. The Redbugs were practicing. As the story goes, a coach noticed big Paul, stopped him, and asked if he wanted to play football. Whether the man was head coach Bob Cowan or assistant coach Dan Walton is unknown.

"Yessir, I guess I do," Bryant answered. "How do you play?"

The coach said, "Well, you see that fellow catching the ball down there?"

"Yeah."

"Well, whenever he catches it, you go down there and try to kill him."[36]

Bryant liked what he heard. He certainly didn't mind hitting people. Moments later, he stood on the field about to take part in a punt-coverage drill. The first punt soared into the air, and Bryant sprinted downfield with the same zest as during his footrace to Smith Chapel, arriving at the same time as the ball. He plowed over the team's punt returner. "The following Friday I played on the team," Bryant mused, "and I didn't know an end zone from an end run."[37]

Football provided the perfect stage for Bryant—an arena, boisterous crowds, bands, cheerleaders, and permission to smash people hard. As fate would have it, Bryant also walked into a highly competitive program with a rich tradition. The town's football roots went back to 1904, when a New Yorker named Tom Meddick organized the state's first high school program at the Clary Training school. Five years later, Fordyce High School fielded its first team. In the mid-1920s, shortly before Bryant's arrival, Fordyce Lumber Company donated land for a new high school field. Workers who cleared the land were attacked mercilessly by chiggers, prompting local football correspondent Willard Clary to suggest Fordyce adopt the "redbugs" as its mascot. The name stuck.[38]

So did Fordyce's passion for football. Despite being small in numbers, the fighting Redbugs were unusually talented and tough. Bryant's team lived up to the tradition. The Jordan twins led the way before eventually going on to star at the University of Arkansas. Bryant gained great respect for the Jordan brothers, hailing them as "the best athletes" to ever emerge from Fordyce. The Redbugs also featured skilled players like Collins Kilgore, Arvel "Chink" Lacewell, and Ike Murry. Bryant anchored the defensive line as tackle and played end on offense, reportedly earning All-State honors as a sophomore.[39]

Larry Lacewell, Chink's son and a longtime scouting director for the Dallas Cowboys, summed up Fordyce's enthusiasm for football when he said, "When I was growing up, nobody asked a boy if he *wanted* to play football—they asked you what position you were *going* to play."[40]

Bryant and his teammates added to the legacy by winning the state championship in 1930 with a perfect record. By then, Bryant had grown into a 6-foot-3, 190-pound senior and a football convert. Football provided him with a sense of pride and purpose, perhaps for the first time in his life. In his autobiography, he counted his first train trip during junior season as "the biggest thrill" of his life. The Redbugs traveled to the state capitol to battle the much larger Little Rock High School. Fordyce shocked Little Rock that season with a 7–0 victory—a first for the small Dallas County town. The next season, Fordyce pounded Little Rock 34–0 under the lights, and Bryant contributed a 70-yard touchdown reception that night. He and his teammates received a hero's welcome upon their return home, being treated to a hearty meal of country ham and hot biscuits at the local hotel.[41]

Bryant began to feel like somebody.

However, Monroe Bryant didn't want his youngest son to play football. The elder Bryant's mind-set was actually quite common for many rural families of that era. Monroe considered football a waste of time and wanted his son farming. Period. He even threatened to whip Paul if he disobeyed. Fortunately for Paul—as well as the football world—Paul's mother, Ida, felt differently. She fought with her husband over the issue until he finally relented. Afterward, there was no more talk of not playing football. Period.

Ida even took her son's black high-tops to a cobbler, who crudely screwed cleats into the soles of the shoes. Paul was so proud of his new cleats that he wore them everywhere he went—on and off the football field. Years later, Bryant remained convinced his mother didn't approve of him making football his life's work. "I think . . . she would have loved for me to have been a preacher," he said after her death in 1954. "I was the only one in the family who got to go on to college, and I'm sure she thought it was a waste of time for me to wind up coaching football. I used to tell her coaching and preaching were a lot alike, but she didn't believe it."[42]

Ida, amazingly, never saw her son play or coach in person. Collins Kilgore contended his aunt's absence from the football field didn't truly express how she felt about her son's chosen profession. Kilgore once recalled how Ida would call his mother and say, "Dru, we've got to get together and pray for Paul to win this game."[43] In truth, Ida took great pride in her son's success.

On the field Paul "Bear" Bryant played with an unbound joy. He displayed an abundance of power and good speed downfield for his size. Naturally, teammates also lauded his extreme toughness and aggression. But not everyone approved of his showmanship.

"Bear was a showman even in those days," Murry recalled. "Crowds loved him. He never caught many passes. His best play was when he went down-field to block a halfback. We played on a field that was half-grass, half-dirt. Bear would rumble down and put a rolling block on that halfback. I don't think he ever blocked him, but he'd always raise a cloud of dust, kicking and scrambling around the guy's feet. The crowd would roar. People loved it."[44]

Even his own cousin conceded that Bryant desperately craved attention. "Paul was a showboat, no doubt about it," Kilgore recalled. "From the time he started playing football at Fordyce High School, every newspaper clipping said Bryant this and Bryant that. He loved every minute of it. I think he loved the attention he got as a coach, too, every accolade that came his way."[45]

Darling remembered one of the games against Little Rock when Bryant played with a bruised knee. Bryant hobbled onto the field for warm-ups with an abundance of tape wrapped around his leg. "You would have thought that damn knee was broken in half," Darling mused. Later, during the game, Bryant rambled downfield "stiff-legged" on a punt and plowed over Little Rock's punt returner. "The crowd went crazy and Bear got up and limped to the sideline like he was in terrible pain," Darling added. "But that's the way Bear played football. He was damn good, tough as nails, but he had a lot of movie star in him."[46]

Bryant also had enough talent on the football field for people to notice. "He was the most aggressive player I ever saw," recalled Jack Benham, another of Bryant's former high school teammates. "The coach liked to use him as a model: 'Here, watch Bryant show you how to block.' And Bryant would knock a guy five yards off the line."[47]

Teammates may not have always agreed with Bryant's theatrics, but no one questioned his loyalty—or fierceness. For what he lacked in athleticism he more than made up for in meanness. No one wanted to cross the youngster who wrestled the bear. Once, in a tight game against Hope High School, Fordyce's quarterback Clark "Click" Jordan absorbed a late hit while running out of bounds. The Redbugs were livid as Jordan hobbled to the sideline with a sprained ankle, unable to return.

"Don't worry, Click, I'll get that sonofabitch," Bryant declared. But he had to bide his time, since time remained in the game. Bryant didn't want to jeopardize the victory by doing something dumb to draw a penalty. So he waited. Back then, referees kept the game time on their watches. Thus Bryant asked an official after every play how much time was left on the clock. Finally, with seconds to go, Bryant lined up opposite the Hope player who had delivered the cheap shot. As soon as the ball was snapped, Bryant pounced on the player and pummeled him to the ground. He didn't stop punching until the officials had peeled him off the player and ejected him from the game.

Jordan remembered the episode fondly, musing, "You could say Bear had more loyalty than judgement in those days."[48]

Football gave Bryant identity, self-worth, purpose, and finally, an opportunity to change his life. Over time, Bryant started to realize football would eventually carry him out of Dallas County, just as he had long dreamed while watching trains depart Fordyce years earlier. His ticket arrived in the spring of 1931, when the popular University of Alabama assistant coach Hank Crisp rolled into town. Crisp, who had lost his right hand in an accident at age 13, offered an inspirational story wherever he traveled. Despite his handicap, he still managed to letter in football, basketball, and track in college. On this occasion, he had driven to Fordyce to recruit the ultratalented Jordan twins, but he soon learned he probably wouldn't be able to pry them away from the University of Arkansas.[49]

Crisp failed to hide his disappointment but remained optimistic that the trip wouldn't be a waste. He asked Cowan if he had any other top college prospects. Cowan said he had one: Paul Bryant—a 17-year-old scrapper who was big, tough as leather, and fearless and hit like a sledgehammer. And, Cowan added, he answered to the nickname "Bear."

Cowan had Crisp's attention. The Alabama coach soon stood in front of the big lad from Moro Bottom. Crisp took one glance at the youngster before asking him if he would like to play football for the Crimson Tide. Bryant smiled, and the two shook hands. Later that fall, Bryant hopped into the rumble seat of

Crisp's car and pulled out of Fordyce—bound for Tuscaloosa, Alabama, and a new life.

Bryant left with a small satchel of clothes, a nickname, and a healthy fear of failure. "All I had was football," Bryant said decades later. "And I hung on as though it was life or death."[50]

Just as he once did with a circus bear.

NOTES

1. *Houston Post*, October 26, 1967.
2. Browning, *I Remember*, 4.
3. Bryant and Underwood, *Bear*, 26.
4. Ibid.
5. Ibid., 19, 26.
6. Ibid., 27.
7. Herskowitz, *Legend*, 42.
8. Browning, *I Remember*, 5.
9. Dunnavant, *Coach*, 24–25.
10. Bryant and Underwood, *Bear*, 28.
11. *Dallas County News*, December 1, 1927, and May 5, 1927.
12. Bryant and Underwood, *Bear*, 28; *Dallas County News*, April 7, 1927, and October 13, 1927.
13. Bryant and Underwood, *Bear*, 29.
14. Browning, *I Remember*, 4.
15. Ibid., 9.
16. Ibid.
17. Ibid., 10.
18. Ibid.
19. Dunnavant, *Coach*, 24.
20. Browning, *I Remember*, 6.
21. Buster Garlington, interview with author, February 10, 2016. Garlington was born November 11, 1938.
22. Bryant and Underwood, *Bear*, 27; Barra, *Last Coach*, 19; Browning, *I Remember*, 4.
23. Browning, *I Remember*, 5; Bryant and Underwood, *Bear*, 27.
24. Mitchell J. Shields, "Stars Don't Just Fall on Alabama—Bear Bryant Recruits Them to Keep His Crimson Tide Rolling," *People*, October 1, 1979.
25. Herskowitz, *Legend*, 42; Barra, *Last Coach*, 21.
26. Herskowitz, *Legend*, 42. Bryant told Herskowitz a no-nonsense version of the event September 14, 1954, in Junction, Texas, after he was hired as the new Texas A&M University football coach.

27. Bryant and Underwood, *Bear*, 27.

28. Browning, *I Remember*, 4.

29. Ibid.

30. Bryant and Underwood, *Bear*, 27. Louise would later echo her brother's sentiment: "You should have seen him jump off that stage when he realized that thing had bit him. He was brave enough to get up there and wrestle that bear, but he wasn't about to let it eat him alive" (Barra, *Last Coach*, 21).

31. Browning, *I Remember*, 4.

32. Herskowitz, *Legend*, 43.

33. Browning, *I Remember*, 5.

34. Roy Blount Jr. "Bear Bryant's Stompin' School," *Esquire*, October 1, 1977.

35. Bryant and Underwood, *Bear*, 27–28.

36. Ibid., 26.

37. Ibid., 26–27.

38. *Encyclopedia of Arkansas History and Culture*, s.v. "Redbug Field," accessed February 1, 2016, www.encyclopediaofarkansas.net.

39. Bryant and Underwood, *Bear*, 26.

40. Barra, *Last Coach*, 6.

41. Bryant and Underwood, *Bear*, 34.

42. Ibid., 24, 31–32; Paul Bryant and John Underwood, "I'll Tell You about Football," *Sports Illustrated*, August 14, 1966.

43. Barra, *Last Coach*, 17.

44. Herskowitz, *Legend*, 43.

45. Browning, *I Remember*, 11.

46. Ibid., 11–12.

47. Dunnavant, *Coach*, 26.

48. Ibid., 27.

49. Ibid., 29.

50. Bryant and Underwood, "I'll Tell You."

CHAPTER 3
The Protégé

I really wasn't a good player. I wanted to be.

—Gene Stallings

A tanned Gene Stallings arose from a worn, wooden bench in downtown Paris, Texas, in July 2015 like the protagonist from an old Western novel—tall, erect, and stately. Then 80 years old, the retired football coach moved with a slow and steady gait but still cut a commanding silhouette with a lean 6-foot-2 frame.

His leathery skin exposed the creases of time.

"Gene Stallings," he said in a deep, gravely drawl as he extended his right hand to a visitor. "I see you finally found the place." His voice sounded as sturdy as his handshake, and strikingly similar to old videos and audiotapes of his former college football coach and hero—the late Paul W. "Bear" Bryant.

The similarities are understandable given their lengthy history together. Ever since 1954, the life and career of Stallings have been intertwined with that of the legendary Bryant. Stallings first played for Bryant at Texas A&M (1954–56), then served as an assistant coach under him at Alabama (1958–64), finally following in his footsteps as Alabama's head coach (1990–96). The legend and the protégé even coached against one another in a storied 1968 Cotton Bowl Classic in Dallas, when Stallings held the head coaching post at A&M.

Bryant's profound influence on Stallings was unmistakable. From his coaching philosophy and leadership style to his authoritative mannerisms and Southern drawl, Stallings became a Bryant disciple in every way imaginable.

The comparisons never bothered Stallings.

"Coach Bryant was my hero," Stallings said. "He was a great man, and I loved him. He taught me so much about coaching and life."[1]

Stallings dared to do what many thought impossible: walking in Bryant's footsteps at Alabama. In Tuscaloosa—no, all of Alabama—Bryant's shadow had long hung over the land. So when the university hired Stallings as the next head coach of the Crimson Tide in 1990, a throng of curious media greeted him at a midmorning press conference in Alabama's multimillion-dollar football complex. Famed Crimson Tide alumni such as Bart Starr and Lee Roy Jordan appeared to welcome Stallings home. As a Bryant protégé and one of his beloved "Junction Boys," the expectations were especially high. Paul Bryant Jr., Bear's son, embraced Stallings at the door that day, loudly proclaiming for all to hear, "This is exactly what Papa would have wanted."[2]

The protégé didn't disappoint. He compiled a combined 70–16–1 record in seven seasons at Alabama, including a national title in 1992 and four trips to the Southeastern Conference Championship game. Stallings built those teams around dominant defenses and conservative offenses, and as Bryant biographer Keith Dunnavant astutely noted in his book *Coach: The Life of Paul "Bear" Bryant*, "The effect was not only to venerate Stallings but also to further strengthen the Bryant mystique's grip on the program."[3]

Of course, no one understood the Bryant mystique more than Stallings. Therein rested the secret to success at Alabama for Stallings, who once pointed out he could exit his office onto Paul Bryant Drive and walk past the Paul Bryant Conference Center next to the Paul Bryant Museum, which was located down the street from the Paul Bryant Dorm. Stallings embraced the mammoth legacy of the "Bear." He was often content to stand in his mentor's shadow, and once famously said, "People in Alabama loved Coach Bryant. They just tolerated the rest of us." Stallings further explained his mind-set during this period when he wrote,

> There's just one Coach Bryant. He set the bar, and the rest of us are just trying
> to do the best we can. . . . There's no comparison. I tried to win some games the
> way he did, but I never tried to compete with Coach Bryant. I knew my place. I
> think that's one reason it was a little easier for me to coach at Alabama because it
> did not intimidate me that he had such a great record and that people loved him
> so much. I loved him, too.[4]

Ironically, the lives of these two men were dramatically different growing up. Bryant rose from a hardscrabble existence in the muddy lowlands of Moro Bottom, while Stallings emerged from a Norman Rockwell-esque setting in Paris, Texas.

Born Eugene Clifton Stallings Jr. on March 2, 1935, to Nell and Eugene Stallings Sr., Gene's earliest memories sprang from a "classic" childhood in the quaint Lamar County town just south of the Red River. By 1940, Paris—the county seat—boasted 18,678 residents with a bustling downtown district that featured five theaters, a county courthouse and jail, a drugstore and soda fountain, a newspaper, and a nearby train depot. Back then, Paris High School was also located downtown, and before Friday night football games, the band and cheerleaders always led a parade around the downtown square to rally the faithful.[5]

The fact that Paris existed—let alone thrived—at this time is a testament to the spirit of the town's forefathers. Fires twice ravaged the town, once in 1877 and again in 1916. Officials estimated the 1916 fire destroyed more than $11 million in property, including 1,400 buildings and most of the downtown district. The "Great Fire of 1916" also claimed four lives. Residents resolutely began to rebuild within four months, and in 1927, an ornate fountain commissioned by local benefactor John James Culbertson was unveiled as a memorial to the town's postfire renewal.[6]

During World War II, the Culbertson Fountain served as the staging area for downtown rallies to sell war bonds. Stallings remembered the patriotic fervor of the day, and how he and other children could get into one of the town's movie theaters for free on Saturday afternoons in exchange for scraps of iron for the war effort.[7]

These war bond rallies were especially inspiring and memorable for Stallings. Once, he recalled, a fourth-grade classmate of his boasted that she was related to the "Singing Cowboy," Gene Autry. Stallings doubted her claim until one Saturday afternoon rally. Suddenly, Autry rode into the downtown square aboard his famed horse, Champion, dressed in studded and fringed cowboy garb. Autry then led the crowd in an enthusiastic rendition of his trademark 1939 hit, "Back in the Saddle Again."[8]

Paris taught Stallings the solid, small-town values of a place where neighbors looked out for neighbors. Friendly waves and warm smiles from familiar faces filled his childhood. At home, his mother and father were models of hard work for him and his elder brother, Jimmy. In fact, Stallings couldn't remember a time when his mother didn't hold a job. Nell Stallings worked for a Paris title company well into her 60s because of her knowledge of title abstracts, still penning letters even at age 90.[9]

Stallings Sr. initially earned a living as a roofer. Circumstances later forced him to take a job as an insurance adjuster—a position that required him to work long hours and travel extensively. His boys, meanwhile, always tried to make their father proud with their work ethic. Jimmy and Gene each found jobs as soon as they were old enough to work. Over the years, Gene mowed lawns, caddied at the Paris Country Club, and bagged groceries at the local Piggly Wiggly. He also worked for his father during some summers, repairing roof shingles in the blistering Texas sun.[10]

No one in Paris ever called the younger Stallings by his first name. Since infancy, family and friends called him "Bebes," because his elder brother couldn't pronounce "Baby Gene."[11] The nickname stuck with him throughout his life, just as did his love of sports.

Stallings grew up obsessed with sports. Some of his earliest memories are of the times he huddled next to the family's RCA radio, listening to the weekly Southwest Conference games on the Humble Oil Football Network. Stallings listened and dreamed of someday playing in the Cotton Bowl Classic on New Year's Day like some of his college football heroes. Despite being deaf in his left ear and nagged by painful infections since birth, Stallings carried his dream onto the field, where he first played football in the fourth grade.[12]

Stallings excelled at every sport he played. By the time he reached high school, coaches considered him a standout in football, basketball, and golf. He also captained each team he played on, obviously a greater indicator of the journey to come. His senior year unfolded as he had hoped, and despite the relative slightness of his 6-foot-1, 165-pound build, he managed to earn a football scholarship as an end to Texas A&M.[13]

As was his habit, Stallings always downplayed his talents as a player.

"I really wasn't a good player," Stallings became fond of saying. "I wanted to be."[14]

At the time, if Stallings could have chosen, he would have played football for Baylor University in Waco, Texas. Baylor, however, wasn't interested. Texas A&M then offered him a scholarship. Stallings didn't have to think long. He jumped at the chance.

"My parents couldn't afford to send me to college," Stallings said. "I was just happy to be going to college."[15]

Years later, Gil Steinke—the Aggie coach who recruited him in the summer of 1953—playfully joked with Stallings about A&M's true interest in him. "Why in the world did you go to A&M?" Steinke joked with his former recruit. "We tried as little as possible to recruit you."[16]

Stallings loved the story because it was self-effacing and humorous. Of course, his greatest love wasn't football but a sweet local girl named Ruth Ann Jack. The two seemed destined for a life together after Gerald Jack—Ruth Ann's cousin and Gene's best friend—introduced them in eighth grade. From that moment on they were inseparable. By their senior year in high school, in 1953, classmates considered them the perfect couple—a Homecoming queen and the captain of the football team.[17] In 1956, Ruth Ann and Gene married as expected and raised five children—Anna Lee, Laurie, John Mark, Jackie, and Martha Kate.

Gene and Ruth Ann returned to their roots in 1997, retiring to their 800-acre Hike-A-Way Ranch in Powderly, Texas—a picturesque quilt of pastures and groves located some 10 miles north of downtown Paris. The couple finds comfort in the familiarity and neighborly warmth of living near their hometown.

Even something as simple as a trip to a local barbershop can be a pleasant experience, as one out-of-towner observed in 2015. Stallings walked into the Royal Barber Shop that day at 116 Bonham Street, a block off the downtown square in Paris. The grayish-silver-haired Stallings has had his hair cut at the same barbershop since age 10.

"Let me tell you about my barber, Jack Abshire," Stallings said to the visitor. "He's ninety-six and has been cuttin' my hair for seventy years. Well, he died last week."

Stallings shakes his head in remorse, adding, "Now I have this young guy cuttin' my hair." He then grinned and nodded toward Bill Haynes, the elderly barber standing in front of him with a pair of scissors in hand.

"He's the young guy," Stallings quipped. "He's eighty-four."[18]

No place brings Stallings more joy and pride than his ranch, though. Cattle graze in the sprawling pastures beyond his grand, antebellum-influenced mansion. Nearby, not far from the home's front doors, is a garden that regularly produces plump tomatoes, peas, and a variety of peppers. Ruth Ann enjoys working in the garden along with her husband, but she especially loves spending time tending to a patch of her coveted rose bushes.

Gene Stallings proudly reminds folks that his place is a "working" ranch. Daily, he tends to the chores of the ranch: feeding cattle, grooming the horses, mending fences, welding, tilling, repairing barns, and maintaining farm equipment. The jobs are never ending, and Stallings will point out that tasks only pile up if ever neglected.[19]

So Stallings never lets up.

"When I was coaching, the money wasn't like it is today," Stallings said. "I had to work forty years to pay off my ranch. That is why I am so proud of it."

Shortly after his retirement in 1997, Stallings ventured out one morning to feed three colts. He was alone and carrying two buckets of sugar feed when an overenthusiastic colt rammed him, knocking him to the ground. He broke his right hip. Various newspapers nationwide reported the accident at the time, but what isn't widely known was that Stallings—then 62—climbed to his feet. He placed one foot on top of the other and hopped to the fence, some 25 yards away, to get someone's attention. He shrugs at the painful memory, bluntly stating, "I had no choice."[20]

Stallings is a hardline man in many respects. He doesn't devote much time to anything other than problem-solving activities, and he has one rule he attempts to always live by: no complaining.

"My complaining days are over," Stallings said firmly. "Why? My son, John Mark."[21]

John Mark Stallings stormed into this world with a profound purpose June 11, 1962, at Druid City Hospital in Tuscaloosa, although at the time, his birth seemed a more tragic event than the blessing it became. Doctors informed Ruth Ann and Gene that their son was "Mongoloid"—a term then used for Down syndrome—and Gene fainted. He awoke to hovering nurses and smelling salts.[22]

"I guess it was the shock," Stallings said later. "We cried a bushel of tears."[23]

John Mark outlived all medical prognoses and proved instrumental in the development and promotion of the Rural Infant Stimulation Environment (RISE) School of Tuscaloosa. Today, the RISE School is located inside the Stallings Center, which John Mark proudly referred to as "my building."[24]

John Mark also became a beloved member of the Crimson Tide football family. He shadowed his father throughout his career, and the two shared a special moment after Alabama defeated Miami 34–13 in the 1993 Sugar Bowl to win the National Championship, and Alabama finished the season with a 13–0 record.

"Good job, Pops," said a grinning John Mark that night, burying his head in his father's chest. Gene savored the moment with his son, knowing the Alabama nation had no bigger fan. The elder Stallings also understood the pain his son had endured over the years as a result of his condition.[25]

With each passing year, John Mark's health became more delicate. He suffered from a congenital heart defect, and his family had to closely monitor his
breathing. Then, one August night in 2008, Gene checked his son's oxygen
saturation level. A normal level registers in the 90s. John Mark's level had hit 62.
Gene leaned into his son and asked, "Johnny, how are you feeling?"

"I fine," John Mark responded. "I fine."[26]

John Mark died the next morning en route to the hospital, at age 46.[27]

"Here's my son struggling to breathe, and he can still say, 'I fine,'" Stallings
said. "Who am I to complain?"[28]

John Mark's words serve as an inspiration these days for the entire Stallings
family. For Ruth Ann and Gene, their son's words—"I fine"—are showcased in
classy frames scattered throughout their home as a reminder of John Mark's
courage. Across the pasture, in a beautifully gated enclosure, lies his grave
marker, inscribed with another one of his memorable quotes: "I love the farm
on a beautiful day."

Ruth Ann and Gene visit the grave daily.

John Mark also held a special place in the heart of the "Bear." Ruth Ann fondly
remembers the time Bryant visited the Stallings ranch. In a quiet moment, on
the family's front porch, someone snapped a picture of the coaching legend sitting with John Mark by his side. The image is cherished.

"Coach Bryant was bigger than life," Ruth Ann fondly recalled. "But he sure
adored Johnny."[29]

Gene remembers the last time he ever spoke to Bryant, in 1983. One of Bryant's first questions was, "How is Johnny?" Stallings bragged about his son's
performance at the Special Olympics. He then shifted the conversation to Bryant's recent retirement, and how his legions of fans were surely "surprised and
saddened" by his sudden announcement. But Bryant ditched the small talk
and continued to ask about Johnny. Stallings finally concluded, "I knew that if
he was asking, he sincerely wanted to know about him."[30]

Stallings swelled with pride.

Two weeks later, on January 26, 1983, Stallings received a call from Linda
Knowles, Bryant's longtime secretary at Alabama. Knowles informed Stallings
that Bryant had died of a heart attack, adding, "I didn't want you to hear this
on the radio or the TV." Stallings was her first call.[31]

Shocked, Stallings asked Knowles to repeat what she had just said. She did:
Coach Bryant was dead.

Stallings hung up the phone and wept. He would later say of his beloved mentor, "We all thought that he would live forever."[32]

In many respects, Bryant did. In the record books and in men like Gene "Bebes" Stallings.

NOTES

1. Gene Stallings, interview with author, July 8, 2015.

2. Gene Stallings and Sally Cook, *Another Season: A Coach's Story of Raising an Exceptional Son* (New York: Little, Brown, 1997), 187; Dunnavant, *Coach*, 325.

3. Dunnavant, *Coach*, 325–26. The National Collegiate Athletic Association (NCAA) officially recognizes Stallings's combined record at Alabama as 62–24–1. The NCAA forced the Crimson Tide to forfeit eight wins from its 9–3–1 record in 1993 after implicating Stallings and athletic director Hootie Ingram in falsifying the eligibility of Alabama cornerback Antonio Langham during the season. In addition to the forfeitures, the NCAA also placed Alabama on a three-year probation and docked it 30 scholarships from 1995 to 1998.

4. Eli Gold, *Bear's Boys: 36 Men Whose Lives Were Changed by Coach Paul Bryant* (Nashville, TN: Nelson Thomas, 2007), 226–27.

5. US Bureau of the Census, *1940 United States Census: Lamar County, Texas*; Stallings and Cook, *Another Season*, 39; Stallings, interview with author, July 9, 2015.

6. *Gazette Telegraph* (Colorado Springs), March 22, 1916.

7. Stallings and Cook, *Another Season*, 40.

8. Ibid., 39–40.

9. Ibid., 30.

10. Ibid.

11. Ibid., 16.

12. Jim Dent, *The Junction Boys: How Ten Days in Hell with Bear Bryant Forged a Championship Team* (New York: St. Martin's, 1999), 2, 5.

13. Stallings, interview with author, July 8, 2015.

14. Ibid.

15. Ibid.

16. Ibid. Steinke played in the National Football League for the Philadelphia Eagles before embarking on a coaching career. He died May 10, 1995, in Austin, Texas, at the age of 76.

17. Ruth Ann Stallings, interview with author, July 9, 2015; Stallings and Cook, *Another Season*, 16.

18. Stallings, interview with author, July 8, 2015.

19. Carolyn Mason, "Life on the Ranch," *Tuscaloosa Magazine*, September 7, 2006; *Thomasville (AL) Times-Enterprise*, May 25, 2015; Stallings, interview with author, July 8, 2015.

20. *Washington Post*, April 21, 1997; *New York Times*, April 22, 1997; Stallings, interview with author, July 8, 2015.

21. Stallings, interview with author, July 8, 2015.

22. Stallings and Cook, *Another Season*, 17; *Birmingham News*, August 3, 2008.

23. *Birmingham News*, August 3, 2008.

24. Ibid.

25. Stallings and Cook, *Another Season*, 10.

26. Stallings, interview with author, July 9, 2015.

27. John Mark Stallings died August 2, 2008 (*Birmingham News*, August 3, 2008).

28. Ibid.

29. Ruth Ann Stallings, interview with author, July 9, 2015.

30. Stallings and Cook, *Another Season*, 163.

31. Ibid., 164.

32. Ibid.

CHAPTER 4

Sing Sing on the Brazos

At first glance, Texas A&M looked like a penitentiary.

—Paul W. Bryant

By February of 1954, Paul W. "Bear" Bryant had earned a reputation as a star among collegiate football coaches after raising the University of Maryland and University of Kentucky programs from the dead. He was also unemployed.

Bryant, in a stubborn fit of defiance—or a perhaps desperate act of survival—abruptly resigned at Kentucky with nine years remaining on his contract. Speculation swirled as the shocking news spread, and the rumors would only multiply in the coming months and years as to why Bryant chose to leave the lush green pastures of Lexington. Theories regarding his sudden departure ranged from the unavoidable shadow of legendary Kentucky basketball coach Adolph Rupp to even whispers of another woman.

Success on the football field certainly wasn't the issue. In eight seasons at Kentucky, Bryant built a top-10 contender that finished in the Associated Press Top Twenty on five separate occasions and compiled a .710 winning percentage (60–23–5). The Wildcats achieved glory under Bryant, capturing their first Southeastern Conference title in 1950 and an 11–1 overall record, topped by a 13–7 upset over Bud Wilkinson's number one–ranked Oklahoma Sooners at the Sugar Bowl in New Orleans.[1]

Prior to Kentucky, Bryant coached one season at Maryland in 1945. He guided the Terrapins to a noteworthy 6–2–1 record—only their second winning season in an eight-year span.

So what went wrong? Questions only intensified when the Kentucky faithful quickly learned Bryant chose to leave Lexington for the isolated outpost of the Agricultural and Mechanical College of Texas—an all-male military school located 95 miles northwest of Houston. Bryant claimed he was "tremendously impressed" by the spirit of A&M's student body during a 10–7 victory by Kentucky over the Aggies in 1952 at College Station.[2] Maybe so, but something didn't quite explain the impulsive nature of his departure.

Some have naively speculated that Bryant's decision had to do with failing to secure Kentucky's top recruit in 1953, halfback Paul Hornung of Flaget High School. "Hornung was the biggest thing to come out of Louisville until Cassius Clay," Bryant said years later.[3] He pursued Horning intensely. Kentucky governor Lawrence Wetherby even visited Hornung and his family on behalf of Bryant, but in the end, the recruit's mother wanted her son to attend the University of Notre Dame. In retrospect, Bryant called Hornung's decision "a good move."[4] Hornung went on to win the Heisman Trophy at Notre Dame and enjoy a Hall of Fame career in the NFL with the Green Bay Packers.

Years later, in perhaps a moment of levity, Bryant introduced Hornung at a banquet as "the reason I left Kentucky."[5] Hornung humbly approached Bryant afterward and stated, "I would appreciate it if you didn't say that. I still have to live in this state."[6]

Though Bryant clearly meant to compliment Hornung with his remark, the coach addressed his failure to recruit Hornung decades later when he wrote, "I've missed on a lot of great players. Losing one more isn't going to make me throw in."[7]

Hornung was never the reason Bryant left Kentucky. Anyone who knows anything about Bryant knows at least that much to be true. Few coaches, if any, won more games as early in their career and with less talent than Bryant. He tried to settle the matter of his departure from Kentucky once and for all in his autobiography, where he offered thoughtful, candid insight into his psyche at the time. In short, he wrote, jealousy fueled his fateful decision.

In those days, Adolph Rupp towered over the Kentucky landscape as arguably the most powerful man in the Bluegrass State. Bryant had witnessed some of that power and influence his first year there during a recruiting trip to Harrodsburg, Kentucky, where a crowd of 20 people and a handful of local reporters gathered. A booster introduced Bryant to the crowd by noting, "I'm sorry we couldn't give Coach Bryant the key to the city, but we have given one to Coach Rupp for all the championships he's had. We'll save one for when Coach Bryant wins as many games."[8]

Bryant fumed. Against his better judgment, Bryant stood before the small gathering and replied, "I don't want a key to the city. When I win as many games as Coach Rupp, I'll be able to buy the damn city and never miss the money."[9] He then sat down.

Another of Bryant's favorite Rupp stories came shortly after his 1950 Kentucky football team won its first Southeastern Conference championship. That same year, Rupp's basketball team won its seventh straight conference title—an accomplishment that prompted boosters to present Rupp with a shiny blue Cadillac with whitewall tires. Bryant related the story at a banquet, reaching into his pocket and adding, "And here's what I got." He pulled out a silver lighter with a Kentucky logo and held it aloft before a laughing audience.[10]

A framed picture in Bryant's den from the banquet of a laughing Bud Wilkinson captured the moment for posterity. Or, more likely, the picture served as motivation for Bryant to always remain hungry.[11]

"The trouble was we were too much alike, and he (Rupp) wanted basketball to be number 1 and wanted football to be number 1," Bryant wrote. "In an environment like that one or the other has to go.

"Rupp and I never had a cross word, actually. I just got tired of seeing the papers full of basketball. . . . Basketball made money in Kentucky, though, and everywhere I went trying to sell the football program it was 'basketball and Rupp, basketball and Rupp,' and I was jealous."[12]

Clearly, the slights to Bryant's football program had gnawed at him since his arrival to Kentucky in 1946. By 1953, his Wildcats had produced their eighth straight winning season, with a 7–2–1 record that included a season-ending 27–21 triumph over rival Tennessee at home. But then came what Bryant biographer and friend Mickey Herskowitz viewed as the final insult. As the story goes, Bryant traveled to Birmingham the first week of February 1954 on a recruiting trip. He picked up a newspaper and read that the university had given Rupp a new contract.[13]

Herskowitz contends that Bryant decided to leave Kentucky at that moment. Nearly 20 years later, however, Herskowitz told fellow Bryant biographer Allen Barra that Rupp wasn't the only reason for Bryant's sudden exodus from Lexington.

"I think it's safe to say that Paul got out of Kentucky just in time to get a grip on his professional and personal life," Herskowitz said. "Texas A&M was a much more difficult row to hoe, but one much more suited to his temperament. There was a lot less—let's say temptation—at A&M. He knew that, and he preferred it that way."[14]

The strongest rumor, Barra reported, involved the daughter of a prominent Kentucky horse breeder who fell in love with Bryant and confronted Mary Harmon. "The story goes that Mary Harmon heard her out and then quietly asked her to leave," Barra wrote. "No names were attached to this story, and a half century later it remains a rumor."[15]

Barra pressed Jones Ramsey—Bryant's publicist and self-professed drinking buddy at A&M—on the rumors. Ramsey confirmed some A&M folks were hesitant to hire Bryant for reasons unrelated to football. "There were some stories," stated Ramsey, who declined to comment further on the matter.[16]

Rumors or not, this period of Bryant's life brought two things into focus: he loved his wife and family dearly, and he fiercely aspired to greatness as a football coach.

Now he simply had to determine his next move. By his own admission, Bryant realized he went "off half-cocked" when he offered his resignation, only to find himself in "a corner."[17]

"My timing was bad," Bryant confessed. By the time he decided to leave Kentucky, he had already turned down lucrative offers from his beloved Alabama as well as the University of Arkansas, Louisiana State University, the University of Minnesota, and the University of Southern California. Each had settled its coaching vacancies; Bryant would have accepted the Alabama offer if Harold "Red" Drew hadn't been the head coach at the time for the Crimson Tide. Bryant refused to bump Drew, whom he held in the highest regard. Drew had mentored Bryant as his tight end coach when unbeaten Alabama (10–0) won the 1934 National Championship.[18]

Bryant harbored too much respect for Drew—and himself—to gain a coaching job that way. He opted for another path. But only one other job offer still remained on the table—at Texas A&M. Bryant momentarily considered sitting out a season to wait for a better coaching gig, only to immediately dash the thought from his mind. Who was he kidding? He wanted to be in the arena. So he picked up the telephone and called Jack Finney, a member of A&M's board of directors. Bryant boldly instructed Finney "to get his pencil sharpened."[19]

"I'll meet you in Dallas tonight," Bryant said. Finney agreed.[20]

The decision to meet in Dallas, as opposed to Houston, helped ensure that the meeting would be a clandestine affair. Two hundred miles and at least three hours of driving separated Dallas from the A&M campus at College Station. The meeting took place near the airport, at the elegant Fairmont Hotel, and when Bryant entered the small room, the drapes were pulled to make it "a real hush-hush deal."[21]

In addition to Finney, board of directors chairman W. T. "Doc" Doherty and board member A. E. Cudlipp were also in attendance. The trio formed A&M's special "advisory" committee in search of a new coach. The *Houston Post* reported that preliminary talks with Bryant had occurred three weeks earlier at the NCAA convention in Cincinnati with A&M athletic director Barlow Irwin and W. L. Penberthy, chairman of the university's athletic council. The duo reportedly offered Bryant a three-year deal worth $11,500 annually at that initial meeting. Another report stated the offer was $12,000. But Doherty, Finney, and Cudlipp realized those paltry sums wouldn't land Bryant, whose contract at Kentucky was estimated to be as high as $17,000 annually.[22]

Bryant, meanwhile, didn't want to talk money at first. He wanted to talk about winning. Money, Bryant surmised, "should always be the last consideration because if you can't win the money's no good anyway."[23]

A simple recruiting question opened the meeting.

"If you could offer a boy the same scholarship deal Texas does, and there were twenty good prospects, how many would we sign?" Bryant asked.[24]

Finney replied, "Ten."

"You mean we could get half?"

"At least."[25]

"Half" impressed Bryant. He knew he could win with half of 20 good prospects. He also knew Finney was exaggerating—grossly. Twenty years later Bryant expressed amusement at Finney's overly optimistic estimation. "I didn't know the Aggies like I know them now," Bryant later wrote. "Old Jack was exaggerating. You couldn't get ten. You would be lucky to get one. The chances were you wouldn't get any. Not then."[26]

Maybe Bryant really knew the answer all along. Maybe he simply wanted to hear it was possible to compete for top recruits at an all-male military school in the middle of nowhere Texas. Or maybe he had no choice. Regardless, Bryant finally moved to the matter of money and the best deal he could possibly negotiate.

If the university's movers and shakers really wanted him to resurrect A&M's football fortunes, he needed money and time. A&M had stopped giving more than a one-year contract to football coaches after alumni paid off the final three years of Homer Norton's contract in 1947. Bryant asked for a six-year contract. The men agreed. Bryant then turned to the matter of money.

"What do the heads of your departments make?" Bryant asked boldly. "I want to make the same, no more, no less."[27]

A figure was provided: $15,000.

"Of course," Bryant said, "you know I can't come for that."[28]

Tensions filled the air momentarily. Minds raced. The Aggies were desperate for a winner and were still living off the glory of 1939—a season in which Norton led A&M to a national championship. The magic of that season probably seemed more like a mirage with each passing season. Finally, Doherty broke the silence with a viable way to sweeten the deal. Doherty, a Houston oilman, offered to place Bryant on his company's payroll for $10,000 a year. In return, Bryant would do some off-season promotional work for Doherty's charitable foundation such as appearances and inspirational talks.[29]

Bryant agreed but pressed further. He wanted as much control as he could obtain. He asked for the title of athletic director, rights to all the game films, a weekly television show aired on Sundays, and an attendance clause for 1 percent of all home gates—a reasonable, yet rare, request at the time.[30]

The committee agreed to each condition. A few days later, on February 4, Texas A&M president Dr. D. H. Morgan formally announced that Bryant had accepted the job with an annual salary of $15,000, making him the highest paid coach not only in A&M history but also in the history of the Southwest Conference. Sportswriter Jerry Ribnick of the *Houston Chronicle* asked Morgan if there was any validity in the rumor that an alumni group agreed to pay Bryant additional money. Morgan angrily replied, "No, I'd have no part of that."[31]

Morgan thought for a moment before calmly adding, "Of course, he may take additional work such as appearing on radio or TV. I understand he did that at Kentucky, and we would pass on that here."[32]

Ribnick and other local sports scribes gushed over Bryant's coaching record and credentials as well as his husky, handsome demeanor—"enough to be given Hollywood movie tests after college," one writer eagerly noted. More important, Bryant became A&M's fourth head coach in eight seasons, and according to Ribnick, the new coach was now charged with leading the once-great Aggies out of the "football wilderness."[33]

Of course, Bryant loved the pressure and spotlight. His first comments regarding A&M were probably scripted in his mind, especially the one about

being attracted to the "spirit of the student body." The Aggie spirit, in fact, probably genuinely impressed Bryant the first time he encountered its fervor in 1952.
But there was something much greater driving the competitive heartbeat of Bryant, who, in a brief moment of candor, acknowledged A&M "presents certain
challenges that appeal to me."[34]

Translation: Bryant saw the Aggies on the scrapheap of college football, and
he wanted to save them or die trying. Legends are built in this manner. By the
sheer magnitude of his presence, a gathering storm of excitement instantly
swirled around this charismatic, 40-year-old coach from Arkansas. A strange
confidence—imagined or otherwise—shadowed him from Moro Bottom to Tuscaloosa, from College Park to Lexington and now to College Station.

"Now that we've got him," a wildly enthusiastic Houston booster proclaimed,
"let's get him the horses to pull the plow."[35]

In Kentucky, meanwhile, sentiments were quite different. The *Lexington
Leader* published a blistering and pious editorial in response to Bryant's resignation. The newspaper especially took issue with Bryant's remaining contract:

> We are, naturally, proud of the record the Kentucky Wildcats have achieved under
> Coach Bryant and of their rapid rise from the conference cellar to national football
> fame, but actually it matters not so much how many games are won and lost, but
> the kind of men the sport develops. And a coach who seeks release from his own
> solemn commitment does not typify the kind of sportsmanship Kentuckians want
> their boys to learn.[36]

Publicly, Bryant said all the right things, thanking everyone for "all the nice
things that happened to me and my family in Kentucky." He intentionally added,
"I assume my resignation will be accepted . . . as soon as practical."[37] Those words
were specifically meant for university president Hermon L. Donovan and athletic
director Bernie Shively, both of whom expressed reservations about releasing
Bryant from his contract.[38]

Bryant anticipated the resistance. So he approached Governor Wetherby, a
friend and supporter who often traveled with Kentucky University sports teams
to events. Wetherby graciously spoke of Bryant to the press, admitting, "I hate to
see Kentucky lose Bryant. I think he's the greatest coach in the country. I also
think he is one of the best builders of young men."[39]

Behind the scenes, the governor told Bryant, "I know why you're here, and I
don't blame you."[40] Bryant asked if he could intercede on his behalf with Donovan

and Shively. Wetherby agreed. As Bryant told it, Wetherby utilized his considerable clout to convince Donovan, Shively, and the athletic board to dissolve the contract. Wetherby needed just one sentence to accomplish his objective: "If this boy's not released by five o'clock today, you all will come by me."[41]

Kentucky released Bryant. Texas A&M now officially had a new football coach, and within 24 hours, he had boarded a plane bound for the Lone Star State.

National and local sportswriters shadowed Bryant's every move en route, even asking him to disembark at Louisville for photographs and questions before leaving for Texas. Bryant obliged for the cameras but declined to talk. By the time the Pioneer airliner landed at College Station's Eastwood Airport at 8:35 p.m. on February 8, Bryant had spent more than 11 hours to reach his destination.[42]

Aggie administrators, students, alumni, and media greeted him like royalty. Two hundred people eagerly welcomed him at the airport, including Chancellor Tom Harrington, W. L. Penberthy, and Barlow Irwin as well as the cocaptains of the football team, Norbert Ohlendorf and Louis Capt. Bryant glanced at Ohlendorf and Capt, and one sportswriter overheard him quip, "I saw too much of you two guys already."[43]

Ohlendorf and Capt were part of the team that had defeated his Wildcats 7–6 in the 1953 season opener less than five months earlier.

Flashbulbs popped and reporters furiously scrawled on their notepads to document every detail of that moment. Also among those present were three assistant coaches from outgoing Aggie coach Ray George's regime—Bill Duncan, Willie Zapalac, and the popular line coach Mike Michalske, whom Penberthy and Irwin had lobbied for as A&M's next head coach. Someone asked whether Bryant had made any decisions regarding his coaching staff, but Bear wasn't biting.

"I'm not ready to announce my staff," Bryant said. "When it has been decided, I'll announce it all at once."[44]

Soon, head yell leader Monte Montgomery and yell leader Jim Tyree whisked Bryant off to the Grove, home of the Aggie spirit rallies. A&M's famed marching band led their way through the outdoor amphitheater with military precision, enthusiastically carving through the throng of frenzied cadets who held aloft torches that flickered wildly in the wind. Waves of cadets crowded excitedly against the stage as the man of the hour reached his destination.

"I do proclaim this Bear Bryant Night," Montgomery screamed from the speaker's podium. "We have got the man here who's going to go the route."[45]

Tyree eagerly added, "Tonight we're having college night because we're on the road to victory."[46]

A thunderous cheer rocked the campus.

Bryant stood in the rear corner of the stage, both inspired and bemused. Ramsey—A&M's colorful sports information director—stood by his side.

"How many ya figure are here?" Bryant asked in his gravelly drawl.

"Best I can tell, about six thousand," Ramsey replied. "Best damn turnout I've ever seen."

"How many we got in school right now?"

"Last count, sixty-two hundred."

"Then where the hell are the other two hundred turds?"

"Don't know, Coach. Maybe we could send a posse out and hang 'em."[47]

Pvt. Gene "Bebes" Stallings, the gangly 6-foot-1, 165-pound sophomore end from Paris, Texas, stood in the crowd. He eagerly waited to catch a glimpse of his new coach. Stallings soaked in the raucous scene that engulfed him. The loud chants and deafening cheers . . . the bobbling torches and spirited Aggie fight song . . . the unharnessed energy of the cadets . . .

Stallings had never experienced anything nearly as exciting back home, not even when Gene Autry rode into town.

"Bebes, we've been saved!" shouted Bill Schroeder, a hulking lad from Lockhart who finished the 1953 season as A&M's starting end.[48]

"I know it looks pretty good!" Stallings yelled above the din. "But I've never heard of this man!"[49]

"Never heard of him—how's that possible?" Schroeder barked in disbelief. "This man's the greatest coach in college football! Shoot, Bebes, he's bigger than Frank Leahy. He's gonna put A&M football back on the map!"[50]

Schroeder tugged on Stallings, and the two youngsters began to shoulder their way through the crowd to join their teammates near the podium.

Onstage, Bryant turned to Ramsey and said, "OK, what should I say to these toy soldiers?"[51]

"My advice is give 'em what they want," Ramsey replied. "Hell, you could bring down the damn house with a loud burp."[52]

In truth, Bryant didn't need any advice. Not for a moment such as this one. If this coach understood anything, it was human nature and the theater of life. He'd understood it as a youngster when he accepted a challenge to run barefoot from Fordyce to Smith Chapel. He'd understood it when he wrestled the bear at the Lyric Theatre. And he'd understood it when the drapes were pulled closed at the Fairmont Hotel in Dallas.

Bryant had been studying people his whole life, but for the Aggie faithful, there really wasn't much to study. They desperately hungered for a savior, and he instinctively stepped from the shadows onto the stage to play his role.

Bryant's famed charisma kicked in. The 6-foot-3, 225-pounder peeled off his beaver hat and coat, violently slamming the larger garment on the stage. He ripped off his tie, rolled up his shirt sleeves, and glared menacingly into the crowd.

Cheers erupted.

"I don't know about you, but I'm ready to play tonight," Bryant bellowed. "What I'm seeing here this evening is the reason why I'm thankful to the Lord I'm an Aggie."[53]

Bryant stared into the audience and warned, "Let's be realistic, we have a momentous task . . ." The coach uncharacteristically stuttered as the word "momentous" left his mouth, quickly scaling back his frankness for "a tough job, I mean."[54]

"It will mean a lot of hard work," he continued. "If we work as a team, we can get the job done. I assure you that I will do everything in my power to control the athletic program in all departments. And remember that the athletic program is only a small part of the whole job at this great school. I hope we can maintain a high standard on and off the campus as well as in sports. . . . If anyone asks me again why I came to Aggieland, I certainly can tell them now.

"Thanks so much."[55]

Stallings stood in awe at the giant man on stage.

"He was a big man." Stallings marveled in the remembrance. "He told us he came to A&M to win, and we believed him."[56]

In the hours and days that followed, the optimism and excitement spread to all corners of the A&M family. Bryant knew he would build a winning team at A&M one way or another. He also knew his first—and possibly greatest—challenge would be recruitment, and not in the typical sense. Recruiting is competitive by nature, whether you are the coach at the University of Southern California or Alabama. College Station offered a unique challenge in this respect, starting with the fact that A&M was an all-male military institution with no women on campus.

College Station also sat in seclusion, surrounded by an ocean of rich, rolling farmland in Brazos County. Both before and after the Texas Revolution, early colonists eagerly sought this land for its fertile soil, access to the Brazos River, and abundance of wild game. Football recruits, however, proved to be a tougher sell.

Privately, Bryant understood the odds of recruiting choice players were stacked against him. On his return trip to College Station with his wife, Mary Harmon, and their children, he studied the campus and mentally assessed those odds at a place Texans referred to as "Sing Sing on the Brazos."[57]

"At first glance, Texas A&M looked like a penitentiary," Bryant said. "No girls. No glamour. A lifeless community. A&M is a great educational institution, but at the time it was the toughest place in the world to recruit because nobody wanted to go there."[58]

Quarterback Don Meredith fit into that category.

Meredith, who later went on to play nine seasons for the Dallas Cowboys, had starred in football and basketball at Mount Vernon High School, some 100 miles east of Dallas. Bryant wanted Meredith "in the worst way," and worked overtime to sell him on A&M. Meredith even made an impression on Mary Harmon, once grabbing a towel and helping her wash dishes after dinner while on a recruitment visit to the Bryant home in College Station.

Coach Bryant and Meredith also connected, and it was clear he wanted to play for "Bear." He just didn't want to play for Bear at A&M.

"I flew up to Mount Vernon and he drove me to his house, and the tears came to his eyes," Bryant recalled. "When I saw those tears I knew I'd lost him."[59]

Meredith sobbed, "Coach, if you were anywhere else in the world except A&M—anywhere in the world . . ."[60]

Southern Methodist University signed Meredith shortly thereafter.

Another of Bryant's favorite recruiting stories involved one of his loyal assistant coaches, Elmer Smith. Bryant dispatched Smith to Alabama in the summer of 1954 to scout for any unsigned players. Smith called from an all-star game, somewhat dejected.

"Are there any who aren't signed, any who can play?" Bryant inquired.

"Yeah, there's one," Smith replied.

"Then sign him."

"Well, coach, there is one thing," Smith added. "He's only got one arm."

"Damn," Bryant said, "the pickin's are slim."[61]

Bryant instructed Smith to sign him anyway. The player was Murray "Stubby" Trimble, who earned All-Southwest Conference honors as guard his sophomore year for the Aggies. Trimble's toughness became legendary, beginning with his first trip to College Station. Trimble famously hitchhiked all the way from his home in Hanceville, Alabama, to begin his collegiate career.[62]

Money certainly played a role in some recruiting after Bryant's arrival at A&M. Decades later, even Bear admitted money changed hands.

"I'm not sure how many of our boys got something," he said. "I guess about four or five did. I didn't know what they got, and I didn't want to know, but they got something because they had other offers and I told my alumni to meet the competition."[63]

A&M's overzealous alumni undoubtedly stepped up to answer the call. In his best-selling book, *The Junction Boys*, author Jim Dent tells an incredible—if not outright untruthful—story regarding the payment of recruits. In one passage, Dent describes Bryant taking center stage in a room full of wealthy Aggie alumni. Bryant placed a silver spittoon on a table and said, "I made my commitment when I took this job. Now it's time for you to make yours."[64]

At first, no one moved a muscle.

"Boys," Bryant continued in Dent's yarn, "just think of this as going to church and dropping dough in the plate. Let's see how much commitment you got in your hearts."[65]

Rubber-banded rolls of 100-dollar bills began filling the spittoon, according to Dent. By the time each alumnus in the room had made his donation, Dent claimed there was $30,000 in the spittoon—enough to lure "two or three good players."[66]

Herskowitz, for one, doubted the silver spittoon story ever happened.

"The alumni spent some money, there's certainly no question about that," Herskowitz told fellow Bryant biographer Allen Barra. "But I don't believe Bryant ever saw any of it. Of course A&M gave money to players; all the Texas schools did, even Rice, which liked to think of itself as the Harvard of the Southwest. For that matter, I seriously doubt if there was a major football program in this country whose alumni didn't get money to its football players one way or the other. But smart coaches didn't want to know the specifics, they looked the other way. It wasn't necessarily something they could control anyway, and in any event Bryant didn't try."[67]

Philosophically, Bryant didn't believe in the widespread payment of players. He generally thought that those who received money didn't play as hard—a fundamental philosophy that was probably based on his firsthand knowledge of certain players.

Bryant also wasn't a fan of alumni butting into his business. Or anyone else, for that matter.

For instance, the pending selection of his coaching staff sparked a lot of chatter from alumni and media. Everyone wanted to know who Bryant might keep, if anyone. Several A&M linemen were asked to weigh in on the fate of their popular line coach, Mike Michalske, for an article in the *Battalion*. "I don't know much about Bryant, but I sure hope he keeps Mike (Michalske) on his staff as a line coach," said Ray Barrett, a senior guard.[68]

Center Fred Broussard, A&M's lone returning All-Southwest Conference player, chose his words for the reporter unwisely: "I don't care who they got for head coach, just so long as they keep Mike."[69]

Bryant retained one assistant coach from George's staff—the energetic Zapalac. He sent everyone else—Michalske included—packing.

Bryant's message became clear to everyone at A&M: he alone was in charge. Broussard, meanwhile, would learn this lesson the hard way.

NOTES

1. Despite the loss, Oklahoma walked away as the consensus national champions thanks to polls by the AP and NCAA coaches. The final polls for both showed the Sooners at number 1.
2. *Battalion*, February 5, 1954. The *Battalion* is the student newspaper of Texas A&M University. The daily newspaper began as a monthly publication in 1893 and continues to this day.
3. Bryant and Underwood, *Bear*, 118.
4. Ibid.
5. Herskowitz, *Legend*, 77.
6. Ibid.
7. Bryant and Underwood, *Bear*, 118.
8. Ibid., 118–19.
9. Ibid., 119.
10. Bryant and Underwood, *Bear*, 120; Herskowitz, *Legend*, 73. Herskowitz further claimed that Bryant used the joke from time to time and always pulled the Kentucky lighter from his pocket for maximum laughs.
11. Bryant and Underwood, *Bear*, 120.
12. Ibid., 118.
13. Herskowitz, *Legend*, 76.
14. Barra, *Last Coach*, 160.
15. Ibid.
16. Ibid. Ramsey died in Austin, Texas, on July 19, 2004—a year before the release of Barra's book. Ramsey's career spanned more than 30 years. He served as University

of Texas sports information director from 1960 until his retirement in 1982, and he once semi-jokingly declared the only sports in Texas were "football and spring football." Prior to his tenure at Texas, he worked for nine years at Texas A&M, including during Bryant's period from 1954 to 1957 (*American-Statesman* [Austin], July 19, 2004).

17. Bryant and Underwood, *Bear*, 122.
18. Ibid., 117–18, 121.
19. Ibid., 126.
20. Ibid.
21. Ibid.
22. *Dallas Morning News*, February 5, 1954; *Houston Post*, February 5, 1954; *Battalion*, February 5, 1954.
23. Bryant and Underwood, *Bear*, 126.
24. Ibid.
25. Ibid.
26. Ibid.
27. Ibid.
28. Ibid.
29. Ibid.
30. Herskowitz, *Legend*, 78; Barra, *Last Coach*, 158.
31. *Houston Post*, February 5, 1954; *Houston Chronicle*, February 5, 1954.
32. *Houston Chronicle*, February 5, 1954.
33. *Dallas Morning News*, February 5, 1954; *Houston Chronicle*, February 5, 1954.
34. *Battalion*, February 5, 1954.
35. *Bryan (TX) Daily Eagle*, n.d., 1954. A copy may be found in the Paul "Bear" Bryant vertical file, Cushing Memorial Library and Archives, Texas A&M University.
36. Republished in the *Bryan (TX) Daily Eagle*, February 8, 1954.
37. *Battalion*, February 5, 1954.
38. Bryant and Underwood, *Bear*, 122; *Battalion*, February 5, 1954.
39. *Battalion*, February 5, 1954.
40. Bryant and Underwood, *Bear*, 122.
41. Ibid.
42. *Junction (TX) Eagle*, February 8, 1954; *Houston Chronicle*, February 9, 1954; *Dallas Morning News*, February 9, 1954.
43. *Houston Post*, February 9, 1954.
44. *Bryan (TX) Daily Eagle*, February 9, 1954.
45. Ibid.
46. Ibid.
47. Dent, *Junction Boys*, 6.
48. Ibid., 5.
49. Ibid.
50. Ibid.

51. Ibid., 6.

52. Ibid.

53. *Bryan (TX) Daily Eagle*, February 9, 1954; *Houston Post*, February 9, 1954.

54. *Houston Post*, February 9, 1954.

55. Ibid.

56. Stallings, interview with author, July 8, 2015.

57. Bryant and Underwood, *Bear*, 125.

58. Ibid., 124.

59. Ibid.

60. Ibid.

61. Ibid., 129.

62. *Cullman (AL) Times*, October 14, 2015. Trimble died October 10, 2015, at the age of 79.

63. Bryant and Underwood, *Bear*, 140.

64. Dent, *Junction Boys*, 13.

65. Ibid.

66. Ibid.

67. Barra, *Last Coach*, 167.

68. *Battalion*, February 5, 1954.

69. Ibid.

CHAPTER 5
Junction

We left College Station on two buses, and returned on one.
—Gene Stallings

Elmer Parrott never expected to be living in Junction, Texas, in 1954. Life had steered the onetime sand and gravel business owner down an unexpected path to his current position as facility manager of the Junction Adjunct—A&M's summer campus for students trying to make the transition from high school to college. Upperclassmen studying geology and engineering also used the facility for fieldwork, and Parrott's task would be the daily oversight of the facilities.

Administrators sent Parrott to the Adjunct in 1950, and what was supposed to be a six-month stopover turned into a 23-year stay. Prior to his arrival in Junction, Parrott served the US Army Air Corps stateside during World War II. At the war's triumphant conclusion, he was assigned to the old Bryan Air Force Base, just west of Bryan, Texas. It was here that he and his wife, Mattie Lee, started a family, and their only child, Wanda, was born in 1946.[1]

Their move to Junction four years later, in 1950, offered the small family a chance to build new memories, and the town didn't disappoint.

Parrott fell in love with Junction and the Adjunct, a 411-acre patch carved from Kimble County's rugged terrain of dense vegetation, cedar brakes, mesquite trees, and sedge grasses. The Adjunct's campus itself offered more than a mile of scenic property on the South Llano River lined by stout oak trees and groves of pecan trees that students studied. The property also featured a long administrative building with classrooms, a library, a mess hall, and a medical clinic constructed with steel frames, concrete floors, and—as one college bulletin boasted—corrugated "concrete asbestos roofs."[2] The student living quarters were a bit more spartan, consisting of a cluster of 20 screened Quonset huts, or "cabins," as they were generously called. Each hut housed as many as 12 students on metal-frame bunks beneath its tin roof. The quarters were located near a tiled bathhouse and offered electricity but no air conditioning.[3]

Parrott took great pride as manager of the facility.

As for the town, its founders originally called it Junction City. They surveyed the area in 1876 and selected a breathtaking grassy valley nestled at the fork of the North and South Llano Rivers—hence the name Junction City. In 1927, the town was incorporated, and its name was shortened to "Junction."

Miles of caliche, cacti, and thorny mesquites separated Junction from the rest of the world. San Antonio—the closest major city—was 114 miles to the east. The nearest border town was 123 miles to the south in Del Rio. Still, Junction's isolation offered solitude and its own unique brand of beauty for the soul. The region teemed with wildlife. Whitetail deer, turkeys, quail, rabbits, coyotes, and mountain lions occupied the landscape, where clusters of lush green vegetation often belied the region's harsh terrain.

Junction's downtown offered a quaint row of businesses, no differently than most small towns of the period. Main Street served as the central thoroughfare for the community and buzzed with six gas stations, seven motels, two saloons, a bank, a grocery store, a theater, a café, three restaurants, an infirmary, a newspaper office, and a department store. A highway billboard outside town proudly proclaimed: "JUNCTION—Front Porch to West Texas."

Parrott certainly had no complaints. Junction had provided a bit of an oasis for him and his small family since their arrival in 1950.

By 1954, however, Junction resembled anything but an oasis.

West Texas was four years into a historic drought by then, one that mercilessly punished Texans until 1957. Insufficient rainfall plunged the entire state into a water shortage and left farmers and ranchers peering helplessly into the skies whenever a hint of dark clouds gathered. Folks in West Texas suffered more than others. Thirsty cattle bawled, creeks turned to powder, old wells ran dry, and crops withered in the dust. The late novelist Elmer Kelton wrote what is generally considered the best account of those parched years in his novel *The Time It Never Rained*. In the book, Kelton writes, "It crept out of Mexico, touching first along the brackish Pecos and spreading then in all directions, a cancerous blight burning a scar upon the land."

The drought forever scarred the landscape as well as the psyches of those who witnessed its wrath.

"The cattle would weaken down, and then the wild hogs would just start eating 'em while they were alive," recalled Eugene Kelton, Elmer's brother. "They'd be laying there bawling, and those wild hogs'd be eating on 'em. So I fell out with hogs right there."[4]

West Texans waited for the drought to break. In the meantime, the buzzards circled from above.

"I've had hailstorms that killed three hundred lambs," former rancher Mort Mertz once recalled. "I've had lightning kill sixty to seventy sheep at one time. I've had lightning kill my saddle horse, my cows. I've had bad fires that burned up all my fences. The drought was a hundred times worse."[5]

It was into this drama that Parrott unexpectedly recorded another bit of history in September 1954 with a new Bell and Howell 8-millimeter movie camera he had recently purchased in Austin. Parrott loved to film the outdoors and his family's excursions, but it's his 3 minutes of color footage—often blurry—of the Texas A&M football team's arrival to Junction for preseason training that will be forever remembered by football historians.[6]

Parrott's film captures the moment A&M's two powder-blue-and-white buses rolled into the drought-plagued town and shows players kicking up clouds of dust as they run across an open field during drills at the Adjunct. The film is the only one known to exist of Paul "Bear" Bryant's immortal Junction Boys in action.[7]

Or, as those Aggies themselves would say, the only known film of them in Hell.

•   •   •

Bryant didn't want to be bothered by meddling Aggie alumni or administrators; by overzealous fans, coddling parents, or snooping reporters. He didn't want to hear their voices. He didn't even want to see their faces. He wanted his players to focus—heck, *he* wanted to focus. He not only had a team to mold for the upcoming season but also had to first separate the wheat from the chaff, the heart from the faint of heart. Who were his fighters?

Bryant wanted to determine whom he could count on in the trenches.

In order to achieve this objective, Bryant believed he had to flee College Station for some remote locale where he could eliminate distractions. He desired a place where he could run his players through fire without interference. He didn't want a preseason training camp as much as a survival boot camp.

So in July, Bryant secretly dispatched assistant coaches Phil Cutchin and Willie Zapalac to search for the perfect site for a preseason camp.[8] Both assistants were typical of the kind Bryant surrounded himself with: tough, gruff, no-nonsense coaches who lived by an old-school code.

Zapalac, then 33, was a World War II veteran who had completed 32 bombing missions in the Pacific as a navigator. He was later promoted to squadron bombardier for the 484th Bomb Squadron, retiring as a captain. Prior to the war, Zapalac had emerged as a heavily recruited running back from Bellville, Texas, where he had led his high school team to the state championship in 1938 with an 11–0 record. "Wild" Willie Zapalac, as he was then known, rushed for 2,189 yards that season and averaged 9.2 yards per carry. He signed with A&M in 1939 and had played in two Cotton Bowls by the time his college career had concluded.[9] In 1947, the Pittsburgh Steelers drafted him, but injuries cut his professional playing career short. He turned to coaching.

Cutchin, slightly shy of 34, was already a veteran of two wars. He initially played two seasons for Kentucky (1941–42) before serving an 18-month, noncombative stint in the US Army in France during World War II. He later returned to the army to fight in the Korean War, where he saw combat as a first lieutenant and received a citation as a company commander. At one point during the fighting, he received a slight wound when a bullet grazed his nose.[10]

In 1946, Cutchin returned from the war to play one final season as Kentucky's quarterback during Bryant's first season at the helm. Cutchin became Bryant's first team captain.[11] He preceded the legendary quarterback George Blanda, who earned a spot in Kentucky's starting lineup in 1947 on his way to a Hall of Fame career. Cutchin, meanwhile, joined Bryant's Kentucky coaching staff in 1952 and then followed him to College Station.

Now Cutchin and Zapalac were being entrusted by Bryant to produce a secretive site for summer training. As one version of the story goes, Zapalac initially told Bryant of a distant place at the western edge of the Texas Hill Country, a remote town where A&M managed a spacious facility with lush green fields on the banks of the South Llano River known as the Adjunct. The frontier town? Junction.[12]

Intrigued, Bryant told Zapalac and Cutchin to acquire more information about the availability of the location, which was some 250 miles east of College

Station. The two returned to Bryant with different opinions. Cutchin remained hesitant because of the Adjunct's spartan facilities and its remoteness on the Texas frontier. Zapalac, however, thought Junction would serve as the perfect location for those same reasons.

"Coach, it kinda looks like an old army base, even though it's pretty new," Zapalac reportedly said. "They didn't waste much money slapping it together, but there's a helluva lot of land. And, Coach, you can just look into those rocky bluffs and still see them Comanches [sic] charging down the hill in war paint. It's kind of exciting, really."[13]

Junction's remoteness is mostly what sold Bryant in the end. What no one seemed to consider—or perhaps respect—was the severity of the drought in West Texas, where thirsty cattle were literally dropping dead on the hardened, sunbaked land. The lush green fields of the Adjunct's recent past were now barren and riddled with prickly goat's head thorns.

Apparently, Zapalac underestimated the region's apocalyptic transformation. But that revelation would come soon enough.

Bryant called a team meeting in late August. The month had already been a tumultuous one for Bryant, who had received an emergency call while he and his family were on vacation. His beloved mother had suffered a stroke. Paul, Mary Harmon, and their children immediately boarded an airplane for Arkansas. They drove to the hospital where Ida was lying in bed, unresponsive and wearing an oxygen mask.

Tears streamed down Bryant's cheeks as he stood at his mother's bedside.

"Sweetheart," he said, grabbing her hand, "this is the first time I've squeezed your hand that you failed to squeeze mine."[14]

Ida Kilgore Bryant—arguably the toughest person Paul ever knew—died August 2, at age 77.[15]

Shadowed by this great loss, Bryant returned to work to mold a new team. More than 100 players gathered for Bryant's meeting. He told them to each grab a blanket, a pillow, and a couple changes of clothing because they were "going on a little trip."[16] Stallings remembered Bryant firmly ordered the players to be packed and ready in front of the dorms in 10 minutes.

They were ready in five.

Suddenly, two empty powder-blue-and-white buses pulled up in front of the dorms.

"We climbed aboard and moved off and nobody knew our destination," Stallings recalled. "And nobody asked. It was that kind of feeling."[17]

Freshman halfback John David Crow, A&M's top recruit, watched the team board the buses in frustration. Assistant coach Elmer Smith told Crow that he and the other freshmen athletes wouldn't be allowed to go on the trip, since NCAA rules forbid first-year players from varsity practices.

Crow felt disheartened.

"Coach Elmer told me it would be just players and coaches and football," Crow once recalled. "He said it was a nice place with a camp on a river, and the only camp I had ever been to was a Methodist camp.

"I thought it would be like a picnic."[18]

Crow's assumption couldn't have been more wrong. He and every other Aggie player were equally in the dark about the team's destination. Bryant later referred to Junction as "a flyspeck on the map out in the hill country near Kerrville."[19] His description was much harsher in the summer of 1954. As the team buses rolled west of Austin, Bryant began to notice the landscape gradually changing from green to brown. Dry creek beds could be seen as they crossed one bridge after another. Buzzards populated the sky.

Bryant grumbled, "I've never seen so many goddamned birds in my life."[20]

"The farther we go, the hotter and drier it gets," Smith painfully noted. "It just ain't gonna get no better."[21]

Miles of desolate terrain increased in the rearview mirror as the buses approached Junction. Zapalac sat uncomfortably in silence.

Finally, after more than 10 hours on the road, the buses cruised down a rocky hillside 2 miles east of town and crossed the Flatrock Bridge over the South Llano River. Ironically, below the bridge gushed clear water. Fed by 700 springs, the flowing river contrasted greatly with the parched land that greeted the team as it entered the front gate of the Adjunct.

There, with rocky bluffs framing the eastern skyline, the Aggies stared out the bus windows at a mostly barren, rocky field littered with goat's head. The hardened, dusty field—broken by green patches of grass watered faithfully by Parrott from a well—resembled a cow pasture more than a collegiate football field.[22]

"I think I'm gonna puke," muttered Bryant, glaring at Zapalac. "Was this your idea, Willie? Or was this just some goddamn prank."[23]

No one laughed.

As for the players, they were still uncertain what this long-distance excursion across Texas meant. So they settled in as young men might do on a leisurely camping trip. They found their assigned Quonset hut, dropped off their pillows and blankets, and searched the grounds for something fun to do. Some engaged in a touch football game, although the sun baked them thoroughly as they played. Eventually, someone found what would fondly become known as the Aggie Swimming Hole and jumped in. Others peeled off their shirts and jeans and gleefully followed.[24]

"See, I told you boys!" shouted Dennis Goehring, a 5-foot-11, 185-pound sophomore guard from San Marcos, Texas. "This place is gonna be fun. Just wait til the girls find out we're here."[25]

Zapalac watched as the boys jumped into the swimming hole one after another. He flew into a rage, hollering, "Hey! Wait just a goddamn minute!"[26]

Bryant stopped him before he could spit out another angry word.

"Let the little peckerheads go," Bryant grumbled. "Let 'em have their fun. They'll be too tired tomorrow to fart."[27]

Unaware of the impending pain, the players continued to splash and romp in the water as if at summer camp. Later that night, they congregated inside their assigned Quonset huts, laughing and telling stories. Stallings remembered his group was playing cards and joking around when Bryant walked in unannounced.

The coach silently looked around the room.

"No more card playing after tonight," Bryant barked in his familiar drawl. "And I won't have to tell you anymore."[28]

Bryant's tone instantly set an ominous mood, just as he had intended. The cards disappeared after that night. So did the fun.

Stallings and his roommates eventually dozed off for the night, some perhaps wondering what the next day might bring. The answer arrived soon enough. Hours later, before sunrise, the players were roused from their bunks when student team manager Troy Summerlin stormed from one hut to the next, blowing his whistle. Summerlin—all 145 pounds of him—yelled as loud as he could for the players to wake up, put on their uniforms, and assemble on the field in 5 minutes.[29]

"I wasn't sure if I was dreaming or not as I jumped out of my bunk, grabbed my pants and jersey, and pulled them on," Stallings said. "Even though it was still dark out, we were all lined up, fully dressed, and out on the field a few minutes later."[30]

Bryant strode onto the field like a general as the sun poked over the nearby bluffs. The conditioning commenced shortly thereafter. No breakfast would be served on this day. Only pain. Players were soon clashing in a controlled scrimmage in full pads on a rocky, open field. Parrott's green patches were mostly mowed weeds and burrs. Stallings recalled, "You'd get down in your stance and you'd come up with a handful of sand burrs."[31]

The sand burrs—also known as goat's head—constantly plagued the players, whose hands and forearms quickly became bloodied.

"They're the worst of grass spurs because they have two horns on them and they puncture the skin and stick to you," Goehring told a reporter decades later.[32] In the same interview, he concluded, "It wasn't a football field. It wasn't any kind of field."[33]

The heat also proved merciless. Each day the temperatures climbed into the triple digits.

"From a heat standpoint, I was a Hill Country guy to begin with," Goehring said. "I didn't feel the impact of the heat that much. I was an old farm boy from a ranch, and you were out there all day in the heat bailing and working.

"The problem was more probably from a lack of water."[34]

Bryant subscribed to a philosophy common in those days: withhold water to develop a tougher athlete. The Aggies were forbidden to take water breaks.

"Times have changed," Stallings said upon reflection. "In those days, they felt like it probably prevented you from getting into shape if you took a little water."[35]

As a result, most of Bryant's players lost significant body weight in the searing heat.

Herskowitz, then a cub reporter for the *Houston Post*, eagerly telephoned his editor from a pay phone to describe in great detail the pain and suffering endured by the Aggies on the first day of training. He spoke of the "bone-crunching tackles" and "helmets clashing." While most college teams set aside the first practice for photographs and paperwork, Herskowitz noted with a sense of wonderment Bryant's desire for militaristic intensity on day one.

Herskowitz began to dictate his story.

Only his editor wasn't the only person listening. The pay phone shared a common wall with the room where the coaches held their meetings, and the walls were thin. Bryant and his staff heard every word. Herskowitz remembered hearing the booming voices of the coaches when he dialed his editor. Then suddenly, he noticed that the voices had gone silent. He glanced at Jones Ramsey, the team's jovial publicity man with whom he shared a room. Ramsey sat on one of the room's beds, "nervously tapping his index finger against his thumb."[36]

When Herskowitz hung up the phone, a student manager—perhaps the whistle-blowing Summerlin—was standing nearby. "Coach Bryant would like to see you," the youngster said sheepishly. By the time Herskowitz entered the meeting room, Bryant's assistant coaches had scattered.

The young reporter stood alone with Bryant.

A restrained Bryant explained that he hadn't meant to eavesdrop on Herskowitz, but he couldn't help but overhear some Herskowitz's conversation with his editor. The words, Bryant said, left him disturbed. Herskowitz sensed tension in Bryant's voice as he frowned and asked incredulously, "Did I hear you say something about bones getting mangled?"[37]

Prior to Junction, Herskowitz had mainly covered high schools and Little League baseball, hoping for the opportunity to display his talents on a bigger stage. He was given his big chance when Clark Nealon, then sports editor of the *Houston Post*, assigned Herskowitz to cover Bryant's Aggies. Bryant fascinated Nealon, himself an A&M alumnus. The *Houston Post* therefore became the first major daily newspaper to dedicate a reporter to full-time coverage of the Aggie football program.

The assignment promised to be the major career break Herskowitz desired. Now he realized he had angered the one man everyone wanted to read about the most on his new beat. He stood quietly as Bryant waited for an answer.

"It does sound familiar, Coach," Herskowitz finally replied. "But I think I said 'crunched,' not 'mangled.'"[38]

"Now, Mickey," Bryant said, "you know that story's going to upset a lot of mamas and papas when they read it."[39]

"Yessir."[40]

"And it's so unnecessary," Bryant shrewdly continued. "That was no full-scale scrimmage. That was no more than a dummy scrimmage. Don't you think you ought to call your paper and tell them what really happened?"[41]

Herskowitz thought for a moment, clearly weighing his journalistic integrity against the intimidation he felt from the charismatic Paul "Bear" Bryant. To be fair, Herskowitz was young—younger even than some Aggie players at the time. "I was too young to realize how shrewd he was being," Herskowitz said years later. "He could see I was prepared to resist him if he came at me too hard. But the way he did it made me think, 'Well, damn, this guy's won a lot of football games and he knows a hell of a lot more about football than I do. What if he's right?' I was afraid that maybe I just didn't know enough about football to know the difference, so I called my editor and persuaded him to do a little—let's call it 'light'—editing."[42]

The aura of "the Bear" had again worked its magic.

Yet Bryant's patience could only extend so far in the stifling heat of the Hill Country. Shortly after the team's arrival, three local businessmen presented Bryant with another challenge. They had the audacity to invite Bryant, his staff, and players to a local barbecue in their honor. J. B. McKinney (owner of the downtown department store), Squirt Newby, and Buckshot Jones—all A&M fans—extended the invitation in person at Bryant's office.

Bryant impatiently listened to the men, surely thinking about why he fled College Station in the first place. Interlopers, or so the coach saw these men, only distracted him and his staff from the dirty work at hand. Bryant realized they only had so much time to essentially build a team—and a culture—from scratch, and time was short.

So was Bryant's patience. He tersely replied, "We didn't come out here to eat, we came out here to play football."[43]

Stunned and likely offended, the three men quietly departed with their hats literally in hand. Word spread of Bryant's surly demeanor and foul mouth. Parrott, for one, would return home after long hours at the Adjunct and refer to the new A&M coach as "a crusty old guy."[44]

Stallings, naturally, defended the memory of the man he grew to respect and love.

"I don't know what kind of language others might regard as offensive, but I didn't hear anything from Coach Bryant on the practice field I hadn't heard a lot of other places. He wasn't *that* foulmouthed—he used his words selectively because he wanted to make an impact."[45]

Jack Pardee, then a sophomore fullback, enjoyed Bryant's cursing.

"To tell you the truth, it was kind of amusing," Pardee told one Bryant biographer. "And believe me, there wasn't much else about those practices that was amusing. I kind of got a kick out of waiting to see what cuss words were going to come out of his mouth next and how creative he was going to be in stringing the expressions together. He never let us down."[46]

Rob Roy Spiller, then a local teenager who worked at the bus station, witnessed Bryant at work several nights during A&M's stay in Junction. Bryant held nightly scrimmages down the road from the Adjunct, under the spotty lights at the high school football field. Those sessions attracted large crowds, sometimes even as many as 100 people in a town of some 2,500 souls.

"Of course, there wasn't much else to do in Junction," mused Spiller, now chairman of the board at Junction National Bank. As for the legendary Bryant,

Spiller said, "No one really thought too much of him. A lot of us felt bad for those players. We were used to a [high school] coach who was strict, but straightlaced. Coach Bryant wasn't. He was kind of like a tyrant. He just cracked the whip."[47]

And withheld water during practices.

In that respect, it's a miracle no one died, although tackle Bill Schroeder came dangerously close one day. The 6-foot-1, 200-pound junior from Lockhart last remembered breaking from a huddle and bending down in a three-point stance for the dreaded punt drills. The drills required the players to run as fast as they could for punt coverage and then run back for another punt. By then, players were moving on sheer will, with lungs burning and mouths that felt like cotton for hours. Players routinely dropped from heat exhaustion. Those who couldn't run, walk, or crawl back to the huddle were quickly dragged to the side by student managers.

Suddenly, before the next punt, Schroeder bent down and toppled to the mostly gravel field. A cloud of dust popped up, but the husky lineman lay motionless.

Billy Pickard, an assistant to head trainer Smokey Harper, rushed onto the field.[48] Pickard's services had been invaluable as players continuously dropped from heat exhaustion, but Schroeder's condition instantly scared him.

"He's dying!" Pickard reportedly yelled. "We gotta get him to Doc Wiedeman. Somebody fetch my Ford!"[49]

Pickard and a few players hurriedly loaded Schroeder into the backseat of the vehicle. But Schroeder was tall. His feet extended beyond the doorway. So Pickard told one of the players to hold his teammate tightly, and they sped away with Schroeder's feet dangling out a partially open door.

Minutes later, they arrived downtown to the infirmary, where Schroeder was placed on a stretcher and wheeled inside for Dr. J. E. Wiedeman to examine. Other Aggie casualties previously taken to the hospital watched the drama unfold with ice packs pressed against their wounds. Vomit began to spout from Schroeder's now-purplish mouth.

Wiedeman immediately diagnosed Schroeder with heatstroke and ordered him packed in ice. Two nurses jumped into action. Schroeder later described an out-of-body experience that day, wondering why he was looking down on his own purple body and seeing nurses pack him in ice. Wiedeman and the nurses watched over Schroeder as his temperature dropped. The doctor never forgot Schroeder's first words as he slowly regained consciousness. Groggy and still disoriented, Schroeder said, "I'm sorry, Coach Bryant. God, I'm really sorry."[50]

Schroeder returned to practice the next day.

A few players were actually jealous of Schroeder. He was given water to drink and packed in ice. "I almost wished I had passed out," Pardee said enviously. "Maybe I'da gotten a drink, too."[51] Goehring echoed Pardee's twisted sentiments. "Most of the time, we were running around cotton mouthed," Goehring said. "Packed in ice? That sounded pretty good to us. We weren't sure we wanted to have a heatstroke in order to get to the ice, but it sure was something we thought about."[52]

The Junction camp soon became a test of mental strength. Even the short periods of rest were trying experiences. Stallings, for instance, remembered trying to get a little rest in his Quonset hut during afternoon breaks. As an underclassman, he received the last choice of where to sleep and got stuck with a top bunk. He lay in the bunk, with a hot tin roof a foot from his face. "I could barely breathe," Stallings recalled, "it was so sweltering."[53]

The dwindling numbers also made the drills tougher.

"In the beginning, we might have fifteen ends," Stallings explained. "You have a chance to rest while other players run through their drills. Then fifteen turned ten, ten turned seven, and finally seven turned to five. Soon, there's no time to take a break."[54]

Coach Bryant certainly wasn't waiting.

"It became a test of your physical and mental endurance," said Pardee, who lost 20 pounds at Junction. "It was hot as hell and it was demanding as hell . . . and some guys just couldn't take it."[55]

Defections were common.

During those afternoon breaks, Stallings frequently watched players approach a water fountain outside. They would walk to the fountain and take a drink. Sometimes, they walked away, only to return a few moments later to mill around. Sometimes, they gathered around the fountain in small groups of two or three.

The players were trying to scrounge up enough courage to knock on Bryant's hut door. Eventually, someone would knock and walk in.

"We'd all be watching through the window," Stalling said. "When they came out they'd look kind of relieved, in a nervous way, and they'd grin and wave at the rest of us."[56]

Summerlin would then be summoned to drive the departing players to the bus station downtown.

Not everyone possessed the courage to face Bryant, though. Numerous defectors left in the middle of the night, either hitching a ride out of Junction or walking downtown to the bus station. Players would generally hear some rustling in the dark or a hut door open and close. After a while, they knew what the noises meant: another casualty.

Spiller worked at the downtown Texaco gas station, which also doubled as the town's bus depot. The teenager pumped gas, fixed tires, and sold bus tickets.

The Aggies kept him hopping.

"I'd get there in the morning, and there would usually be two or three A&M players waiting at the station to catch a bus out of town," Spiller recalled. "I'd always ask, 'Which way ya headin'?' A few replied, 'Where's the first bus goin'? I'll take that one.'

"They didn't care which way it was going. They just wanted out of town."[57]

Junction also became the site of an inevitable showdown between Bryant and center Fred Broussard, A&M's lone returning All-Southwest Conference player and only obvious professional prospect. Bryant saw an arrogant sense of entitlement and a laziness he despised in Broussard. But the coach also thought he could mold Broussard into a fine player if he first taught him about humility, discipline, and hard work.

The experiment didn't work. One afternoon, in the middle of a workout, Broussard decided he'd had enough of the fiery Bryant and his camp. The 6-foot-3, 235-pounder simply walked away.

"Young man," Bryant called out incredulously, "where you going?"[58]

Broussard refused to answer.

"You better think about it now," said Bryant as Broussard reached a gate at the far end of the practice field. "If you go through that gate, you're gone."[59]

Broussard hesitated for a moment, opened the gate, and continued to walk.[60]

Later that evening, in the mess hall, Bryant was equally stunned to see Broussard in line for dinner. "Young fella, you must be making a mistake," Bryant said to Broussard. "A&M football players eat here."[61]

"You mean I can't eat here?"[62]

"I mean exactly that. You can't ever eat here again."[63]

Team captain Bennie Sinclair approached Bryant soon afterward and asked if he would take Broussard back. "Bennie," Bryant replied, "I'm not going to take him back. He's quit before, hasn't he?"[64]

Sinclair said, "Yessir, lots of times."[65]

"This is the last time," Bryant said. "We want players we can count on. We've got a long way to go, and we don't want anybody laying down once we get started."[66]

Jones now had the dubious job of informing the media that A&M's lone All-Southwest Conference player wouldn't be suiting up for the Aggies. Ever. He asked Bryant what he should tell the Associated Press.

"Just say Broussard quit," Bryant snapped. "Q-U-I-T. That's all"[67]

By day nine, the number of players still in uniform had dramatically dwindled. Bryant counted heads. Seventy-six players had quit, including the team's last center—Broussard. Bryant turned unflinchingly to Summerlin (his 5-foot-8, 145-pound student manager) and told him to suit up. He was now the team's new center.

Summerlin's improbable journey from student manager to player gave a rebirth to a cherished Texas A&M tradition—the Twelfth Man.

Two days later, the A&M players boarded a bus for College Station, ending 10 hellish days in Junction. For those who survived the goat's head, sweltering heat, and painful bouts of thirst, there was a profound sense of accomplishment. Herskowitz observed the growth of "an extraordinary fellowship" and "bonding of men."[68]

"Looking back at Junction," Bryant said years later, "there were times when, if you hadn't been so well raised, you would have wished you were dead."[69]

Stallings, for one, never entertained the thought of quitting. He needed football. Or, more precisely, he needed the football scholarship to pay for his education.

"I did want to die, though," Stallings said. "I remember one day we were riding on the bus, and we went over the bridge. I remember thinking we could ride off this bridge and all drown. At least that would be an honorable way out.

"But quitting? Never gave it a thought."[70]

For players like Stallings, quitting simply wasn't an option.

"A lot has been made about the ones who stuck it out being stronger or whatever," said Bobby Drake Keith, a halfback who was among the survivors. "But I think most of us survived because football was important to us for whatever reason, and it was in our nature to do whatever we had to do to stay on the team and stay in school. Our instinct was survival."[71]

In the end, 29 Aggies were among the Junction survivors—barely enough for a scrimmage. As the years passed, the legend of Junction grew. Stallings has often been asked about Junction, repeatedly summing up the experience with his now-famous sentence: "We left College Station on two buses, and returned on one."[72]

The fruits of Junction didn't truly come into focus until two years later in 1956, when A&M won the Southwest Conference championship with a 6–0 record (9–0–1 overall). The Aggies compiled a combined 8–11–1 record during the previous two seasons, including a dreadful 1–9 record in 1954. A&M went winless for six in-conference games that season before rebounding the following season with a respectable 4–1–1 slate against conference foes.

Then in 1956, the Aggies clinched the Southwest Conference title with a 34–21 victory over the rival Texas Longhorns at Texas Memorial Stadium in Austin. Ten of the Junction survivors—including captains Stallings, Pardee, and Lloyd Hale—were among those who celebrated that day. Bryant credited his beloved "Junction Boys" for forming the foundation of that championship squad. "I don't think I'll ever be as proud of another crowd as I am of this group," Bryant uncharacteristically confessed to the press.[73]

In 1979, the A&M Club of Junction held the first reunion of the Junction Boys to commemorate their 25th anniversary of the camp. Twenty-two of the 29 survivors attended the reunion and walked in their own long-ago footsteps. The Adjunct was now lush with green vegetation—signs of life.

Bryan Booth, a lifelong resident of Junction and an A&M club member, remembered that what made the occasion so special was Bryant's arrival at the tiny Junction International Airport at the edge of town. Bryant arrived in a private jet as his former players laughed and joked and reminisced on the ground below.

"The plane made a pass over the airport and then landed," Booth recalled. "All the joking stopped. All the laughing stopped. It was like they all came to attention. There was a respect there—a sense that here's 'The Man.'"[74]

Bryant still wielded a powerful aura.

Later that night, Bryant and his former players met in private to share the moment together. The Aggies presented Coach Bryant with a diamond ring commemorating their unique place in college football lore as Junction survivors. Bryant died less than four years later. At the time of his death, his family noticed he was wearing only one piece of jewelry—his Junction ring.[75]

NOTES

1. Wanda Teel, interview with author, June 30, 2018. Elmer and Mattie Lee were married in 1928.

2. *Bulletin of the Agricultural and Mechanical College of Texas for the Junction Adjunct, Fifth Series* 9, no. 2 (February 1, 1953).

3. Ibid. The author is indebted to Robert Stubblefield, the present director of the Adjunct—now called Texas Tech University Center at Junction. The Texas State Legislature transferred the 411-acre facility to Texas Tech University in 1971. Stubblefield graciously gave the author a golf cart tour of the grounds during an April 2017 visit, providing important background on the facility and its history.

4. John Burnett, "When the Sky Ran Dry," *Texas Monthly*, July 2012.

5. Ibid.

6. Wanda Teel, interview with author, April 20, 2017, and June 30, 2018.

7. Teel, interview with author, April 20, 2017.

8. Dent, *Junction Boys*, 41.

9. *American-Statesman* (Austin), May 20, 2010. Zapalac was inducted into the Texas A&M Football Hall of Fame in 1991. He died May 18, 2010, at age 89. Once he was asked by his son, Jeff, and brother, Bill, if he had ever read Dent's best-selling book, *The Junction Boys*. "I was there," Zapalac reportedly replied in a gruff tone. "Why would I want to read it?"

10. *Tulsa World*, January 8, 1999. Cutchin died January 7, 1999, at age 78.

11. Ibid.

12. Dent, *Junction Boys*, 40.

13. Ibid., 41.

14. Browning, *I Remember*, 279.

15. *Junction (TX) Eagle*, August 3, 1954.

16. Stallings, interview with author, July 8, 2015. No one ever reportedly recorded the exact number of players who left College Station for Junction that day. Eyewitnesses generally estimate the total number to be around 100 players.

17. Herskowitz, *Legend*, 23.

18. Tommy Deas, "A Look Back at Bryant's Junction Boys at Texas A&M," *BAMAInsider.com*, September 14, 2013 (accessed February 1, 2016).

19. Bryant and Underwood, *Bear*, 129.

20. Dent, *Junction Boys*, 47.

21. Ibid., 48.

22. Teel, interview with author, April 20, 2017.

23. Dent, *Junction Boys*, 48.

24. Stallings and Cook, *Another Season*, 48; Stallings, interview with author, July 8, 2015.

25. Dent, *Junction Boys*, 52.

26. Ibid.

27. Ibid.

28. Stallings, interview with author, July 8, 2015.

29. Stallings and Cook, *Another Season*, 48.

30. Ibid.

31. *Houston Post*, October 6, 1968.

32. *Junction (TX) Eagle*, August 15, 2014.

33. Ibid.

34. Deas, "A Look Back."

35. *Junction (TX) Eagle*, August 15, 2014.

36. Herskowitz, *Legend*, 23.

37. Ibid., 24.

38. Ibid.

39. Bryant and Underwood, *Bear*, 130.

40. Ibid.

41. Ibid.

42. Barra, *Last Coach*, 171.

43. Ibid.

44. Teel, interview with author, April 20, 2017.

45. Barra, *Last Coach*, 174.

46. Ibid., 175.

47. Rob Roy Spiller, interview with author, April 20, 2017.

48. Wilford F. "Billy" Pickard Jr. died March 9, 2015, in College Station, Texas, at age 81 (*Bryan [TX] Daily Eagle*, March 11, 2015).

49. Dent, *Junction Boys*, 120.

50. Barra, *Last Coach*, 175.

51. Ibid.

52. Ibid.

53. Stallings and Cook, *Another Season*, 49.

54. Stallings, interview with author, July 8, 2015.

55. Dunnavant, *Coach*, 103.

56. *Houston Post*, October 6, 1968.

57. Spiller, interview with author, April 20, 2017.

58. Bryant and Underwood, *Bear*, 133.

59. Herskowitz, *Legend*, 27.

60. Ibid.

61. Bryant and Underwood, *Bear*, 133.

62. Ibid.

63. Ibid.

64. Ibid.

65. Ibid.

66. Ibid.

67. Herskowitz, *Legend*, 28.

68. Ibid., 30.

69. Dunnavant, *Coach*, 103.

70. Stallings, interview with author, July 8, 2015.

71. Dunnavant, *Coach*, 106.

72. Stallings, interview with author, July 8, 2015.

73. *Houston Post*, November 30, 1956.

74. Bryan Booth, interview with author, April 20, 2017. Booth graduated from Texas A&M in 1968.

75. Dunnavant, *Coach*, 112; Herskowitz, *Legend*, 234.

CHAPTER 6
Alabama

My plan was to bleed 'em and gut 'em.

—Paul W. Bryant

Few ever wanted to say good-bye to Paul W. "Bear" Bryant.

The faithful of Kentucky certainly didn't. Nor did the dedicated folks at Texas A&M, where Bryant would be forever known as the architect of the legendary Junction Boys and the 1956 Southwest Conference championship. But nothing—and no one—lasts forever. Not even a stubborn coach nicknamed "Bear."

Bryant's final days at A&M were shadowed by rumors of his departure for beloved alma mater Alabama University.

Twenty-six years earlier, Bryant had left Fordyce for Alabama and played end for the Crimson Tide from 1933 to 1935. He was a member of Alabama's 1934 National Championship team under Frank Thomas and then served the legendary coach as an assistant in the ensuing four seasons—a stretch in which the Crimson Tide compiled a combined 29–5–3 record.

By the fall of 1957, however, memories of Alabama's glory days seemed almost mythical. Alabama's program had fallen into disarray by then, logging a combined 8–29–4 record between 1954 and 1957. The previous three seasons under head coach J. B. "Ears" Whitworth painted an even more dreadful portrait. Under Whitworth, the Crimson Tide won only 4 of 30 games.

Alabama fans now impatiently awaited the return of their prodigal son—Paul W. "Bear" Bryant.

But not everyone thought Bryant would return to Alabama. Some Texans didn't. In retrospect, the denial might have been wishful thinking in Texas. Regardless, Bryant's path became clear after A&M's heartbreaking 9–7 loss to rival Texas on November 28, 1957, at Kyle Field in College Station. The loss was the Aggies' second straight conference defeat and left them a combined three points shy of a conference title. In two weeks, A&M dropped in the Associated Press poll from the number one–ranked team to number four. As a result, the Aggies were forced to accept an invitation to the Gator Bowl in Jacksonville, Florida, rather than to the more coveted Cotton Bowl appearance in Dallas.

Bryant added to the sting of the moment.

As reporters huddled around him in his tiny office after the Texas loss, Bryant began to speak in measured but candid words about the rumored Alabama job. Herskowitz, A&M's beat writer at the *Houston Post*, listened intently with other scribes to what became known as Bryant's "Mama Called" speech.

"I'd like to think I haven't considered [the Alabama job] yet," Bryant said. "I'd like to think I have been preparing for Texas. There is one and only one reason that I would consider it.

"When you were out playing as a kid, say you heard your mother call you. If you thought she wanted you to do some chores, or come in for supper, you might not answer her. But if you thought she *needed* you, you'd be there in a hurry."[1]

Bryant didn't confirm the rumors directly. He still had a Gator Bowl to win and his professional integrity to preserve, but as Herskowitz would later write, for those "who knew him best, that sentiment said it all."[2]

The Bryant era at A&M would soon end.

Herskowitz, for one, already sensed Bryant's days in College Station were numbered. Rumors of Bryant's departure from A&M had been heavily reported a week earlier in the aftermath of a 7–6 loss to Rice—the team's first of the 1957 campaign. Unidentified sources were being quoted in the *Birmingham News*, confirming Bryant would be the new Alabama coach. In private, Herskowitz asked Bryant why he wouldn't just squash the rumor with a denial on the record.

"No, I wouldn't want to say that," the coach replied, "because I might do it."[3]

Herskowitz knew then that Bryant was gone, but he convinced himself that the coach he'd come to admire might change his mind. Bryant's aura possessed that kind of pull. Memorable moments and colorful stories trailed him wherever he traveled. Life seemed more vibrant in his presence. And the football games he coached seemed to mirror life's sometimes epic struggles.

Bryant's departure from A&M would leave only a sense of loss and nostalgia.

Bryant's arrival in Tuscaloosa, however, would ignite a football revival reminiscent of the one experienced by A&M cadets four years earlier in College Station. And now—as then—Bryant's presence would forever change lives.

. . .

Gene Stallings became one of the first people Bryant contacted after he agreed to take the Alabama job. The coach had grown fond of Stallings, who was one of his beloved Junction Boys, captain of A&M's 1956 championship squad, and an overachiever who never showed a trace of quit.

Stallings possessed one other character trait Bryant greatly admired: loyalty.

So one day, Bryant summoned the 22-year-old Stallings to his office. Stallings entered, and Bryant wasted no time in getting to the point. "Now, I'm going to offer you a job on my staff at Alabama," said Bryant, his voice growing stern, "but if I hear of it before I'm ready to announce it, then you don't have it."[4]

Stallings could hardly contain his excitement. He vowed silence.

"Actually I wanted to run out and shout it from the rooftops," Stallings later confessed. "To be able to coach in a place like Alabama, well, that kind of thing doesn't happen very often, especially to a twenty-two-year-old, just out of college. . . . I was tickled to death to have such a wonderful job."[5]

And with an annual salary of $4,500. Life was grand.

The Alabama faithful in 1957 felt a similar sensation. Bryant brought instant cachet as the new head coach in Tuscaloosa. His resume spoke for itself in wins and losses, having amassed a .659 winning percentage (91–39–8) with a reputation for being able to resurrect a dying program at each new stop.

Charles H. Land was 25 the first time he saw Alabama's savior. The Tuscaloosa native grew up watching the Crimson Tide in the "stands of the old thirty-thousand-seat stadium when it wasn't even half full." Back then, Land said, "we could only dream of what it would be like to be in a bowl game."[6] In high school, Land worked as a stringer for the *Tuscaloosa News*, earning 10 cents for every inch of copy he produced for managing editor Ben Green. He later graduated from the University of Alabama and by the time Bryant arrived in 1958 had been promoted to sports editor of his hometown newspaper.[7]

Land couldn't help but be impressed by Bryant.

"He walked into a room, and you knew he was there," Land recalled. "He was larger than life. He was a big, charismatic guy—physically imposing."[8]

Land made one other observation as the days and weeks passed: "Coach Bryant controlled everything."[9]

Bryant brought his stubborn, albeit successful, way of conducting business to Tuscaloosa. As usual, he wasted no time in establishing clear and firm boundaries for everyone in and around his football program. He sent his message, in a variety of ways, that he—and he alone—would be in charge.

· · ·

Merrill "Hootch" (or "Hootchman") Collins may have been the only man on the Alabama campus exempt from Bryant's wrath. He was born in 1888, the son of a former slave (although Collins never clarified his family roots). He began working for the university in 1900 at the age of 12 as a janitor and in time became a locker room attendant for the football program.

Former players and coaches remember Collins as living in a boiler room in the basement of a building next to the athletic department. In earlier years, he traveled with the team and often held valuables for the players during games. As the years progressed, the elderly Collins could usually be found sitting on a pillow in a cane-bottom chair in the breezeway that led to the athletic department offices. An Alabama baseball cap sat atop his bald head.

Trainer Jim Goostree claimed both Hank Crisp and Collins were present for his formal job interview, which was fittingly held in the breezeway. Later that summer, Goostree said, he was trying to clean a training room and turned on a giant fan to cool his work space—the room's marble floor sat directly above the boiler and caused the room to overheat. But when Goostree turned on the fan, it blew clouds of red clay dust from the parking lot into the room.

"Hootch was sitting out back in that breezeway, and I just needed help bad," Goostree recalled. "I decided to go out and ask him to help me. So I went out there, and I said, 'Sir, what do you do around here?'"[10]

Collins calmly replied, "I is retired. In the summer time around here, everybody is retired."[11]

By 1958, Collins had been connected to the Alabama football program longer than anyone in its history, having served the coaching regimes of Zen Scott, Wallace Wade, Frank Thomas, Red Drew, and J. B. Whitworth.

"He was a heck of a guy," remembered Clem Gryska, a former player, assistant coach, recruiter, and administrator who died in 2012. "He was one of the few who didn't call Coach Bryant 'Coach.' In fact, he was the only one who called him 'Boy.' I think he was the only one still there who remembered him as a boy."[12]

Land, for one, never saw Collins do much of anything by the time he started covering the team for the *Tuscaloosa News*. "I'd always see him sitting in the breezeway on a chair," Land remembered. "I think he was sort of inherited."[13]

In reality, Collins was typical of many elderly African Americans who lived alone in the segregated South of that era. Akin to orphans of a formerly enslaved society, some were paternalistically cared for by various families and institutions or simply remained with a piece of land from one generation to the next. The University of Alabama community genuinely cared about Collins, who regularly received food from the dining hall and money from students who pooled together their laundry change. Bryant later assigned James Booth—an Alabama basketball player (1960–64) the task of bringing Collins a hot meal every day. Bryant also ordered business manager B. W. Whittington to escort Collins to the Social Security Administration to ensure he received his "pennies."[14]

Collins died in 1968—three years before the first African American football player broke the color barrier at Alabama. Shortly before his death, however, former halfback Richard Strum of Mississippi traveled through Tuscaloosa and decided he would visit Collins. He brought him a bottle of Jack Daniels as a gift. By then, Bryant had moved Collins into some old "negro" housing nearby. Strum knocked on the door.[15]

"Come on in," a voice said.[16]

Strum entered an entirely dark room. He would later recount, "I couldn't see anything, didn't know what he looked like but I gave him that bottle and shook his hand . . . and that was the last I ever saw of Hootchman."[17]

• • •

Aside from Collins, everyone else served as fair game for Bryant's wrath. The need for a culture shock became apparent even before he stepped one foot on campus. Benny Marshall, a sports columnist for the *Birmingham News*, made that abundantly clear when he cornered Bryant at his first conference as Alabama's new head coach.

"Coach," Marshall said, "the alumni are expecting your team to go undefeated next season."[18]

"The hell you say," Bryant replied. "I'm an [alumnus], and I don't expect us to go undefeated."[19]

Marshall's comment had struck at the heart of Bryant's greatest challenge. Attitudes needed to change, and that required everyone involved to begin dabbling in reality. The 1958 Alabama Crimson Tide would not go undefeated. Bryant knew that long before even taking the job. He had to change everything about the Alabama program, starting with an inherited roster he described as "a fat, raggedy bunch."[20]

Bryant used every occasion to set a new tone. Throughout January, when he wasn't watching film on players, he carved out time for personal appearances to chat about his coaching philosophies with an eager Alabama fan base. On one memorable occasion, Bryant attended a banquet honoring freshmen players. The purpose of the banquet amused Bryant. Morris Childers, a freshman running back at the time, remembered Bryant's attitude bordered on rudeness.

"We hadn't won a game, and Bryant . . . was rather insulting," Childers recalled. "I do remember that he jokingly said that he had never seen anyone celebrate a team that hadn't won a game."[21]

Organizers never hosted another freshman banquet.

Bryant also delivered a stern warning that night to the alumni. He wanted to avoid the problems he had encountered at A&M when Southwest Conference officials placed the Aggies on a two-year probation for recruitment violations involving cash and gifts. The probation cost A&M trips to the Cotton Bowl in 1955 and 1956.

"I have heard some bad stories," Bryant told the alumni in the room. "If anything is wrong, come and tell me.

"If you are giving anybody any money, for anything, I want you to stop right now. I've done it, and I found out if you pay 'em, they'll quit on you."[22]

Bryant wasn't finished. On January 10, he called a team meeting for 1:15 p.m. At exactly 1:15 p.m., Bryant tapped his watch and yelled for his quarterback prospect, Jerry Gilmer. Someone hollered back that Gilmer wasn't present. Bryant immediately ordered assistant coach Carney Laslie to go to the dorms upstairs and pack Gilmer's belongings.

"He's off scholarship," Bryant barked.[23]

A tense silence stifled the room. Bryant commanded the space and then arguably delivered one of the greatest speeches of his illustrious career. He told his players he had come to Alabama "for one reason. To build a winning football team. We are going to do two things. We are going to learn to play football, and we are going to get up and go to class like our mamas and papas expect us to. And we are going to win."[24]

Bryant's voice deepened with resolve. Now his words seemed inspired by some place deep within, perhaps the same place where he and his mother were still rolling out of Moro Bottom with a wagon full of vegetables on an icy morning. "Ten years from now, you are going to be married with a family, your wife might be sick, your kids might be sick, you might be sick, but you will get your butt up and go to work," Bryant said emphatically. "That's what I'm going to do for you. I'm going to teach you how to do things you don't want to do."[25]

Then Bryant issued a sober warning.

"We don't plan to discuss the past coaching staff," Bryant said. "We don't plan to discuss anything in the past. I'll advise you to be ready when spring practice starts. I'm telling you now to get into shape. You haven't been through anything like you're going to go through."[26]

The legend of Junction, Texas, had yet to take flight nationally with fans, but stories were already making the circuit in Tuscaloosa since Bryant's hiring. Word of Bryant's ruthless training regimen quickly escalated into tall tales. Lineman Billy Neighbors—a freshman in 1958—recalled one such wild yarn: "One of the stories that went around was that while [Bryant] was at Texas A&M, they'd dig a pit and throw one or two players into it, and the ones who came out got to play!"[27]

Tall tales aside, one thing now remained clear to Bryant's new players: he intended to implement the same hellish training practices he employed four years earlier at Junction. His first meeting had left no doubts about what they could expect. Bryant wanted to know who really wanted to wear an Alabama uniform, who would fight for one.[28]

"My plan was to bleed 'em and gut 'em, because I didn't want any well-wishers hanging around," Bryant said.[29]

Scholarships were no longer seen as guaranteed entitlements. Bryant didn't want anyone to feel comfortable. He even issued a letter, dated July 15, to emphasize the importance of reporting for camp in shape—in "racehorse condition."[30] He also addressed players who had already been deemed overweight.

"We realize also how difficult it is for some to lose weight," the letter read. "On the other hand we know that you cannot play without getting your weight down, so in fairness to you and the team, we are requesting some to be down to a certain weight before reporting here."[31]

Bryant's letter delivered a gut-punch in the next sentence: "If you are in this category, and fail to make the weight, we will assume that winning means little to you and there will be no place for you here."[32]

Land remembers a conversation with one player's father prior to the fall practice that season. His son was one of the linemen whom Bryant had deemed overweight. The father revealed to Land that his son hadn't reached the goal weight.

"You don't think Coach Bryant will hold him to that, do you?" the father asked Land.[33]

"Well," Land replied, "if that's the weight Coach Bryant wanted, I imagine he meant what he said."[34]

The father and son soon received their answer. All the players who reported overweight on the first day of practice were told they would not get a uniform. According to Land, they were informed by Bryant that if they wanted to play, they could lose the required weight and ask to return. Otherwise, they could go home and never come back.

Some players never returned.[35]

Prior to the first fall practice on August 30, Bryant met with each player individually. The players dreaded the meeting, especially after his fire-and-brimstone speech a few months earlier. Marlin "Scooter" Dyess, a halfback from Elba, Alabama, never forgot Bryant's colorful words from his first encounter.

Dyess had run track with some success in high school but was small for the football field, even for his era. He stood 5-foot-6 and weighed 150 pounds. Bryant remembered Dyess as weighing 140 pounds in his autobiography, perhaps a result of his enthusiasm for a good story.[36]

"Coach," Dyess said, "you indicated you wanted to have a meeting with each of the players."[37]

"Yes, I did," Bryant replied.[38]

The diminutive Dyess amused Bryant. Dyess wore a crew cut like most young men then. Bryant playfully rubbed Dyess's head and asked, "What the hell are you, the water boy?"[39]

Later, Dyess nervously waited for Bryant in his office. He didn't know what to expect. Bryant walked in and fired off his first question: "Do you think you're good enough to make this team?"[40]

Dyess humbly replied that he would try.

"Let's get something straight right off the bat," Bryant shot back. "We either are or we are not. We're not going to have any triers."[41]

Dyess made the team and became one of Bryant's favorite players by the end of the season.

Players like Dyess were pushed to their physical and emotional limits under Bryant from the start, though. Those unable to perform to an expected standard were sometimes cut on the spot. If the coaches suspected a player of being a quitter, they weeded him out quickly. "I had one boy saying he was going to quit," Bryant recalled in his autobiography, "and I wanted to nip that in the bud so I went to his locker and took all his things out and threw them into the street."[42]

Beneath the brutality, however, there existed a gentler side of Bryant few would believe and fewer ever witnessed. A typical story of Bryant's kindness emerged years after his departure from Texas A&M, involving former assistant coach Elmer Smith—another fierce taskmaster from Arkansas. Occasionally, before sunrise, Bryant would say to Smith, "Coach Elmer, let's go get a cup of coffee."[43]

Bryant respected Smith's input on various subjects. So the two men would climb into Bryant's car and embark on an early morning drive down Wellborn Road, past the Aggie practice field and into the country. They simply drove and talked. In those days, Wellborn Road offered nothing more than solitude, except for an occasional small shack.

One morning, Bryant felt a bump as he drove down the road. He felt he'd hit something but wasn't sure. He backed the vehicle up and drove around. He saw nothing and returned to the office. Later that day, he said to Smith, "Elmer, let's go take a ride."[44]

Bryant and Smith drove down Wellborn Road.

"Paul," Smith said, "what are you doing?"[45]

"Well, I hit something this morning," Bryant answered. "I thought it might be a dog."[46]

Bryant proceeded to stop at a few of those roadside shacks to inquire if any families had lost a pet. Finally, one woman said, "Yes, my son's dog was laying by the side of the road this morning."[47]

The next day, Bryant personally delivered a puppy to the child.[48]

Gestures of this kind were often done in private by Bryant, who maintained a no-nonsense persona as coach. There were layers to his personality, though. For instance, class distinction meant nothing to him—a noteworthy stance in Southern post-antebellum society, where segregation reigned as stubbornly as the extreme privileges of wealth. Bryant knew white Alabamans weren't ready to address racial issues at the time, but he deemed class an entirely different matter.

"I don't care who you are, where you come from, whether you played last year or not," Bryant stated. "I don't care if your folks are rich or whether they don't own the farm they live on. I want people who want to win and who want to be part of the tradition of Alabama football."[49]

Bryant also surrounded himself with loyalists who would help him carry out his grueling plan to "bleed 'em and gut 'em." In addition to Stallings, fellow Junction veteran Bobby Drake Keith also joined his coaching staff at Alabama that first season. Keith was 23, one year older than Stallings. Together, along with fellow coaches like Pat James and Dee Powell, they provided the aggressive, youthful energy Bryant demanded.

Yet no drill or instruction was done without purpose. Contact, for instance, wasn't simply done for the sake of contact. Stallings earned praise for teaching the "9 Technique" to defensive linemen—a technique in which the defender delivers "a hand or forearm shiver to the head of the offensive end" with his first move. The objective is to momentarily stun the end and free the defender to locate the ball carrier.[50]

Crafty pugilists have employed a similar tactic throughout boxing history, intentionally missing a hook to deliver a more devastating forearm to an opponent's jaw. Whether Stallings learned this technique from watching boxers is unknown, but the concept is the same and one Bryant would have appreciated in or out of the ring.

In raw terms, Bryant clearly viewed football—and life—as a fight. Hence, he harbored a distaste for quitters. Drake once insisted Bryant "hated to see kids quit. He felt, though, that if you quit in practice, you'd quit in a game. What he wanted to see was a kid fight, to hang in there, to take what he dished out and come back for more. He wanted to see who wanted that uniform the most."[51]

Sometimes, in his blind quest for toughness, Bryant pushed a player too hard.

Alabama end Bud Moore of Birmingham witnessed Bryant's wrath firsthand during one practice. Moore, a rugged player who loved contact, ate too many turnip greens one afternoon at lunch in the dining hall. He later became nauseated at practice and drew the attention of Bryant, who overlooked the practice field from his now legendary tower.

"The coaches and players were always looking up at the tower to see if he was watching," Stallings recalled. "Everyone wanted to please Coach Bryant."[52]

No one wanted to see what they saw that day—Bryant descending from his lofty perch. He angrily marched down the tower and over to Moore.

"Coach Bryant got down off his tower, and said, 'I'm going to show you how it's done,'" recalled James Beall, a team manager. "And [Bryant] went one on one with [Moore] and didn't have any pads on him. Telling Bud to hit him, hit him . . . Bud was sick . . . he said, 'Coach, I got sick at lunch today . . . because of turnip greens.' . . . Bryant was, 'I don't give a damn, you hit me, hit me' and he actually drove him into the ground."[53]

Moore began to vomit. Bryant called a break as all the players gathered around, but Moore couldn't stop puking. Growing impatient, Bryant's temper flared and he snapped, "Well, if you can't handle it any better than that, you are through."[54]

A shaky Moore obediently trudged off the field to the showers. Shortly afterward, Stallings retrieved Moore from the showers. "Come with me," Stallings said mercifully. Moore followed, wrapping a towel around his waist as he walked. He was still shaky and trembling.

"Just say, 'Yessir' or 'Nossir,'" Stallings advised Moore en route to Bryant's office.[55]

"So I knocked on the door," Moore recalled years later. "He opens the door, big old rascal standing there, still in his coaching clothes, and he says, 'Boy, what do you want?' and I said, 'Well, Coach Stallings said you wanted to see me.' And he said, 'Yeah, these coaches tell me I'm making a mistake by running you off. I don't know about it myself, but you've got a uniform if you want it.' And I said, 'Yessir.' And he slammed the door."[56]

Moore survived that first season and later enjoyed a storied coaching career in which he served as an assistant under two legends—Oklahoma's Bud Wilkinson and Bryant. Others weren't so fortunate.

"We lost about twenty-two people that [first] spring," Dyess remembered. "When they were quitting, you kept wondering, 'This guy is a maniac. How is he going to build a team with what we have left?' When we came in, in the evenings, and three of his first-teamers would be gone, he'd move the second ones to the first team. He didn't care. He was going to play with what he had left."[57]

Fall practices trimmed even more players from the roster. The real hell began September 16—a date that marked the start of two-a-day practices. For the next 16 days, Bryant and his staff relentlessly pushed players through grueling practices that tested the limits of their resolve in the sultry Alabama mornings and afternoons. The AP quoted Bryant after the first few practices: "The riffraff are fast eliminating themselves and we had two real good scrimmages."[58]

Bryant disputed the use of the word "riffraff" in his autobiography, contending that he was referring to the hangers-on around the program. The claim doesn't make sense, though. Bryant oversaw his program with an iron fist and even locked the gates for each practice. No one was allowed in or out of the practice field without his permission.[59]

On at least one occasion, a player vaulted the fence to escape. The player—Eugene Harris, a sophomore from Cleveland, Tennessee—reportedly brushed past the noseguard on one play and bolted for the fence.

"Come back here, boy!" cried Laslie, an assistant coach.[60]

Harris never broke stride, hopping a 4-foot-high chain link fence in a single bound. He stripped off his gear as he ran. By the time he reached the locker room, players said he wore only a jock strap.

No one saw him again after that day.[61]

Other players had to be carried out. During one infamous afternoon session, a large thundercloud ominously rolled in over the practice field. Bryant called his players together and, sensing an early end to practice, a few cheered. Their joy was premature. Bryant instead said, "I'm going to let you take your shoulder pads off, we're going to do a little running to see what kind of shape y'all are in."[62]

The players were divided into smaller groups, and the running commenced. They ran full speed and nonstop. They ran distances of 10, 20, 30, and 40 yards and repeated the required distances with each whistle. There were no breaks. Only constant motion.

Nearly every player was crawling on their knees from exhaustion and throwing up. "I thought really that day that I was going to die, and I was in good shape," said Walter Sansing, a fullback. "I saw coaches grab players by the seats of their britches and throw 'em because they were throwing up [. . .] they'd just make 'em go a little bit more [. . .] I'll always remember that [. . .] you'd be on your fours trying to finish and your buddy over there would be throwing up, and the coaches would be yelling, 'you're not going to quit, you can't quit, you'll quit in the fourth quarter if you quit here.'"[63]

By the end, players were dizzy and blacking out.

"We ran thirty-one fifty-yard sprints," recalled Duff Morrison, a halfback and another camp survivor. "When we ran the thirtieth one, down to Coach Stallings, he let us get a knee [. . .] he says, all right, if you can make it through the gate, you can go in [. . .] there were eleven of us [. . .] eight of us made it through the gate, three of us didn't make it [. . .] they got the fish eye and just rolled back and passed slap out."[64]

Alabama broke camp with 46 players on the roster. At A&M, Bryant broke camp at Junction with 29 players. But each team earned the respect of Bryant and his coaching staff. Despite missing a bowl game, Bryant's 1958 squad surprised a lot of critics with a 5–4–1 overall record. The season marked the only time a Bryant-led team at Alabama didn't play in a bowl game. But this group—like his Junction Boys—laid the groundwork for the success to come.

Decades later, Stallings gave the 1958 Crimson Tide their proper due.

"Listen, the guys that started in fifty-eight were the toughest sons of bitches that ever walked on a football field," Stallings said. "I was in College Station when Coach Bryant came to A&M, and I went through hell, but let me tell you, the hell that I went through plus what these guys went through, we put it on these guys, we were sent there to run people off [. . .] the guys that were there at the end of that spring [. . .] they did well, they were tough."[65]

•   •   •

The 1958 Crimson Tide ushered in change. Quarterback Pat Trammell and the class of 1961 ushered in championships.

Trammell, a doctor's son from Scottsboro, Alabama, led a highly talented freshman class in 1958. For Bryant, those freshmen eventually held a special place of reverence. They formed the nucleus of Bryant's first national championship team, and he later described them as "the best freshman group I ever had, too, in terms of character and dedication."[66]

"I could just sense they were something special," wrote Bryant in his autobiography, recalling his first meeting with that freshman class. With typical cunning and bravado, Bryant seized the moment to issue the group a challenge:

> I said, "What are you doing here?" And I waited. It was so quiet in there you could hear a pin drop.
>
> I said, "What are you doing here? Tell me why you're here. If you're not here to win a National Championship you're in the wrong place."
>
> Then I told them what I thought it would take to do it, and they believed me. They believed every word . . .
>
> When I walked out that day I knew we were going to win the National Championship with that group.[67]

He wasn't alone.

Neighbors, a powerful, 248-pound guard who grew up in Tuscaloosa, had been "scared to death" of Bryant until then. Suddenly, he felt inspired.[68]

"National champions!" recalled Neighbors, who earned All-American honors as a senior and then played eight seasons professionally. "I was just stunned when I heard that. We all were. We'd heard so much about this man and what he could do, we all knew how awful Alabama had been before he got there, and here he was telling us that we could be national champions. We would be national champions by 1961 if we did what he told us and believed in ourselves. I got goosebumps. I started believing that every minute."[69]

Trammell, for one, didn't need any confidence. He arrived at Tuscaloosa as if he had been destined to lead. One story now entrenched in Alabama lore is that of a young Trammell bursting into a room filled with fellow freshman teammates. He strode to a table of quarterbacks, flashed a switchblade, and stuck it in the middle of the table.

Then with the knife still quivering, he loudly declared, "I aim to be the quarterback of this team. Does anybody else here think they're quarterbacks?"[70]

No one uttered a word.

"Right then," said Bill Oliver, a running back on the 1961 title team, "they all became halfbacks."[71]

Bryant came to respect—and love—Trammell as a player and person. "Pat would have played in the NFL if he hadn't decided to be a doctor," Bryant said. "He couldn't pass and he couldn't run; all he could do was put points on the board and win games. He called plays better than the coaches could, and he instinctively knew what the defense was trying to do. He was a tremendous leader [. . .] the players followed him around like they were following their mamas."[72]

In reality, Trammell was a gifted athlete who could run and pass with accuracy. He stood 6-foot-2 and weighed 195 pounds—bigger than most of his lineman. Bryant tended to play down Trammell's athleticism in order to highlight his character, work ethic, and extraordinary leadership. Trammell also possessed one other quality Bryant greatly admired.

The quarterback feared no one.

"I think Coach Bryant was always a little in awe of people who weren't in awe of him," Gryska said. "Pat loved him, but he wasn't in *awe* of him."[73]

Once, during lunch, Bryant approached Trammell in the dining hall to show him a new play he wanted to implement for an upcoming game. Trammell studied the playbook for a minute and replied, "Coach, I think it's crap. It'll never work." Bryant smiled and walked away satisfied with Trammell's assessment.[74]

By his senior season, Trammell stood poised to lead the Crimson Tide to their first national championship under Bryant and a return to glory. Alabama had a combined 15–3–4 record with Trammell at the helm the previous two seasons. But in 1961, Trammell and his teammates were unstoppable, posting an 11–0 overall record (7–0 in the Southeastern Conference). Of the more than 100 freshmen who tried out for the team in 1958, only 11 survived the entire four seasons to savor the title.[75]

Alabama completed its perfect season with a 10–3 victory over Arkansas in the Sugar Bowl on New Year's Day 1962—four weeks after trouncing rival Auburn 34–0 in the Iron Bowl and being declared national champions by the major wire services. Trammell established a new school passing record in the process with 1,035 yards on 133 attempts.

Trammell's leadership, as well as Bryant's confidence in him, were revealed again years later in a story from the Auburn blowout. At one point during the game, Trammell shocked his coach with a quick kick on a second down near midfield. Bryant marched up to his quarterback and asked him what he was thinking. The coach didn't have to wait long for an answer.

"Coach," Trammell replied, "we're just not blocking worth a crap, so I figured I'd see what our guys can do on defense."[76]

Bryant shrugged and walked away. He couldn't argue with sound reasoning.[77]

By the end of the 1961 season, Bryant had entered the realm of a genuine living legend. Or at least, his credentials as a legend had been greatly enhanced with a national championship finally on his resume after 17 seasons as a head coach. Members of the American Football Coaches Association added to the luster of his star when they voted him Coach of the Year—an honor long overdue. In the spring of 1962, Bryant's supporters held a special dinner in his honor in Fordyce. Sportswriters from throughout the nation attended. Friends of Bryant thought it would be interesting to escort a group to the coach's old family homestead at Moro Bottom.

Joe Sheehan of the *New York Times* joined the group. Upon seeing the weather-beaten shack of Bryant's youth, Sheehan said, "Why, Bear, I've been hearing for years that you were born in a log cabin."[78]

"Naw, Joe," Bryant replied without hesitation. "That was Abraham Lincoln. I was born in a manger."[79]

NOTES

1. Herskowitz, *Legend*, 115.
2. Ibid.
3. Ibid.

4. Stallings and Cook, *Another Season*, 13.

5. Ibid.

6. Charles H. Land, interview with author, January 23, 2016.

7. Land, interview with author, March 30, 2018. Land was born December 20, 1932, and became an institution in Tuscaloosa. He served as the newspaper's sports editor before becoming its managing editor on November 1, 1970. He retired from the newspaper in July 1995.

8. Land, interview with author, January 23, 2016.

9. Ibid.

10. Tom Stoddard, *Turnaround: The Untold Story of Bear Bryant's First Years as Head Coach at Alabama* (Montgomery, AL: River City, 2000), 99.

11. Ibid.

12. Barra, *Last Coach*, 218.

13. Land, interview with author, March 30, 2018.

14. Stoddard, *Turnaround*, 99; Kurt Edward Kemper, *College Football and American Culture in the Cold War Era* (Champaign: University of Illinois Press, 2009), 121; Paul W. Bryant, letter to Frank Rose, 2 April 1958, "Athletic Department," Merrill Collins vertical file, Box no. 1, FR1, Papers of Frank Rose, University of Alabama Archives, Tuscaloosa, Alabama.

15. Stoddard, *Turnaround*, 99.

16. Ibid., 100.

17. Ibid.

18. Barra, *Last Coach*, 209.

19. Ibid.

20. Bryant and Underwood, *Bear*, 161.

21. Stoddard, *Turnaround*, 38.

22. Ibid., 39.

23. Barra, *Last Coach*, 212.

24. Ibid.

25. Ibid.

26. John Forney and Steve Townsend, *Talk of the Tide: An Oral History of Alabama Football Since 1920* (Birmingham, AL: Cane Hill, 1993), 79.

27. Forney and Townsend, *Talk of the Tide*, 76.

28. Ibid., 78. Marlin "Scooter" Dyess, a halfback on Bryant's first Alabama team, said, "We had heard of his exploits at Texas A&M, and we just didn't think he was the guy for the job."

29. Bryant and Underwood, *Bear*, 165.

30. Stoddard, *Turnaround*, 116.

31. Ibid., 115–16.

32. Ibid., 116.

33. Land, interview with author, March 30, 2018.

34. Ibid.

35. Ibid.

36. Bryant and Underwood, *Bear*, 167.

37. Forney and Townsend, *Talk of the Tide*, 79.

38. Ibid.

39. Ibid.

40. Ibid.

41. Ibid.

42. Ibid.

43. Curley Hallman, interview with author, October 9, 2018.

44. Ibid.

45. Ibid.

46. Ibid.

47. Ibid.

48. Ibid.

49. Barra, *Last Coach*, 212.

50. Stoddard, *Turnaround*, 69.

51. Barra, *Last Coach*, 215.

52. Stallings, interview with author, July 8, 2015.

53. Stoddard, *Turnaround*, 94.

54. Ibid.

55. Ibid., 95.

56. Ibid.

57. Forney and Townsend, *Talk of the Tide*, 79.

58. Stoddard, *Turnaround*, 124.

59. Stoddard didn't buy Bryant's explanation of "riffraff" is his book, *Turnaround*. "There were no 'riffraff' followers at practices that fall," Stoddard wrote. "'Riffraff' was indisputably Bryant's word for players not willing to meet expectations."

60. Stoddard, *Turnaround*, 126.

61. Ibid.

62. Ibid., 122.

63. Ibid., 123.

64. Ibid.

65. Ibid., 216.

66. Bryant and Underwood, *Bear*, 161–62.

67. Ibid., 163.

68. Forney and Townsend, *Talk of the Tide*, 76.

69. Barra, *Last Coach*, 219.

70. Ibid.

71. Herskowitz, *Legend*, 125.

72. Ibid., 149.

73. Barra, *Last Coach*, 224.

74. Ibid.

75. Forney and Townsend, *Talk of the Tide*, 76; Barra, *Last Coach*, 244.

76. Barra, *Last Coach*, 243.

77. Trammell died December 10, 1968, at the age of 28 from complications of metastatic testicular cancer. He left behind a wife and two children. In his autobiography, Bryant described the hope and ultimate heartbreak in the months leading to Trammell's death—a moment he called "the saddest day of my life." Bryant loved Trammell. On the day he died, Bryant and Mary Harmon drove to Scottsboro to comfort Trammell's mother and father. Bryant wrote in his 1974 book, "Pat's funeral was the most moving I've ever been to. I escorted his mother. [Auburn] Coach [Ralph 'Shug'] Jordan was there, and a lot of the Auburn players as well as ours. President [Richard] Nixon and Governor [George] Wallace sent telegrams of condolence. Everybody loved him . . . I still miss him" (Bryant and Underwood, *Bear*, 179).

78. Ibid., 245.

79. Ibid.

CHAPTER 7
The Namath Episode

I thought he looked like a hoodlum. I thought, "We are scraping the bottom of the barrel."

—Linda Knowles, Bryant's secretary, after meeting
Alabama recruit Joe Namath

On a fall day in 1961, an 18-year-old quarterback strode onto the Alabama practice field for the first time as if fresh from a Hollywood movie lot. Assistant coach Howard Schnellenberger would later say the freshman recruit looked like "he was from another country."[1]

Translation: He wasn't from Dixie.

"He looked like a street hustler," Schnellenberger noted to one biographer, "with a checkered sport coat and his pocket watch and chain."[2] A toothpick dangled from the corner of his mouth, and he donned blue jeans and zippered boots, a fashion rarely—if ever—seen in Tuscaloosa. "I thought he looked like a hoodlum," recalled Linda Knowles, Bryant's longtime secretary. "I thought, *My goodness. We are scraping the bottom of the barrel.*"[3]

Long, black hair hung to the youngster's shoulders, poking out from beneath a stylish flat cap—the kind commonly worn by professional golfers. Only no one had ever seen any professional golfer wear his flat cap the way this young man did. "Tilted," remembered Clem Gryska, Bryant's chief recruiter. "Just the right way."[4]

Alabama players snickered and sneered at the sight of the flashy stranger, shaking their heads in disbelief. Then, like a bolt of lightning, Bryant interrupted, "frowning and yelling" from atop his observation tower, and beckoned the new recruit to join him. Until then, the two had never met in person.[5]

Joseph William Namath—the talk of Beaver Falls, Pennsylvania—climbed the tower to visit his new coach. The practice field fell silent.

"Everybody was just shocked," recalled Jack Hicks, then a student manager.[6] Only an honored few had ever been invited to join Bryant in his tower—men such as Governor George Wallace and Dr. Frank Rose, university president. Now a freshman named Joe Namath could add his name to that short list. He would go down in history as the first and only player to ever ascend Bryant's legendary tower.[7]

"Joe was up there thirty, forty minutes, and Coach Bryant talked the whole time," Hicks marveled. "Joe said he could only understand one word: 'Stud.' The whole time, 'stud' is the only word he could understand."[8]

And Namath later confessed he didn't even know what "stud" meant.[9]

"I was always at practice, but I wasn't there when Namath was up in the tower," said Land, who doubled as the team's sports information director in 1961. "I heard about it, though. That was very rare for anyone else to be in that tower besides Coach Bryant. . . . You know, Alabama didn't just have Southern boys playing for them. But Namath was from Pennsylvania. He was a Yankee, and for some people in Alabama, that was enough cause for suspicion."[10]

Indeed.

But Bryant clearly didn't harbor such sentiment where Namath was concerned. Frankly, he could have cared less how Namath dressed and talked or where he grew up. The young man could play football. Stallings, then the defensive coordinator, explained Bryant's success at its unvarnished core. "Coach Bryant was a good coach, but he knew you won football games with good football players," Stallings said simply. "And some players are better than others."[11]

Namath measured better than most.

Bryant himself once called Namath "the best" athlete he had ever seen. "He is blessed with that rare quickness—hands, feet, everything—and he's quick and tough mentally, too," Bryant wrote in his autobiography. "Anybody who ever watched him warm up could tell that football comes easy for Joe."[12]

Not everyone related to the gifts bestowed upon Namath.

Stallings, for one, had to scratch and claw for everything he achieved as a football player. In many respects, he and Namath were complete opposites. Namath possessed an enormous amount of natural athleticism, a cocky-confident attitude, and a flashy demeanor on and off the field. Stallings possessed moderate talent, an iron will to succeed, and a profound sense of humility on and off the field.

Namath was heavily recruited. Stallings was nearly overlooked by recruits.

Namath once looked down from Bryant's tower. Stallings always looked up at the tower.

The contrasts are numerous, and yet for all their differences, they would someday share the common ground of cherished memories in the presence of a beloved mentor. Destiny would also thrust them together at a pivotal moment in Namath's storied career in December 1963—an episode that would ultimately define the characters of both men.

·   ·   ·

Namath hailed from a steel town on the Beaver Falls some 40 miles northwest of Pittsburgh. He was the youngest of five children born to Rose and John Namath, a steelworker who strongly encouraged his three boys to play sports. But before entering the seventh grade, Joe's parents divorced, and he went to live with his mother on a full-time basis until he graduated from high school. From a young age, the scarcity of money led Namath to hustle where he could for a dime, sometimes running errands at a pool hall, shining shoes, and shooting pool.[13]

By the time Namath entered high school, he had earned a reputation as one of the best football and baseball players in Pennsylvania. Scouts from the Oakland A's, Baltimore Orioles, and Chicago Cubs all courted Namath in the days before an amateur baseball draft. The Cubs offered $50,000 for his services. On the football field, Namath attained glory with his golden arm and brash leadership. He was a cocksure gunslinger who propelled Beaver Falls to the Western Pennsylvania Interscholastic Athletic League Championship, and in the aftermath of the title run, he reportedly had no less than 50 schools recruiting him to play football.

Namath's extracurricular activities also attracted much attention in Beaver Falls and created an abundance of fodder for the nasty business of town gossip. As Namath biographer Mark Kriegel wrote in his 2004 best-selling book, *Namath: A Biography*, "In the minds of most adults, Namath dwelled at the epicenter of bad influences. He bet. He smoked. He drank. . . . And of course, he was out to screw everyone's daughter."[14]

Beaver Falls taught Namath that being a football hero attracted both admirers and detractors. In Namath's case, his sins—real or perceived—eventually became town news. On November 15, 1960—three days after his final high school football game—local sportswriter Joe Tronzo of the *Times-Tribune* felt compelled to address the controversy that swirled around the talented Namath. He wrote a column he never imagined he would have to write about one of the prep athletes he covered. The column read in part:

> Probably more rumors have cropped up about Joe Namath than any other high school kid since I have been covering sports . . .
>
> Among the stories are that he sawed a cow in half in the auditorium of the high school, punched a pregnant woman, punched a school administrator, bombed school board members' houses, poured gasoline on a fifth grader and set him afire, threw eggs at Richard Nixon . . .
>
> There are some who have said I have made a hero out of the worst juvenile since Cain took a sling to Abel.
>
> Actually, even if Joe did all the above plus a few others, I would write him up in the same way. I am not interested in what a kid does off the field.
>
> I mean that my primary job is to report what goes on in the sport scene. If he is a hero on the field he is a hero on the sport page.
>
> If a kid has bad habits that is up to his parents, teachers and preachers to correct. Certainly it is not our job. It must be remembered that in Beaver Falls there are more parents, teachers and preachers than there are sports writers.
>
> However, I do want to defend this Namath lad . . . he is not the ogre that he has been made out.[15]

Fortunately for Namath, his days in Beaver Falls would soon end. The recruiting frenzy around him quieted greatly when it became clear he wanted to play for Maryland or Notre Dame. Bryant, for one, understood Maryland to be a lock and informed Gryska to recruit elsewhere. Alabama dropped out of the Namath chase.

Then one day, Alabama assistant coach Charlie Bradshaw received a call from Bernie Reid, a friend on the Maryland coaching staff. Reid informed Bradshaw that Namath failed to pass his entrance exam and would not be attending Maryland. The coach hoped Alabama might sign Namath before a team on Maryland's schedule did. No one on the Maryland coaching staff wanted to play against Namath.[16]

Bryant quickly dispatched Schnellenberger to fly to Beaver Falls in hopes of wooing Namath to Tuscaloosa for an official visit before one of the eastern schools discovered his availability. Schnellenberger, a Louisville native, played for the Kentucky Wildcats under Bryant and was a senior when Namath's elder brother, Frank, played on the freshman squad.[17]

Informed of Alabama's interest before Schnellenberger's arrival, Namath coolly replied, "Alabama? That's Bear Bryant, isn't it?"[18]

The response was classic Namath. Luckily for Schnellenberger, he won over the one person who mattered most—Rose, Namath's mother. Rose liked Schnellenberger. One night, she invited Schnellenberger to dinner for some homemade chicken and dumplings. Afterward, Rose excused herself from the room. As Namath would later remember, "My mother went upstairs, packed my bags and said, 'Take him.'"[19]

Namath became an Alabama football player at that moment.

Namath's elder brother, Frank, also liked the idea of his talented, wayward kid brother playing for a disciplinarian like Bryant, and soon Namath would be exposed to the memorable hospitality—as well as the unforgettable demands—of his new coach. His first encounter with Bryant's legendary temper occurred not long after his visit to Bryant's tower, and unlike that day, the freshman clearly understood every word his coach uttered. The encounter took place during a Monday night scrimmage between the freshman team and the varsity reserves. Namath rolled to his left on one play and was tackled as he started to make a pitch. The ball squirted loose.

"I didn't make a scrabble for the ball," Namath recalled. "Hell, I couldn't; the guy who'd tackled me was still holding me."[20]

An angry Bryant stormed onto the field and yelled, "Goldarn it, Namath, it's not your job just to pitch the ball out and lay down there on the ground and not do anything. You don't just lay there."[21]

Namath began to walk back to the huddle with his head down as Bryant continued to grumble. Suddenly, Namath felt a strong yank on his facemask—Bryant grabbed his facemask so hard the freshman thought he had been lifted off the ground.

"Namath," Bryant barked, "when I'm talking to you, boy, you say, 'Yes, sir,' and look me in the eye."[22]

"Yes, sir," Namath immediately replied. "Yes, sir."[23]

Bryant and his new quarterback and protégé understood each other from that day forward. By the next season, Namath's extraordinary talents were on full display. Alabama opened the 1962 season with two dominating performances against Georgia (35–0) and Tulane (44–6). Broadcast on national television, audience members watched Namath's varsity debut against Georgia on September 22 at Legion Field in Birmingham before 54,000 fans. He didn't disappoint.

A few minutes into the game, Namath dropped back for a play-action pass. Georgia's defenders collapsed on the fullback as Namath lofted a perfect spiral over the left shoulder of receiver Richard Williamson, who caught the ball in stride and sprinted 52 yards for a touchdown 3:14 into the first quarter. Namath threw two more touchdown passes that day, finishing with 179 total passing yards. He also rushed for 36 yards. "Pat Trammell couldn't throw like that," said Williamson, then a senior. "We hadn't seen anybody who could throw like that . . . Joe was a whole different deal."[24]

Namath also brought his wit as well as a fierce competitive spirit to Tuscaloosa. Bryant witnessed both of those traits two weeks later in a game against Vanderbilt. Namath remembered having a "miserable day" when Bryant yanked him from the game after a series of bad downs. Angry and frustrated, Namath slammed his helmet to the turf as he walked off the field. Bryant calmly walked over to Namath without expression, sat beside him on the bench, and draped an arm around his young quarterback's neck.[25]

"There were about fifty thousand fans in the stands and it must have looked as though he was giving me some fatherly advice, or cheering me up," Namath said. "But what he was doing was squeezing the back of my neck with one of those big hands of his."[26]

Bryant leaned into Namath's ear and said, "Boy, don't let me ever see you come out of a ballgame acting like that. Don't you ever do that again."[27]

"Dammit, Coach," Namath replied. "I'm not pissed off at you or at anybody else. I'm just pissed off at myself for playing so damn bad. I deserved to be taken out of the game."[28]

Satisfied, Bryant walked away. Bryant later told another memorable story from that game—one that emphasized Namath's gift for what the coach defined as "street talk." A Vanderbilt defender smashed Namath on one tackle, and then tauntingly asked, "Hey, number twelve, what's your name?"[29]

"You'll see it in the headlines tomorrow," Namath shot back. On the next play, Namath threw a touchdown. Namath went on to lead Alabama to a 17–7 victory over Vanderbilt, completing 7 of 13 passes for 142 yards and two touchdowns.[30]

Namath eventually broke Trammell's single-season passing record in 1962 with 1,192 yards. Alabama finished with an overall 10–1 record, its lone loss being a 7–6 defeat against Georgia Tech in a Southeastern Conference clash. The Crimson Tide felt as though they had redeemed themselves on New Year's Day with a 17–0 triumph over Bud Wilkinson's powerful Oklahoma team in the Orange Bowl. All-American linebacker Lee Roy Jordan carried Alabama against the Sooners that day with an amazing 31 tackles in a performance witnessed firsthand by President John F. Kennedy.

Somehow, Alabama managed to finish with a number five national ranking in both the Associated Press and coaches' polls. Whether Alabama's status as an all-white team hurt them in the final rankings may be open for debate. What isn't a matter of conjecture is Alabama's defiant approval of segregation in 1962. By then, the national cries of racial injustice increasingly gathered over Bryant's program, the university, and the entire state of Alabama like mammoth storm clouds.

Jim Murray, the Pulitzer Prize-winning columnist for the *Los Angeles Times*, delivered some of the most stinging criticism of Alabama's stance on segregation in a series of columns in 1961. The editorials struck a nerve with Alabamans, probably because they were mostly true. Murray claimed to have traveled to Birmingham to cover Alabama's November 18 matchup with Georgia Tech, but the sportswriter's claim proved disingenuous. His real intention was to delve into Alabama's all-white roster and its anticipated invitation to the upcoming Rose Bowl—a legitimate news story framed by the South's continued institutional racism a century after the start of the Civil War.

"A writer—even a sportswriter—is supposed to cover the news," Murray wrote. "The real news of the game I covered had very little to do with the score. It had to do with the smell of roses and the color of the players."[31]

Bryant, as usual, held court with a group of reporters the day after Alabama's 10–0 victory over Georgia Tech. He hosted the gathering in his downtown suite at Birmingham's swank, 15-story Bankhead Hotel, where bourbon flowed in a festive atmosphere. Bryant enjoyed the banter, but not as much as he enjoyed what awaited his unbeaten squad. If the 9–0 Crimson Tide took care of business the following week against Auburn as expected, it was commonly thought they would receive an invitation to play UCLA at the Rose Bowl. Privately, Bryant probably savored the notion of Alabama's return to the Rose Bowl and the site of its 1935 victory over Stanford, when he had donned a Crimson Tide uniform.[32]

Regardless, Bryant felt proud of what his team had accomplished thus far, and his easy smile spoke volumes to those gathered. Then an unfamiliar voice arose from the pack as a man with thick, black glasses perched studiously on a long nose asked the coach a question.

"Coach Bryant," Murray said, "what did you think of the announcement out of UCLA that the colored players would not take the field against your team if it got to the Rose Bowl?"[33]

Silence suffocated the room. Bryant glared intensely at the stranger for a few uncomfortable moments. Murray stood his ground, waiting with a notepad and pen in hand. Bryant didn't appreciate being shown up by anyone, let alone a sportswriter from Los Angeles. Finally, Bryant replied in a raspy, southern drawl, "Oh, I would have nothing to say about that. Neither will the university I am sure."[34]

One local reporter, whose name has seemingly been blotted from history, angrily blurted, "Tell them West Coast Nigger-lovers to go lick your boots, Bear." The reporter didn't speak for everyone in the room, and a few other local scribes whispered their disapproval to Murray: "That's not the attitude."[35]

Murray returned to Los Angeles and unleashed a series of acidic columns meant to shame Southerners and Alabamians for their institutional racism. He openly called out any collegiate football program that fielded an all-white team in any corner of the United States, and he began with Bryant's Alabama squad. "It's worse than un-American, it's unhuman," Murray wrote in one column. "An all-white team has no business being #1, it's a denial of democracy."[36] In another column—bluntly titled "Bedsheets and 'Bama"—he called Birmingham the "gateway to the Ku Klux Klan," where an "evening dress" meant nothing more than "a bedsheet with eyeholes."[37]

Alabamans were livid.

So was Bryant, but not for what some might assume. Bryant's silence certainly made him complicit in Alabama's segregation policy, but in reality—and the historical record is clear on this point—Bryant worked behind the scenes as Alabama's head coach to bring about racial change as it pertained to his football program. In 1959, for instance, Bryant pushed the boundaries of Southern tolerance by insisting on playing an integrated Penn State team at the Liberty Bowl in Philadelphia, as opposed to the Bluegrass Bowl in Kentucky. Bryant's plan prompted immediate backlash in the forms of official protests and veiled threats of violence.

At least one Alabama board of trustees member publicly stated he would boycott the Penn State–Alabama game if it were played. Meanwhile, James Lester, chairman of the Tuscaloosa Citizens' Council, sent a telegram to Alabama

University president Frank Rose: "We strongly oppose our boys playing an integrated team. . . . The Tide belongs to all Alabama and Alabamians favored continued segregation."[38] As Bryant biographer Allen Barra so wittingly noted nearly half a century later, "Black Alabamians were not consulted on the issue."[39]

Rose also received another chilling telegram from a staunch segregationist who referred to the enrollment of Autherine Lucy at the university three years earlier. On February 3, 1956, Lucy had become the first African American student to attend the university. Three days later, riots erupted on campus, and the house of then president Oliver Carmichael was pelted with stones. As a result, trustees expelled Lucy from school. The telegram to Rose read:

> Dont [sic] you realize the consequences of a most certain repitition [sic] of trouble and a very probable unhappy return to such trouble to your doorstep. . . . May God have mercy on you at this Christmas season and the days to follow.[40]

Despite the protests, Bryant received his wish, and Alabama headed north to play Penn State. The decision wasn't entirely selfless on Bryant's part; he wanted Alabama to be viewed as a national power, not simply a regional one. Yet he also saw the game as a chance to shatter stereotypes. Billy Neighbors, Alabama's standout guard, recalled Bryant's careful instructions prior to taking the field against Penn State.

"They had a really good black lineman named Charlie Jones, and he lined up against me," Neighbors said before his death in 2012. "He was one of the best players I ever faced. All Coach Bryant said to me about playing against a black guy was, 'Now Billy, a lot of people are going to be watching us and watching how you behave yourself. You play hard, you play clean. You knock him down, you hold out your hand and help him back up.'"[41]

Penn State won the bowl game 7–0. Still, the game itself signified progress, even if that progress was moving at a glacial pace.

President Rose clarified Bryant's position on segregation in a 1983 interview with *New York Times* reporter Ira Berkow. In the article, which appeared seven days after Bryant's death, Rose told Berkow, "It's true that Bear worked very closely with me behind the scenes to bring about integration and to follow the court orders."[42]

Rose conceded that Bryant "wasn't contemptuous" of Governor Wallace, "but like me, differed on his racial position."[43] Rose also provided Berkow with something all journalists value—context. "You must remember," Rose empha-sized, "these were dangerous times, fearful times."[44]

The former university president recounted a trip he took to Montgomery to visit with Wallace. Prior to his arrival, someone fired a gunshot through a win dow of the governor's mansion. Even Wallace feared for his life.

"He told me, 'Some of these people are going to kill me, and going to kill you,'" Rose said. "It was not the climate for getting up [on] a public rostrum and lecturing people on the racial issue. Nowhere in the South. I don't think even Bryant could have done it and not have [had] a negative effect."[45]

Wallace, for his part, did nothing to soothe the racial discord. Instead, he stroked the flames of hate and division with his 1963 inaugural speech, in which he infamously declared, "In the name of the greatest people that ever trod this earth, I draw the line in the dust and toss the gauntlet before the feet of tyr-anny, and I say segregation now, segregation tomorrow, segregation forever." Five months later, Wallace defiantly stood in the doorway of Foster Auditorium at the University of Alabama to block the entry of two African American students wanting to enroll. Wallace was eventually ordered to step aside by the Alabama National Guard, which President Kennedy had federalized with an executive order.[46]

Amid this racial turmoil, in 1963 Bryant tried to build another national cham-pionship team on the strength of Namath's arm and a stingy defense. Yet the issue of race shadowed Bryant at every turn. Prior to one game at Legion Field, Rose said an exasperated Birmingham Police Chief Bull Connor contacted him. The chief asked if Rose could meet him at the mayor's office on an impor-tant matter. Rose agreed, and Bryant accompanied him from Tuscaloosa to Birmingham.

Upon their arrival, Connor told them tickets would not be sold to black fans.

"Bear and I told him we'd never play any more football games in Birming-ham," Rose recalled. "Connor said, 'Well, I guess I really didn't mean it.'

"Bear said to him, 'And if any black person is hurt or a rock thrown at him, we'll never come back.' The game was played, and blacks came and there were no incidents."[47]

Namath never felt comfortable with the dismissive way Southerners treated African Americans or the disparaging language used to describe them. In Beaver Falls, diversity reigned. Namath's hometown friends ran the spectrum of racial and ethnic backgrounds. Tuscaloosa, therefore, presented a culture shock.

During his freshman year, while studying, another student wandered into his dorm room. The student grabbed a picture Namath had on his desk of his girlfriend—a photograph of her as homecoming queen, surrounded by her court.

"That your girl, Joe?" the student asked.[48]

Namath never looked up, and muttered, "Yeah."[49]

Unbeknownst to Namath, the student had pointed to another girl in the picture—a black girl. Word quickly circulated that Namath had a black girlfriend, and other students began calling him "a Nigger-lover." Some simply called him "Nigger."[50] One teammate even told his parents, "You ought to see this nigger we got playing quarterback. This nigger's somethin' else."[51]

The player's parents thought Namath had broken Alabama's color barrier until they saw him remove his helmet one day on the sideline. "I wasn't a crusader or anything," Namath said. "Those people down there were just raised one way and I was raised another. I didn't care if a guy was black, white or purple. It made no difference to me."[52]

On the field, Namath continued to grow as a quarterback. His greatest challenge in 1963 ultimately proved to be himself and some old habits that shadowed him off the field. His troubles, though they certainly had nothing to do with racism, were nonetheless destructive. In a state searching for its soul, Namath now found his own cause for introspection.

One bad choice in particular left him at the crossroads of his Alabama football career. And in that defining moment, Namath encountered two men of integrity—Bryant and Stallings.

•   •   •

Word reached Bryant the week of Alabama's regular-season finale at Miami. Namath had been seen drunk and directing traffic in Tuscaloosa's downtown district. "When I heard it I was sick," Bryant said. "Nauseated."[53]

If true, Namath had violated Bryant's sacred in-season training rules about drinking alcohol and would have to be suspended. The coach sought Namath in his dorm that Monday morning to learn the truth but couldn't find his star quarterback. So Bryant sat in the nearby dining room to drink a cup of coffee. Namath suddenly appeared, plopped into a chair next to his coach, and began talking game plans.

"Joe, let's go back to my room," Bryant interrupted. "I want to talk to you."[54]

Bryant sat Namath down and wasted no time with small talk. He told Namath about the disturbing story he had heard, and asked, "Is that true?"[55]

"No, sir," Namath replied. "That's a lie. I wasn't drunk and I wasn't directing traffic downtown Saturday afternoon. I was watching the Army–Navy game on television."[56]

"Were you drinking at all Saturday?"[57]

"Well, yes, sir," Namath said. "I had a drink Saturday night."[58]

Bryant appeared upset and reflexively said "Oh, no," before pausing to think. A few seconds passed without a word. "Joe," he finally said, "I've got to suspend you."[59]

A visibly shaken Bryant then instructed Namath to report back to him later that day in his office. Alabama, then 7–2 overall, sat at a critical point in its season, with two nationally televised games to play—one at Miami and another against number seven-ranked Ole Miss in the Sugar Bowl. Namath's absence would leave both games in doubt.

Bryant gathered his assistant coaches to garner their input on Namath's punishment. He started with Dude Hennessey, who voiced empathy for the youngster. Hennessey didn't want Namath suspended.

"Aw, Dude," Bryant growled, "you're worried about your bowl bonus."[60]

One by one each assistant weighed in on the issue, and one by one, each offered an alternative form of punishment. No one wanted Namath suspended. No one except Stallings. The 28-year-old coach sat and shook his head.

"Nah," Stallings said to Bryant, "if it had been me, you would've kicked me off the team, right?"[61]

Bryant nodded.

"Well, then," Stallings firmly added, "let him go."[62]

Stallings found no satisfaction in his conviction, only a sense of what was right and wrong. Personally, he liked Namath. He simply believed no one should be above the team rules, and by letting one player slide on an infraction, it would be detrimental to the team as well as the player. Stallings stood firm in this belief, a belief seasoned by years of hard knocks as arguably one of Bryant's all-time greatest team players.

Once, during his senior season, Stallings found himself in a battle for his starting end position with a talented junior, Bobby Marks.

"Coach Bryant pulled Gene aside one day and said, 'Bebes, you gotta pick it up out there or else I'm gonna have to bench you,'" Herskowitz recalled. "He said, 'You're one of my captains, and I don't want to have to do that. So pick it up.' To

Gene's credit, he never complained. Not one word. He just scratched and clawed his way into the lineup."[63]

Stallings shared his thoughts at the time about his starting position with fellow receiver Bobby Drake, who was shocked by the depth of his teammate's unselfish attitude.

"Bobby Marks is just better than me," Stallings told Drake.[64]

"Nah."[65]

"Yeah, he is," Stallings added. "And if it makes the team better, so be it."[66]

Drake looked at Stallings and said, "You're crazy, Bebes."[67]

Hard work and self-sacrifice weren't simply phrases to Stallings. During one spring practice his sophomore year, he nearly ripped a finger off when it got caught on a helmet. Stallings returned to practice the next day after a few stitches.[68]

Unlike Namath, nothing came easy for Stallings on the football field. So he ran every drill and played every down as if his life hung in the balance. In the 1954 season opener against Texas Tech—the first game for the famous Junction Boys—A&M was taking a pounding as Stallings watched from the sideline. Finally, early in the third quarter, Bryant instructed Stallings to take the field. Texas Tech ended up posting a 41–9 victory in a game with few bright moments for the Aggies, but Stallings still managed to make an impression on his new coach. During Monday's practice, Bryant gathered his team and sternly lectured them on the numerous ways in which they must improve. He then stared at Stallings and said, "My biggest mistake was not playing that skinny kid over there."[69]

"That was a proud moment for me," Stallings said with a broad smile. "I thought, *Coach Bryant has singled me out in front of the whole team.* From that moment on, I would have run through a brick wall for him."[70]

By the time of the Namath episode in 1963, Stallings's life had also been framed by a different perspective. He would later credit that gift to his son John Mark, who was born June 11, 1962, with Down syndrome. Society then attached a stigma to children with Down syndrome, and Stallings and his wife, Ruth Ann, struggled to accept the fact that their child had a disability. They even wondered if they had done something wrong.

"I threw myself into my work," Stallings recalled. "It seemed like the only thing to help me cope."[71]

Stallings buried himself in every aspect of his job—recruiting trips, new coaching techniques and drills, media interviews . . . anything to distract him from the reality of his son's condition. Then, four weeks into the 1962 season,

Stallings and his wife noticed a "bluish tint" on their four-month-old son's face. They rushed him to the local hospital, praying he wouldn't die. The next morning, a cardiologist sat the couple down in his office and delivered the bad news: John Mark suffered from a life-threatening heart defect. The gravity of the doctor's words left them breathless:

> Johnny has a condition called Eisenmenger's syndrome. Essentially he has a hole in the wall of the heart which separates the heart chambers. The flow of blood between the heart and lungs meets with resistance. As Johnny gets older his resistance will increase. The oxygenated blood and nonoxygenated blood get mixed up, and for the rest of his life he will have trouble getting enough oxygen.[72]

Suddenly, without warning, Stallings started to evaluate his own life. His passion and commitment to caching football never wavered, but his infant son reminded him of what was truly important in this world. He began to cherish every moment of every day.

"Now I was slowing down, taking my time a little more with my family, my friends, and my work," he said. "I wasn't concentrating on the future so much, because I didn't know from one day to the next if my son was going to live or not."[73]

Stallings discovered a newfound perspective.

So when Bryant asked him what kind of punishment he thought would be fair for Namath a year later, Stallings answered with an honest heart. In that moment, he wasn't thinking about bowl bonuses or wins and losses. His evaluation of the situation sprang from a much loftier plane, perhaps even a spiritual one. At the very least, he wanted to stand on the solid mantle of integrity. Without it, what was the point?

Bryant, like his young coaching protégé, subscribed to the same conviction. He realized Namath had to be suspended. The coach dismissed his assistants, shut the door to his office for two hours, and cried.[74]

Finally, Bryant called his coaches back into his office. Someone retrieved Namath, who found the entire coaching staff waiting for him. Only Bryant spoke. "You're suspended, and I don't give a damn what anybody here says," Bryant said. "You're not going to play. The university could change this decision if they wanted to, or I could. But if they change it or I change it I'll resign."[75]

"Aw, no, coach, I don't want you to do that," Namath replied.[76]

Bryant stuck to his decision. Namath didn't play the final two games of the season, and through sheer grit, Alabama responded with a 17–12 victory over Miami and a 12–7 triumph over Ole Miss in the Sugar Bowl to finish with a 9–2 record. Years later, Hicks—the team manager and Namath's devoted friend—said a lot of Alabama players were also partying that night and drank until they were drunk. To Namath's credit, he never implicated anyone else.[77]

By the next season, Namath had earned both Bryant's trust and a way back onto the team through hard work and commitment. He then led Alabama to a national championship with a 10–1 record, showing discipline and maturity to accompany his amazing talents. After the season, his reward came in the form of a $400,000 contract to play for the New York Jets in the fledgling American Football League. Upon signing his first professional contract, Namath approached Bryant and said, "I want to tell you, you were right. You did the right thing, suspending me. And I want to thank you."[78]

And no one took more pride in those words than Stallings.[79]

NOTES

1. Mark Kriegel, *Namath: A Biography* (New York: Penguin, 2004), 72.
2. Gold, *Bear's Boys*, 164.
3. Ibid.
4. Kriegel, *Namath*, 72.
5. Joe Namath and Dick Schaap, *I Can't Wait until Tomorrow . . . 'Cause I Get Better Looking Every Day* (New York: Random House, 1969), 133.
6. Ibid., 73.
7. Kriegel, *Namath*, 73.
8. Ibid.
9. Gold, *Bear's Boys*, 165.
10. Land, interview with author, March 30, 2018.
11. Stallings, interview with author, July 8, 2015.
12. Bryant and Underwood, *Bear*, 199.
13. Ibid., 200.
14. Kriegel, *Namath*, 52.
15. *Times-Tribune* (Beaver Falls, PA), November 15, 1960. Also quoted in Kriegel, *Namath*, 53.
16. Bryant and Underwood, *Bear*, 200.
17. Ibid.

18. Kriegel, *Namath*, 67.

19. Ibid., 68.

20. Namath and Schaap, *I Can't Wait*, 133.

21. Ibid.

22. Ibid.

23. Ibid.

24. Kriegel, *Namath*, 61.

25. Namath and Schaap, *I Can't Wait*, 134.

26. Herskowitz, *Legend*, 147.

27. Namath and Schaap, *I Can't Wait*, 134.

28. Ibid.

29. Bryant and Underwood, *Bear*, 201.

30. Ibid.

31. *Los Angeles Times*, November 29, 1961.

32. Ibid., November 20, 1961.

33. Ibid.

34. Ibid.

35. Frank A. Rose, letter to Daniel J. Haughton, November 29, 1961, Rose Papers.

36. *Los Angeles Times*, November 20, 1961.

37. Ibid.

38. Dunnavant, *Coach*, 241.

39. Barra, *Last Coach*, 227.

40. Dunnavant, *Coach*, 252.

41. Barra, *Last Coach*, 228.

42. *New York Times*, February 2, 1983.

43. Ibid.

44. Ibid.

45. Ibid. In 2008, the Associated Press reviewed documents obtained under the Freedom of Information Act that revealed the FBI tracked Bryant for nearly two years. The FBI opened a file on the Alabama coach after US federal judge U. W. Clemon—then a prominent Birmingham attorney who fought the state's all-white establishment—filed a lawsuit in July 1969 against Bryant, the University of Alabama, and others for violating the Civil Rights Act of 1964. The act outlawed racial segregation at public educational institutions, and the lawsuit claimed violations on the grounds that Alabama had no African American football players on scholarship.

   In both a sworn statement and in interviews, Bryant insisted he had been trying to recruit African American athletes for years prior to the lawsuit. The lawsuit was dismissed in 1971 after the university issued a few scholarships to black athletes, thus also ending the FBI's surveillance of Bryant.

   Clemon suspected the monitoring of Bryant might have had more to do with him. In a 2008 interview, he said, "Bear Bryant was a god in Alabama in those days; maybe it was just a matter of keeping up. And you have to recall the thinking of some of the southern FBI agents at the time. Maybe they thought I was doing something illegal. Maybe they just wanted to pursue it because black people were suing Bear Bryant" (Associated Press, November 15, 2008).

46. A fascinating postscript to George Wallace's life can be found in a powerful September 1994 column written by Jay "Sweet Tea" Grelen for the *Mobile Register*. Grelen spent the day in Montgomery with the former Alabama governor, who was then 75 years old and wheelchair-bound from a would-be assassin's bullet. "He lives in a world of silence now," Grelen poetically wrote, "stone deaf, and at moments he seems adrift in the silence." Grelen noted that nearly all Wallace's needs were handled seven days a week by three caretakers—Eddie Holcey, Jimmy Dallas, and Robert Jackson. All three men are black. Later that day Benny Maynor—a member of the governor's security staff—drove the entourage to a local restaurant where Grelen profoundly observed, "The six of us plant ourselves under one table for lunch—two white hands, three black hands and Governor Segregation's hand, all snagging bread from the same straw basket."

   Wallace died four years later on September 13, 1998.
47. Associated Press, November 15, 2008.
48. Namath and Schaap, *I Can't Wait*, 110.
49. Ibid.
50. Ibid., 111.
51. Ibid.
52. Ibid.
53. Bryant and Underwood, *Bear*, 202.
54. Ibid., 203.
55. Namath and Schaap, *I Can't Wait*, 136.
56. Ibid.
57. Ibid.
58. Ibid.
59. Ibid., 136–37.
60. Kriegel, *Namath*, 102.
61. Stallings, interview with author, July 8, 2015.
62. Ibid.
63. Mickey Herskowitz, interview with author, August 20, 2018.
64. Dent, *Junction Boys*, 233.
65. Ibid.
66. Ibid.
67. Ibid.
68. Ibid.
69. Stallings and Cook, *Another Season*, 50.
70. Stallings, interview with author, July 8, 2015.
71. Stallings and Cook, *Another Season*, 29.
72. Ibid., 35.

73. Ibid., 43.

74. Bryant and Underwood, *Bear*, 203.

75. Ibid.

76. Ibid., 204.

77. Kriegel, *Namath*, 102. Charles H. Land recounted the trip to New Orleans for the Sugar Bowl that season and how he and few other sportswriters ended up at one of the big parties. "Joe and his friend, 'Hoot Owl' Hicks went to New Orleans on their own, and we sneaked them into the party with us," Land recalled. "I remember Joe wearing his shades. We probably shouldn't have done it, but we did."

78. Namath and Schaap, *I Can't Wait*, 137.

79. Stallings, interview with author, July 8, 2015.

CHAPTER 8
Make Something Happen

He threw himself into the task with the abandon of a Bryant-trained general.

—*Houston Chronicle*, on new Texas A&M head coach Gene Stallings

Whispers of Gene Stallings's return to Texas A&M first reached Mickey Herskowitz's tidy desk at the *Houston Post* on a clear, chilly December afternoon in 1964. Tipsters informed the popular sports columnist that the 29-year-old Stallings had been hired as A&M's new head coach.

For Herskowitz, the news felt like the return of the prodigal son to College Station. Ten years earlier, Herskowitz—then a cub reporter—had watched a tall, skinny Stallings survive the hell of Bryant's first training camp at Junction with 28 other determined Aggie players. Over the next three seasons, Herskowitz and Stallings developed a friendship, and in later years, the sportswriter would note that Stallings was one of his "immediate favorites" among the Junction Boys.[1]

Now Herskowitz had to verify the rumors.

Since Stallings would be unable to confirm the reports until his contract had been formally approved, Herskowitz instead reached out to numerous sources at College Station from his newsroom at the corner of Polk and Dowling in downtown Houston. He soon received confirmation of the hire from well-connected A&M contacts—the type of wealthy alumni who routinely supplement a football coach's official salary in private.[2]

• • •

In Tuscaloosa, meanwhile, Stallings tried to absorb the last 48 hours. On Sunday, he received a telephone call from Pete Peterson, a Texas A&M board of trustees member, on his way out the door for church. Peterson asked Stallings if he would be interested in interviewing for A&M's vacant head coaching position. Stallings eagerly agreed, and by the next morning, he was aboard a private jet headed for College Station.

The trustees offered Stallings the job that same day, after a few "short and direct" questions. Stallings, in turn, accepted the job on the spot.

Money hadn't even been discussed.[3]

Upon his return to Alabama, Stallings questioned whether the job made sense for his family, especially Johnny. Ruth Ann often drove Johnny to his cardiologist's office an hour away in Birmingham, and the couple had grown to trust and respect their son's medical team. Gene shared his reservations with his wife, who smiled and replied, "This is the opportunity of a lifetime. We've got to go for it."[4]

Ruth Ann's words meant everything. They always had.

Stallings then picked up the telephone to call Coach Bryant, who was attending the College Football Hall of Fame dinner in New York City. He wanted his mentor to hear the news from him before reading about it in the newspapers or seeing it on television.

"Coach Bryant, this is Bebes," Stallings said when Bryant answered. "I just wanted to call and tell you they've offered me a job as head coach at A&M and I've accepted it."[5]

Bryant didn't say a word.

"You know, I've always appreciated the opportunity you gave me coaching in college and getting me started at Alabama," Stallings continued. "I have really enjoyed working for the very best and I just wanted to thank you."[6]

Bryant haltingly offered a few words before saying good-bye. Afterward, Stallings felt confused by Bryant's relative silence. A few days later, someone in the hotel suite told Stallings that Bryant was crying.[7]

• • •

Shortly thereafter, Herskowitz sought to contact Bryant for a comment about the departure of his beloved protégé. He learned Bryant was in New York.

"I knew Coach Bryant liked to stay at the Waldorf Astoria whenever he was in New York," Herskowitz recalled. "So I dialed the hotel, and asked for Paul Bryant's room." Amused, Herskowitz added, "Coach had registered under his own name."[8]

The desk clerk promptly patched him through to Bryant's room.

Bryant openly shared his feelings with Herskowitz, perhaps one of the few reporters he trusted. The coach confessed the news had hit him hard emotionally.

"It's the first time I've cried in twenty or thirty years, and believe me, I really did," Bryant said. "I cried because I'm so proud that one of my little Junction Boys is going back there to take over. And second, I cried because I'm upset over losing him. Shoot, with Stallings gone I may have to go back to work."[9]

Bryant continued as Herskowitz scribbled on his notepad, "A&M could go back to [Knute] Rockne, and they could not have picked a better man. He will be the best football coach the school ever had, and that includes father [Bryant]."[10]

The older, mellower Bryant now spoke in paternalistic terms when talking about former players. Herskowitz understood Bryant's genuine affections for Stallings as well as anyone, but even he dismissed some of Bryant's comments that day about crying as "hyperbole" or some of the coach's "unique hokum."[11]

Several years later, Herskowitz learned otherwise when fellow sportswriter Bob Curran of the *Buffalo News* shared a humorous sequel to that day. In December of 1964, Curran was working as a freelance writer in his native Boston and was in New York to cover the College Football Hall of Fame dinner. He walked into Bryant's hotel suite and as he entered, Alabama assistant coach Dude Hennessey raised his index finger to his lips: "Shhh." Hennessey pointed to Bryant, who at that moment was on the phone, probably talking to either Stallings or Herskowitz.

Curran noticed tears on Bryant's cheeks.

"What's the matter with Paul?" Curran asked quietly.

"He lost one of his coaches," Hennessey replied.

"Oh, my God," Curran said. "How old was he?"

"Twenty-nine."

"Oh," Curran said shaking his head, "that's terrible."

"Oh, no," said Hennessey, realizing Curran misunderstood. "He didn't die. He just went to Texas A&M."[12]

. . .

Stallings walked into a mess at Texas A&M.

The celebrated gains under Bryant's leadership were already ancient history around College Station as the calendar flipped to 1965. Since Bryant's departure in 1957, the Aggies had played a dismal brand of football, if any brand at all. A&M had compiled a combined 10–33–4 record in the Southwest Conference and an 18–47–3 mark overall since Bryant's exit for Alabama.

In the three previous seasons, the Aggies won a total of only five conference games under head coach Hank Foldberg. The Aggie faithful were starved for a return to glory—a theme that had once greeted Bryant in February of 1954.

"I feared for him (Stallings) because I knew they didn't have any talent," Herskowitz said of the Aggie roster. "On the other hand, I knew that was as close as they were going to get to having Coach Bryant back. And I thought if anyone could turn that around and make them a winner, Coach Stallings could."[13]

At least one man in Alabama believed in Stallings.

The new Texas A&M coach—now the youngest collegiate head coach in the nation—spent his final days in Tuscaloosa saying his good-byes. He saved his last farewell for Bryant, who motioned him into his office. Bryant plopped one of his burly hands on Stallings's shoulder, and said, "Bebes, I'm going to give you three pieces of advice: Don't look back. Don't lose your guts. And go out onto that field and make something happen."[14]

Stallings unflinchingly vowed to do all three.

Bryant's words had long ago cast a spell over Stallings. As a player, he'd famously carried a small notebook on him during practices and meetings. Teammates playfully ribbed him about his notetaking habits, but he remained unfazed by the jokes. Stallings meticulously wrote down everything Bryant said and later copied it into a gigantic notebook that remained in his possession.[15]

Stallings's original notebook also became the foundation for Bryant's 1960 book, *Building a Championship Football Team*, which Stallings himself had ghostwritten in time for Christmas. Stallings never received public credit for penning the book and when asked about his literary endeavor shrugged with indifference. Loyalty for Bryant coursed through his veins.[16]

Stallings ventured to College Station with a determination to earn the praise of his legendary mentor and "make something happen." He immediately dove into his work by hiring a coaching staff filled with Bryant disciples. His first order of business was to rehire the person who would be the lone remaining member of Bryant's A&M staff—Elmer Smith—as his offensive line coach. Smith had been fired along with Foldberg, but Stallings harbored great respect for the Arkansas native that dated back to his earliest days at Junction.

Smith, whom the players called "Coach Elmer," fit every description of a rugged, no-nonsense man from another era. During his playing days, he lettered in basketball, baseball, football, and track and field at Hendrix College. On the football field, he earned a reputation as a punishing fullback. Hendrix football coach Ivan Groves once said Smith was "one of the hardest runners ever to come out of the state of Arkansas. He could make yardage through a concrete wall."[17]

Smith coached like he ran a football.

Like a lot of standout athletes, Smith possessed enormous hands, and whenever he grabbed a player, the coach instantly had their attention. Smith presented an intimidating presence as a large-framed man with cutting eyes. He wore a signature brown felt hat tilted to one side and baggy shirts and shorts that flapped in the wind. Players usually heard him approach before they saw him, although he wasn't one for small talk. Stallings loved everything about Smith, whom he described as a "hard-nosed man with a lot of common sense . . ."[18]

Coach Elmer also knew the Paul W. Bryant way. He would not be alone. Stallings also hired former A&M teammates Dee Powell, Don Watson, Loyd Taylor, and Jack Pardee as assistants. He additionally brought in former Alabama quarterback Jack Hurlbut, who had played under Bryant and respected his coaching philosophies.

Bryant's fingerprints were once again all over A&M's program, and the *Houston Chronicle* took note in an article titled "Young Bear Growls at Grid Foes." The piece praised Stallings for his early decisions, while fully embracing the romance of Bear's mammoth shadow:

> He threw himself into the task with the abandon of a Bryant-trained general, appointing the lone remaining member of Bryant's staff—Elmer Smith—as his assistant and filling his staff with men who know the Bryant system and are devoted to victory.[19]

Yet for all the superlatives and optimism, even Stallings knew he couldn't win without recruiting talent. And Texas A&M was never a harder place to attract recruits than at the dawn of 1965.

Anti-Vietnam protests raged on college campuses across the country, but the military confines of Texas A&M remained relatively quiet under university president James Earl Rudder, a retired US Army major general who commanded over 1,000 Rangers during the D-Day landings at Normandy. Rudder lost half his battalion while storming the beaches at Pointe du Hoc, where he and his men scaled 100-foot cliffs under enemy fire to reach and destroy German gun batteries. Rudder led the charge.

Rudder and his men then held off German counterattacks for two days before reinforcements arrived. The major general himself received two wounds during the fierce fighting. So he had no stomach for antimilitary fervor and no time for any sort of perceived collegiate nonsense. Once, in 1963, a large group of cadets marched on Rudder's residence at night, outraged that A&M had voted to allow female students on a limited basis. Incredibly, the cadets stood outside and burned the general in effigy.

"I just saw the flames out there and you could hear the kids," recalled Margaret Rudder, the general's wife. "It liked to have scared me to death."[20]

General Rudder rolled over and went back to sleep.

Recruits who didn't appreciate a military atmosphere in 1965 therefore quickly scratched Texas A&M off their lists. In addition, the university also continued its unspoken policy of segregation and refused to give scholarships to African American football players. Stallings received public criticism in some quarters for A&M's dearth of African American scholarship players, although those who knew him best contend that the issue deeply bothered him at the time.

"That was a touchy point for Gene, and he got some bad press out of it," recalled Herskowitz, whom Gene and Ruth Ann regularly invited into their home for dinner in those days. "But he was operating within an old system of rules, and there wasn't much he could do. I'll say this, I don't think there was a biased bone in his body."[21]

Stallings recounted a time when a representative of the National Association for the Advancement of Colored People (NAACP) visited his office at A&M. The representative pointedly asked Stallings why he had not given a scholarship to any African American football players since his arrival at College Station.

"I reached into my drawer and pulled out a list of the top African American recruits in the nation," Stallings recalled. "I said, 'If you can get any of these players to come play for me at A&M, I'll give them a scholarship.' The man put the list in his briefcase and left my office. I never heard from him again."[22]

In truth, the segregation issue soared far above Stallings. The problem was institutionally embedded at A&M as well as throughout the Southwest

Conference. Loyd Taylor, who coached offensive backs in 1965, once told a story that profoundly revealed the depth of resistance to desegregation in Aggieland.

Taylor's story occurred during A&M's first recruiting forays under Stallings. As the story goes, Taylor received a tip about a phenomenal linebacker at the all-black Dunbar High School in Temple, Texas. Determined to find the best talent Texas could offer, Taylor pulled into Temple on a trip to meet the youngster and his coach. He wanted to do his due diligence.

Taylor waited in a room while someone retrieved the young man from class. Moments later, the youngster walked into the room and Taylor marveled at the physique of the player standing before him—6-foot-4, with broad shoulders and bulging muscles. "Here, I hadn't even seen him play," Taylor would later recall, "but if I could have offered him a scholarship on the spot, I would have."[23]

In an effort to be thorough, Taylor watched game films of the young man before leaving Temple. As the film rolled, Taylor couldn't believe his eyes. He rushed back to College Station and told Stallings, "We need to offer this kid a scholarship. He's *that* good. Best high school player I've ever seen."[24]

Stallings initially balked at the suggestion, fully aware the player was African American.

"Well, Loyd," Stallings replied. "It's just not the right time."[25]

Taylor insisted Stallings watch the game films. Stallings obliged and became equally enamored of the player's power, speed, and prowess. Finally, Stallings turned to Taylor and said, "Let's go talk to General Rudder."[26]

The general listened to Stallings's pitch to make this recruit Texas A&M's first African American scholarship football player—a move that would have generated a flood of media coverage nationwide in 1965. Rudder allowed Stallings to finish making his case and then replied, "Well, Gene, I just don't think it's the right time."[27]

Rudder's word was final.

Afterward, Taylor telephoned a friend who worked as an assistant coach at North Texas State College in Denton. He urged his friend to sign the player to a scholarship—immediately. The friend relayed the message to his head coach, Odus Mitchell. Taylor's account concluded with Mitchell telling his friend to sign the player and adding, "But if that kid can't play, I'm gonna fire your ass."[28]

The player hardly disappointed, switching to defensive tackle and earning consensus All-American status for the North Texas Mean Green squad. He then became the fourth player selected in the National Football League draft by the Pittsburgh Steelers and enjoyed a Hall of Fame career.[29]

The player? "Mean" Joe Greene.[30]

Upon hearing Taylor's story, Herskowitz added, "The [Texas A&M] board would have never allowed it then."[31]

Stallings simply arrived at A&M at a challenging time. As if institutional segregation wasn't enough of a hurdle, the Aggie coaching staff also had to compete with their rivals at University of Texas for talent. The Longhorns had long cornered the market on the state's top white high school prospects, usually signing whoever they pleased at a time when there were no limits on the number of scholarships a university could offer. Everyone else fought for the scraps. Or so lingered the perception.

Stallings, however, remained undeterred by the numerous challenges. He saw what Bryant accomplished in three seasons at A&M with grit and tenacity, and in that sense felt buoyed by hope. On the issue of recruiting, he unsurprisingly embraced another Bryant maxim: "Coach Bryant didn't tell you how to load the truck, he just told you to load it."[32]

By the time Stallings and his coaches first fanned out across Texas, the Aggie "truck" looked empty. That soon changed. Stallings dug into his bag of hope. He and his coaches sold the dawn of a new era in Aggieland, speaking of future championships as a reality and not a dream. They spoke with conviction and sincerity. Stallings also brought cachet as a Bryant protégé and Junction survivor whenever he walked into a prospective recruit's home.

Suddenly, talented players started to listen. Texas A&M once again appeared relevant.

But nothing came easy on the recruiting trail. Stallings and his assistants remained on the road for days and weeks at a time, working tirelessly to catch up with other schools and land top recruits. One of Stallings's first recruiting stops carried him to Cass County in the far northeastern reaches of the state. Cass County bordered the Louisiana state line and was home to Edd Hargett—an intelligent, strong passing quarterback who played for Linden-Kildare High School.

The 5-foot-11, 175-pound Hargett had grown up on a farm and was the youngest of four sons to Otto and Mary Edna Hargett. The family grew watermelons, corn, and cotton, but by the time Edd was old enough to help on the farm, the Hargetts were primarily raising cattle. Sports filled the time between chores. All three of his brothers—Ottis, James, and George—played college football at various levels. George played as fullback for Texas A&M between 1961 and 1963, when losing was as commonplace at College Station as military attire.

Prior to A&M's hiring of Stallings as part of Foldberg's staff, Elmer Smith had courted Edd. Smith couldn't hide his waning enthusiasm, though, as the expected dismissal of Foldberg left Smith uncertain about his own future employment. George, meanwhile, discouraged his younger brother from signing with his alma mater. Frankly, George had lost all faith in Foldberg's ability to coach.[33]

The University of Arkansas was simultaneously vying for Edd's services, and after numerous trips to Fayetteville to watch the Razorbacks, he began to view Arkansas as his first choice.

The arrival of Stallings dramatically changed the landscape, especially in the Hargett farmhouse. The tall, lanky Junction legend entered the Hargett home with an intensity and confidence captured in his motto, "Make something happen." Edd Hargett sensed Stallings deeply believed in what he was saying and admitted, "He pretty much sold me that first visit."[34]

One hundred and sixty miles to the west, at 334 East Main Street in Richardson—a town just north of Dallas—Stallings entered the home of running back Wendell Housley with the same passion and conviction. The 6-foot-2, 190-pound Housley had earned a reputation as a bruising runner who was difficult to bring down. Several colleges were recruiting him at the time, including the University of Oklahoma, Texas Tech, University of Texas, Oklahoma State University, the University of Houston, the University of Tulsa, and the US Naval Academy. The list went on.[35]

"It was a blur," Housley recalled. "Everything was so fast and furious. . . . I'd get off one call and get another call from another coach."[36]

In high school, Housley and his buddy Steve Higgins (a fullback) provided a potent backfield duo for Richardson, but the Eagles competed in the same district as annual powerhouse Garland. Legendary high school coach Charles "Chuck" Curtis led Garland in back-to-back Class 4A state championships during Housley's junior and senior years. Housley, meanwhile, also proved to be a competitive sprinter for Richardson's track and field team.

Robert and Etna Housley also provided Wendell with a strong work ethic away from his athletic endeavors. Robert worked as a general contractor and custom home builder, and co-owned and operated a custom harvesting business with a friend. In addition, the Housleys ran a farm in nearby McKinney, where Wendell and his three siblings shared in every aspect of the operation, from administering vaccinations to the maintenance of tractors.[37]

Yet it was Wendell's ability to run a football that ensured he would receive a top-notch education. "If you get an education at any of these universities, you're gonna be OK," Robert Housley told his son. "This is your decision to make."[38]

Wendell didn't take his responsibility lightly. He weighed what each college offered and studied what each coach said and even how they said it. Stallings instantly stood out. The new Texas A&M coach entered the Housley home with a natty sports coat and alligator boots, but his words were far from those of a "slick-talker" or hustler. Housley remembered Stallings as "just an ol' country boy" who delivered his recruitment pitch matter-of-factly, passionately, and with a slow drawl. "Of course," Housley added, "my folks are just country folks and they liked that."[39]

"We've got some folks we're looking at that hopefully we can bring in, including you," Stallings told Housley. "And in a couple years, I hope to win the South-west Conference and then after that shoot for a national championship."[40]

Housley was sold but told the coach he wouldn't sign until after he visited other campuses and heard what other coaches had to say. Stallings understood Austin to be one of those stops, to visit Longhorn coach Darrel Royal.

"Now you might go over there, and you might find all these talented players at Texas," Stallings warned. "But if you go to A&M, you're gonna play."[41]

If Stallings coveted Housley at that moment, he surely wanted him more after the young man's response.

"Coach," Housley replied without hesitation, "I don't care where I go, but I'm gonna play."[42]

Fortunately for Stallings, Housley chose to don the maroon-and-white jersey of the Aggies.

Perhaps the greatest steal of A&M's 1965 recruiting class hailed from Ama-rillo, although no one would have predicted it at the time. Aggie assistant coach Ralph Smith certainly had no idea what kind of player he would encounter the first time he set eyes on Willie Glenn "Billy" Hobbs, a 6-foot-1, 175-pound tight end who played for the smashmouth Amarillo Tascosa High School program and earned honorable mention on the All-State team.[43]

Hobbs started on a Tascosa squad loaded with talent. The Rebels reached the state semifinals in both his junior and senior years, only to be eliminated by Class 4A buzz saw Garland both years. In 1963, Tascosa posted a 10–1–2 record after Garland defeated them 7–6, one game shy of the state title game. Garland eliminated Tascosa once again the next season with a 21–7 victory in the state semifinals. The Rebels finished with a 13–1 record in 1964, while Garland rolled to its second straight state championship.[44]

Hobbs also excelled on the track for Tascosa, where he finished second in the state in the low hurdles and mile relay. Therein lied his greatest athletic asset: speed.

Ironically, Hobbs almost dismissed the idea of playing football at A&M. "I hadn't even considered A&M," Hobbs once said. "None of my friends wanted to go to A&M and I didn't know anything about it."[45]

Aggie assistant Ralph Smith, who scouted and recruited in the Texas Panhandle, tried to sell A&M one afternoon to Hobbs and several of his teammates. Before getting too detailed, Smith bluntly told the group, "If any of you have no wish to visit A&M, I guess we might as well know it right now."[46]

Several Tascosa players walked away. Hobbs remained. Momentarily, he thought about leaving with his friends. But something told him to stay and hear what Smith had to say. A few years later, Hobbs would call it "the best decision I ever made."[47]

Hobbs still almost signed with Texas Tech.

Amarillo oilman Joe Richardson Jr. heard about Hobbs's intention and interceded. Richardson had graduated from Texas A&M in 1949 with bachelor of science degrees in petroleum engineering and mechanical engineering. He convinced Hobbs to visit with Stallings in person and flew him down to College Station in his private airplane.

The visit sealed the deal, and Hobbs signed with A&M.[48]

Aggie fans would someday celebrate his decision.

Stallings found another gem in his hometown of Paris, Texas, in two-sport standout Bob Long. The Paris High School quarterback earned All-State honors despite his team's 2–8 record. Bob was the son of Poss Long, a hard-nosed taskmaster who coached basketball, baseball, and track and field at nearby Delmar High School in Lamar County. The young signal-caller also played baseball for the Wildcats, anchoring the infield as an All-District shortstop for his Paris ball club.[49]

Long's combination of athleticism and skill ensured he would play both football and baseball in college. Stallings hoped he could entice Long to bring his talents to College Station and drove to his hometown to make his pitch in person. He had undoubtedly heard rave reviews about Long from longtime friends who lived in Paris.

The coach's visit proved to be as memorable for Long as it was humorous.

"You wanna be a football player?" Stallings asked in his slow, deep drawl.

"Oh, well, not exactly," Long answered in a moment of honesty. "I wanna play baseball."

A few moments later, Stallings tried to steer the conversation in a positive direction by asking the youngster, "Are you a winner?" Long thought the coach was asking whether his Paris football squad enjoyed a winning season.

"No, not really," he replied sheepishly. "We only won two games."

Fortunately for Long, his father interceded on his son's behalf

"Yeah, he's a winner," Poss Long quickly interjected. "He didn't have much of a team around him."[50]

Stallings still offered young Long the scholarship.

"Yeah," said Long, recalling that first meeting with a laugh, "I imagine he wanted to get up and walk out."[51]

Fortunately for Stallings, he didn't.

Another hidden gem for Stallings emerged from Houston's Jesse H. Jones High School, in receiver Tommy Maxwell, who managed to cram football, basketball, baseball, swimming, and track and field into his extracurricular schedule. Maxwell received All-City honors for Jones on the football field, where his versatility and supreme conditioning would later prove invaluable for the Aggies.

"With Tommy, you thought of ol' Atlas holding the globe," Housley said. "He had the perfect athletic body."[52]

Rolf Krueger garnered the attention of A&M and several other schools with his brute strength as well as his family bloodline. The 6-foot-3, 210-pound lineman from Bryan, Texas, was the youngest brother of Charlie Krueger, a two-time All-American lineman at A&M under Bryant. By the winter of 1965, Charlie was playing for the San Francisco 49ers as his younger brother made the rounds as a recruit.

Yet Rolf Krueger hardly needed anyone's help to gain notoriety. Coaches selected Krueger as one of the top high school seniors statewide to represent Texas in the Big 33 Football Classic in Pennsylvania. The noted all-star game pitted the best 33 Texas players against the best 33 from the Keystone State (hence the name "Big 33").

Wendell Housley also represented Texas in the Pennsylvania all-star game.

"We all called Rolf Baby Huey," recalled Housley, referring to the popular cartoon character of the day with superhuman strength. "He never knew his own strength."[53]

Krueger's reputation stretched all the way to Alabama, where Bryant invited the powerful lineman to Tuscaloosa for a recruiting visit. Charlie Krueger played no role in arranging the visit, although he did offer his younger brother a bit of advice before meeting the legendary coach: "Just be careful down there.

These guys are pros and they know how to manipulate or influence a young person."[54]

Charlie Krueger wanted his brother's decision to be his own. The elder Krueger actually held Bryant in high esteem, and he wasn't alone—in Texas, especially around College Station and neighboring Bryan, the legend of Junction and the championship glory of 1956 were still spoken of with all the luster of Travis, Bowie, and Crockett's heroic deaths at the Alamo.

Coach Bryant left an indelible impression on the 18-year-old Krueger.

"I'm sure a lot of Bear Bryant's opponents had different things to say about him, but he was an extremely intelligent person and very charismatic," Krueger said. "Whenever you were in his presence, it was special."[55]

Eventually, Bryant pressed Krueger to sign a letter of intent. Krueger balked at signing any document until he was certain where he wanted to attend college. He had already visited University of Texas—a "serious" contender—but A&M also still loomed large in his mind.

"Oh, it's not gonna make a difference," Bryant told Krueger. "It's just for the Southeastern Conference."[56]

"Well, if I sign something than that does make a difference," Krueger replied. "I'm not gonna sign that."[57]

Bryant asked about the letter of intent "two or three" more times, but Krueger held firm. The coach finally dropped the issue and continued to be a gentleman the remainder of Krueger's visit to University of Alabama. "To be honest, I didn't feel like I could play at Alabama and they had just won a national championship," Krueger confessed. "You're walking down the dormitory and seeing the names on the doors like Joe Namath . . . it's kind of overwhelming."[58]

In the end, Krueger felt A&M offered the best opportunities for him to play, win, and receive a top-notch education. He essentially committed to A&M without much persuasion other than the reality of "change" and the promise of "hope." He actually only first met Stallings after he had already made his final decision, stopping by his office one day inside G. Rollie White Coliseum to introduce himself. Stallings struck him as a "pleasant" and highly "positive" coach with an obvious gift for recruiting. Assistants Dee Powell and Loyd Taylor were equally impressive to Krueger, although each displayed a restless energy at the time.[59]

An organized chaos prevailed throughout the football offices.

"They got into the recruiting a little bit late, and everyone was rushing around," Krueger remembered. "They didn't have to spend a lot of time with me, and I think I let them know that, too."[60]

Another fateful decision unfolded simultaneously for a recruit who lived 714 miles away in Northport, Alabama.

Quarterback Hudson "Curley" Hallman grew up dreaming of playing for Paul W. "Bear" Bryant's Crimson Tide. He was the youngest of eight children to Sam and Lola Hallman and lived less than 3 miles from the Alabama campus, across the Black Warrior River in Northport. As a child, Hallman and a few of his pals used to regularly hitch rides along Highway 82 into Tuscaloosa to watch the Crimson Tide practice. They would sneak over to the practice field and try to peer through the large, green tarps that draped the fences to watch the players run through drills and plays. Occasionally, they would spot the legend himself—Bear Bryant.[61]

On game days, Hallman used to hitchhike into Tuscaloosa to sell programs or peanuts or popcorn at Denny Stadium—anything to see some of his college heroes in action for free. Later, in high school, he and other teenagers worked as ushers on game days.[62]

Those were magical times for Hallman, back when Alabama's coaches and players were larger than life.

"Naturally, growing up across the river, you just love the University of Alabama," Hallman fondly recalled. "There might have been something about the name Bear Bryant. . . . We certainly looked at him as a football god."[63]

Hallman clung to the dream of donning the Crimson Tide jersey throughout his childhood and into high school. He lived for the competition of sports, making it a point to engage in an athletic endeavor every day of the year whether it was football, baseball, or basketball. In fact, his favorite sport might have been boxing.

Moody Hallman, his older brother by 17 years, taught Curley how to properly hit a speed bag at age six. Moody supplied his siblings with boxing gloves, headgear, and a heavy bag, and in a house with seven other siblings, boxing matches were always plentiful. Over the years, Moody became a father figure to the younger Hallman children, foregoing college and a career in the US Air Force to return home to help his family avoid financial hardships.

Curley looked up to his elder brother, who always encouraged him to pursue the positive path of athletics. The younger Hallman also had the good fortune of playing at Tuscaloosa County High School, where he was exposed to a number of young, talented coaches who had played for Bryant at Alabama—men like Mickey Andrews, Bill Oliver, Jack Hurlbut, and Mal Moore.

Hurlbut—a backup of Namath's for two seasons—admired Hallman's spunk and grit. He also knew of Hallman's deep desire to play at the collegiate level, despite being a 6-foot-1, 164-pound quarterback soaking wet. Hurlbut often buoyed Hallman with a few words of encouragement and would sometimes say, "Look at your skinny self, you keep working and you might be a college player someday."[64]

By the time Hallman reached his senior year at Tuscaloosa County High School, recruiters generally considered him to be the fifth-ranked quarterback in the state. Bryant signed the top four. Interest in Hallman fizzled by the time the calendar turned to May. The last day of school loomed near. Hallman read about Texas A&M's hiring of Stallings and saw that the new Aggie coach had added Hurlbut to his staff.

Hallman then made a fateful decision—one that would reverberate across two states three years later on the biggest stage of his life. He sat down at his homemade desk and wrote Hurlbut a heartfelt letter. He told his former coach he had initially received interest from recruiters, only to watch his prospects run dry. He also reminded Hurlbut of his unwavering commitment to hard work and promised to earn his way if given a chance to play football at A&M.

Hallman asked for the one thing that often eludes too many—opportunity.

Hurlbut responded to Hallman (after conferring with Stallings) in a letter with one message: "One semester. Make Good."[65]

A few months later, Hallman hitchhiked from Northport to College Station, naively thinking his football scholarship hung in the balance his first semester. But Hurlbut and Stallings were playfully toying with the eager Alabama freshman, fully aware Hallman didn't need any incentive to fight for his keep.

Partial scholarships didn't exist in 1965.

"They were all four-year scholarships back then," Hallman said with a laugh. "But I believed what they told me."[66]

Hallman may have been the last player Stallings signed to his first recruiting class at A&M. Stallings added his name to a list that now featured the likes of Edd Hargett, Wendell Housley, Billy Hobbs, Bob Long, Tommy Maxwell, and Rolf Krueger. The list included a total of 63 high school prospects, but in time, only a handful of those players would survive to wear the Aggie jersey on Saturdays.

"I don't know how well we did," Stallings admitted at the time, "but we signed a lot of boys that other schools wanted."[67]

And some of those "boys" would become Aggie legends. Yet first, they would be required to run through hell.

NOTES

1. Herskowitz, interview with author, August 20, 2018.
2. Herskowitz, interview with author, September 9, 2018.
3. Stallings and Cook, *Another Season*, 52.
4. Ibid., 54.
5. Ibid., 55.
6. Ibid.
7. Ibid.
8. Ibid.
9. Herskowitz, *Legend*, 162.
10. Ibid.
11. Herskowitz, interview with author, August 20, 2018.
12. Ibid. Curran became an institution at the *Buffalo News*, where he worked as a sports columnist for 32 years. He died March 13, 2003, at the age of 80 at a veteran's home in Long Island, New York. In its obituary, the *Buffalo News* called Curran "the Boston Irishman who lost his heart in Buffalo."
13. Herskowitz, interview with author, August 20, 2018.
14. Stallings and Cook, *Another Season*, 55.
15. Stallings, interview with the author, July 8, 2015; Herskowitz, interview with author, August 20, 2018; "If They Charge to the Right, Everything Goes Right," *Sports Illustrated*, September 11, 1967.
16. Paul "Bear" Bryant, *Building a Championship Football Team* (Englewood, NJ: Prentice-Hall, 1960); Stallings, interview with author, July 8, 2015.
17. James F. Willis, *Southern Arkansas University: The Mulerider School's Centennial History, 1909–2009* (Magnolia, AR: Southern Arkansas University Foundation, 2009), 180.
18. Stallings and Cook, *Another Season*, 59.
19. *Houston Chronicle*, May 9, 1965.
20. Brent Zwerneman, *Game of My Life: 25 Stories of Aggies Football* (New York: Sports Publishing, 2003), 66.
21. Herskowitz, interview with author, August 20, 2018.
22. Stallings, interview with author, July 8, 2015.
23. Edd Hargett, interview with author, March 22, 2018. Hargett heard the story from Taylor years after his playing days at Texas A&M.
24. Ibid.
25. Ibid.
26. Ibid.
27. Ibid.
28. Ibid.
29. "Mean Joe Greene," *Texas Monthly*, January 1, 1998.
30. Hargett, interview with author, March 22, 2018.

31. Herskowitz, interview with author, August 20, 2018. Hugh Thomas McElroy Jr. became the first African American to receive a football scholarship at Texas A&M in 1970, a year after playing sparingly on special teams as a walk-on receiver.

"I've had several public speaking opportunities where the consensus of the crowd mistakenly thought that I was the first black to play for A&M," McElroy once said. "I always try to publicly acknowledge that J. T. (Reynolds) and Sammy (Williams) were on the team and sweated and bled just like everybody else, they just didn't get the opportunity to play. I must lay a lot of recognition at their feet, because if they hadn't gone through what they did, I may not have had the character and stamina to last. My part was easy, because I got to play for my practice. They had the tough part. They toiled in anonymity" (Zwerneman, *Game of My Life*, 85).

Reynolds and Williams became the first African Americans to play at A&M in 1967 as walk-ons. Both played sparingly. Reynolds claimed in an interview that he and Williams were subjected to harsher treatment—physically and verbally—than white players by coaches who desired to run them off the team (J. T. Reynolds, interview with author, April 10, 2016).

Williams made a similar claim once about Stallings.

"A reporter called me once and said Sammy told him Stallings had treated him much worse because he was black," Hargett said. "Verbally, maybe. But I told him if they treated them any worse, there's no way they would have made it and gone through—black, white, or whatever. Because if it was any worse than what the rest of us went through, that would be hard to imagine" (Hargett, interview with author, March 22, 2018).

32. Herskowitz, *Legend*, 163.
33. Hargett, interview with author, March 22, 2018.
34. Ibid.
35. Wendell Housley, interview with author, August 28, 2018; *Texas Aggies 1997 Football Press Book*.
36. Housley, interview with author, August 28, 2018.
37. Ibid.
38. Ibid.
39. Ibid.
40. Ibid.
41. Ibid.
42. Ibid.
43. *Texas Aggies 1967 Football Press Book*.
44. *Amarillo Globe-News*, October 2, 2014.
45. *Houston Post*, October 22, 1967.
46. Ibid.; Stallings vertical file, Cushing Memorial Library and Archives, Texas A&M University.
47. *Houston Post*, October 22, 1967.

48. Kristi Hobbs, interview with author, February 5, 2019. Kristi is Billy's widow. The couple was married November 18, 1989, in San Antonio.

49. Bob Long, interview with author, August 23, 2018. Long also played basketball at Paris High School.

50. Ibid

51. Ibid.

52. Housley, interview with author, August 28, 2018.

53. Ibid.

54. Rolf Krueger, interview with author, September 5, 2018.

55. Ibid.

56. Ibid.

57. Ibid.

58. Ibid.

59. Ibid.

60. Ibid.

61. Hallman, interview with author, September 14, 2018.

62. Ibid.

63. Ibid.

64. Ibid.

65. Ibid.

66. Ibid.

67. *Bryan (TX) Daily Eagle*, July 4, 1967.

CHAPTER 9

Tuscaloosa West

The offseason training would challenge you down to the bone marrow.
—Curley Hallman, Texas A&M defensive back

Rick Rickman wanted to embrace the college experience as an incoming fresh-man at Texas A&M in the late summer of 1966. The Terrell resident loved foot-ball like most native Texans but didn't think he was talented enough to play for the Aggies.

So he instead accepted a job as a student manager for the football team, eager to be part of the athletic program and collect a few memories along the way. Rickman encountered far more than he ever imagined. He witnessed a colorful chapter of Aggie history firsthand.

"I have warm memories of those days," Rickman said. "Those were definitely amazing times."[1]

They were times often defined by the intense leadership of Aggie head coach Gene Stallings, then in the second year of a four-year contract. Stallings roamed the practice fields and training rooms with a relentless commitment to produc-tivity. He sought to squeeze positive results out of every minute of every day.[2]

Idle moments were viewed with disdain.

"Never confuse activities with accomplishments," Stallings often said of his fundamental philosophy. "People will always say how hard they work or how long they work. I'm not interested in how hard you work on something or how long it took you. I just want to know if you got results. We live in a results-driven society. Period.

"A lot of people don't understand that concept."[3]

Everyone associated with the Aggie football program became steeped in this philosophy. Those who failed to comprehend it were sent packing.

Rickman clearly understood Stallings's demands the first time he saw the coach stride across a practice field. He detected it instantly in the coach's piercing eyes.

"I will never forget the intense look he had in his eyes," Rickman recalled. "He could give you a stare that would make you melt. It was just kind of sending the message, *I'm gonna hold you accountable. Either you meet the standards, or you are done.*"[4]

Stallings carried himself with the same force as his famous mentor. In fact, echoes of Bryant were everywhere at College Station. Prior to the 1965 season, Stallings ordered a tower installed between the two practice fields, similar to the one Bryant used at Tuscaloosa. From this observation tower, Stallings barked instructions in Bear-like fashion from a bullhorn. Maintenance crews also covered the fences that surrounded the practice fields with large, green tarps at Stallings's request, to discourage onlookers. The tower and tarps would have looked familiar to Hallman, who had watched Alabama's practices studiously throughout his childhood.[5]

Hallman also noticed the similarities between Stallings and Bryant that stretched far beyond the cosmetics of the practice field.

"Both were tough as nails," Hallman observed. "Both were very demanding. Both were very organized. And both of them had a special gift when they spoke. . . . And neither one of them had any patience for the lack of effort. If you really wanted to get headed in the wrong direction—if either one of them saw you didn't give great effort—then your days were numbered."[6]

The truth is, Stallings emulated Bryant in every way imaginable, from the style in which he coached to the manner in which he walked and talked. He even developed a habit of jingling his change and keys in his pocket like Bryant. "You'd close your eyes, and they sounded alike," Hargett noted decades later. "And every little mannerism that Coach Bryant had, Stallings had imitated."[7]

Herskowitz called the similarities between the two men "uncanny," but never felt the resemblances were deliberate by Stallings. For 11 years, Stallings either played for Bryant or worked under him as an assistant. He grew to love and respect the man who grew to love and respect him.[8]

"They had such a great affection for one another, and I think it started when Coach Bryant saw how serious Gene was," Herskowitz said. "Their relationship was akin to a father and son. I think Coach Bryant really felt like Gene was a part of him. The affection was special to see."[9]

Like any star pupil, Stallings adopted many of his teacher's sayings. Stallings regularly repeated Bryant's mantra of "make something happen" to his players and staff, and as a constant reminder, he even had the phrase posted on a sign above his office desk. He also frequently used another favorite Bryant quote: "Show your class," meaning, "always do the best with what God has given you."[10]

Anything less equated to a waste of time.

Essentially, Stallings became a master disciple of arguably the most successful coach in the college football industry. No one knew Bryant's most closely guarded strategies or philosophies better than Stallings, and no one believed in them more. Stallings knew intimately of Bryant's rise from impoverished country boy to celebrated head coach of a national champion, because he had heard and witnessed the story firsthand.

And as far as Stallings was concerned, all roads of that improbable journey eventually led through Junction.

Bryant had tested the physical and psychological limits of his players at Junction in 1954. He drove them relentlessly under the most extreme conditions in order to discover who truly wanted to play football for Texas A&M. Four years later, he repeated his intense training regimen in his first year at the helm in Alabama, later explaining, "My plan was to bleed 'em and gut 'em, because I didn't want any well-wishers hanging around."[11]

Bryant's purging at each stop led to championships.

Naturally, Stallings sought to replicate his mentor's intense training regimen with his own program. Which meant plenty of blood, sweat, and tears for his Aggie players, many of whom never survived to don a uniform on game day. In fact, Stallings's reputation as a Junction survivor and ardent Bryant disciple alone sparked an immediate exodus. The *Houston Chronicle* reported how a number of prospective players quit when Stallings announced much more would be demanded of each player under his charge. The newspaper predicted there would be more defections before the 1965 season opener.[12]

The prediction proved accurate.

"I don't know how many we had on scholarship, but it was like one hundred twenty, one hundred thirty," Hargett recalled of that first season. "By the time we got here as freshman, there were probably sixty left."[13]

As expected, Stallings ran a grueling, merciless training camp upon his arrival. Rickman defined it as "Tuscaloosa West."[14] Hallman, for one, fully expected to be physically and psychologically pushed to the edge after watching how Bryant, Stallings, and the rest of the Crimson Tide staff ran practices at Alabama. Hallman therefore arrived at College Station in "great shape," but admitted the workouts and practices were still "as tough as a human being can imagine."[15]

Stallings essentially brought Junction to College Station.

"Loyd Taylor once told us we did everything they did at Junction," Long said. "They just didn't bother putting us on a bus."[16]

Aggie players were introduced to a militaristic regimen meant to strip them physically and emotionally in order to rebuild them with a champion's mindset. The immersion had all the subtlety of a blacksmith tossing scrap iron into a furnace. Housley remembered the "chaos" of those first days. "They wanted to shock you into submission," said the heavily recruited running back from Richardson. "It was a culture shock—a reality check. I remember thinking, *What have I gotten myself into?* But I figured if this is what it takes to win a national championship, then this is what we're gonna do."[17]

Players sprinted at all times in an environment of perpetual motion. A sense of urgency shadowed every drill, wind sprint, and play. Stallings demanded all business all the time on the field. Coaches jerked players by the facemask or hoisted them up by their shoulder pads to get their attention—all customary acts from that era.

"Do another one!" a coach often shouted during a drill. "Do another one!"[18]

Once, during his sophomore campaign of 1966, Hallman provoked the ire of Stallings by failing to perform to the coach's standards at practice. Stallings grabbed Hallman's jersey and ripped it from his body, holding the shreds of the maroon material in his clutches.

Stallings discarded the shredded material on the ground in disgust, barking to a nearby equipment manager, "Get him a green jersey!"[19]

Hallman had been demoted to the second team.

"I think he wanted to see how I'd respond," Hallman said. "Well, I was gonna respond. I was gonna get that maroon jersey back somehow."[20]

For Housley, three-on-three drills were by far the toughest challenge he encountered during camp. For the drill, three linebackers lined up on one side of the ball while a quarterback and two running backs lined up on the opposite side. The quarterback took the snap and then handed the ball to a running back, who was required to run through a specified lane.

Violence ensued.

"Man, it was brutal," Housley recalled. "It was tough . . . close quarters. And it wasn't like you could go around anyone. You had to run through a certain lane, and that lane was gonna be full of linebackers when you got there. If you got the ball, you were gonna get dogpiled and hit standing up. It was a collision."[21]

Drills such as the dreaded three-on-three exercise usually evoked another favorite saying of Stallings: "People say football is a contact sport. Dancing is a contact sport. Football is a game of collision."[22]

Proof of A&M's punishing practices and workouts could also be found in official player press photographs. Many of the Aggies—Robert Cortez, Billy Hobbs, and Tom Buckman, to name a few—were each photographed with cuts and scars on their foreheads and the bridges of their noses. The flesh wounds were revealing in more ways than one, namely, the changing culture.

"If their nose was not bloody on that bridge, sometimes they would scratch 'em to make sure they were bleeding because they did a lot of facemask-to-chest kind of drills in their blocking and tackling," Rickman said. "If you didn't have marks on your face, then you weren't hitting hard enough or the right way. So it was kind of a badge of honor."[23]

Another custom of the times required players to practice three and a half or four hours a day with virtually no water. Each player received one Dixie cup of water midway through practice. In those days, coaches were convinced that depriving a player of water made him less sluggish and ultimately tougher.

"By my senior year, they invented this great stuff called Gatorade," Long mused. "So then we got a Dixie cup full of Gatorade."[24]

Players, of course, were expected to sprint to the water trays if they desired to quench their thirst. Water breaks could therefore also be a challenge at times. At the very least, Hallman found them sometimes frustrating. By his sophomore year, Hallman had been moved from quarterback to safety. He recalled how defensive backs drilled at the farthest point from the water trays, a field and a half away. The distance meant he and his fellow defensive backs had a longer run than their teammates.

So one day, Hallman bypassed the water break to remain where he stood.

Coach Stallings approached the lanky safety after practice.

"Hall-a-man," Stallings said his deep, gravely drawl, "why didn't you go over to that water break boy?"[25]

"Coach," Hallman answered, "I really didn't need any."[26]

Stallings sternly looked at Hallman and replied, "Well, let's see if you need this."[27]

The coach punished Hallman by making him run on the spot. Hallman never skipped another water break.[28]

This is the world to which Rickman was introduced, at the outset of his freshman year in 1966. As a student manager, his boss required him and other managers to arrive two weeks prior to two-a-day workouts for extra labor. Once the workouts began, Rickman stood in awe at the intensity and brutality he beheld—so much so, he instantly became concerned for a friend back home in Terrell. The friend had received a scholarship to A&M as a lineman and was waiting to report with other freshmen.

Rickman scurried to a telephone the first chance he received to break free. He informed his buddy of all he had witnessed.

"You better run extra laps and everything," Rickman warned. "If you're not in shape, you better get there real quick."[29]

In the spring, Rickman witnessed a whole new level of intensity with offseason workouts. The dreaded, 45-minute sessions were held in DeWare Field House, an old brick building outfitted with wooden bleachers that had originally opened in 1924 as home to A&M men's basketball team. DeWare was eventually replaced for practice purposes by the new G. Rollie White Coliseum in 1954, and within 12 years, had become most useful for intramural sports.

For the football players, DeWare Field House represented a special kind of hell from January to March. Each day, they walked from their locker room to the field house as if marching to the gallows. Strain marked each face as the players trudged toward DeWare in anticipation of pain and suffering. The Aggies first stopped by the weight room, but nobody bothered lifting in order to save their strength for what soon awaited. Finally, they entered the main gymnasium, where they were greeted by high-energy, vocal coaches and several workout stations, including one designated for the infamous stick drill.

Players rotated from station to station in rapid succession without breaks—a grueling process that led to the formation of the "Bucket Brigade." Rickman and his fellow managers formed the brigade, which lined the hardwood floor with several metal trash cans beforehand, in anticipation of the endless streams of vomit.

"The players would puke like hell," Rickman recalled. "We'd haul puke out, and it was just kind of a relay. We'd dump a bucket and bring it back for more puke. One after another after another."[30]

Occasionally, a player would hang his head over the edge of a trash can and feign throwing up for a momentary break. The desperate act usually invoked the rage of a coach who would shout, "You better put something in that trash can real quick!"[31]

"Offseason" to Stallings meant survival training.

"I always made sure I was in great shape because I knew what to expect," Hallman said. "That said, the workouts tested you beyond imagination. The offseason training would challenge you down to the bone marrow.

"Still, I never thought of quitting. I'll tell ya what would have been far tougher than anything I was going through at A&M . . . is what would have been waiting for me at home in Moody Hallman. So I was not gonna quit."[32]

Nothing tested a player's will more than the notorious stick drill. Players remembered the stick drill by several names. Hargett described it simply as "wrestling" with a stick. Hallman called it "the fightin' drill." And Housley remembered squaring off with an opponent on the "take-away mat." Regardless of the name or description, everyone agreed on the brutality of the combative matches.[33]

Each player clutched the stick—or sometimes a rubber hose—with a hand at the commencement of action. The objective was simple: rip the stick from your opponent's hand. And as Housley remembered, "almost anything goes" defined the ground rules.[34]

The last man standing with the stick didn't have to run afterward.

Hargett never forgot the first time he watched the stick drill. Tight end Tom Buckman, his roommate, desperately held onto the stick while his opponent pinned him to the mat. Coaches hovered over Buckman, screaming, "Get up! Don't let that guy keep you down there! Get up!"[35]

Buckman struggled to his feet. But as he stood, Hargett noticed his room-mate's "shoulder was down below his armpit." Buckman had dislocated his shoulder.[36]

Rolf Krueger, the powerful lineman from Bryan, laughed at the recollection of the stick drill. "You made sure to hang on to that stick," he said. "If they jerked it out of your hands, they'd whack you in the head with it."[37]

Few, if any, avoided a "whack" on the head.

No one thrived more in the stick drill than Billy Hobbs, the speedster from Amarillo. Hobbs would crouch in a football stance and then violently yank his opponent forward and butt him with his head. The tactic generally resulted in a knockout victory.

Hobbs would then sit down and rest with the stick in his hands.

Hobbs's tough-man reputation gained notoriety almost immediately after his arrival in 1965. The Aggies originally recruited him as a tight end, but his days on offense ended on the third day of practice his freshman season. Hobbs recalled wiping out a defender with a block. Hargett remembered Hobbs "killing" a defender trying to return an interception. Regardless, Hobbs claimed an observant student coach grabbed him by the shoulders and declared, "This boy should be on defense."[38]

Hobbs quickly emerged as the anchor of the Aggie defense as linebacker. The fleet-footed West Texan proved to be a ferocious, intimidating hitter with an innate instinct for the football. As for the student coach, his name has seemingly been lost to history. Hobbs couldn't even remember his name. But whoever he was, or wherever he ended up in life, Stallings and the A&M faithful owe him an immense debt of gratitude. His fateful decision that day gave birth to the legend of Billy Hobbs.[39]

Hobbs graduated four years later as a two-time All-American linebacker and National Defensive Player of the Year. In truth, even his potential for greatness had been hard to miss.

Stallings, for one, recognized it right away. Once, hours after practice, Hobbs returned to his dorm room in an excited, hyper state of mind. He hollered at Hallman—his roommate and best friend—to wake up. Exhausted, Hallman opened his eyes to find Hobbs sitting on the side of his bed as if ready to take the field.

"Where ya been?" Hallman asked groggily.

"Visiting with Coach Stallings," Hobbs answered.

"Well, that's good."

Hallman rolled over to go back to sleep only to hear Hobbs continue. "Coach Stallings wanted me to come by," he said. "We met and he told me that I had a chance to be as good [as], if not better than, any football player he had ever coached."

"Good," Hallman replied. "Real good."

"Who's he talking about?" Hobbs inquired.

"Billy, he's talking about Lee Roy Jordan, OK?" Hallman said. "Now go to sleep."

"Are you kidding me?"

"Hell no," Hallman said. "That's who he's talking about. Now leave me alone. Let me go to sleep."[40]

The legend of Billy Hobbs flourished throughout College Station.

Tall tales of his wild exploits beyond the football field also began to circulate during this period, some of which carried the scent of urban legend. Yet several former teammates contend that many of the most outrageous stories about Hobbs are indeed rooted in fact.

"Few people like to fight," said Hargett, trying to explain his fabled teammate. "There are people who will fight if they have to. Billy was one of those who liked to fight. He was a very, very physical guy and player. He had a mean streak. Not a dirty streak, but a mean streak."[41]

Hargett stressed how Hobbs saved his mean streak "strictly for game day," but half-jokingly added, "Or the bar, whichever the case might be."[42]

Freshmen who ventured near the football team's dormitory at Henderson Hall reportedly feared encounters with Hobbs, who would sometimes also demand a 25-cent toll for walking on the grass outside the Memorial Student Center. Hobbs also craved physical contact and in moments of pent-up energy would burst into a teammate's room unannounced to practice his wrestling. These impromptu forays usually ended with a pinning by Hobbs, a smile, and a quick exit.

One night, Hobbs turned his playful rage toward Rickman as the student manager studied in his dorm room. The two shared a physical education wrestling class and had become friends. But on this night, Hobbs paced in the hallway outside Rickman's room and yelled, "Rickman, come out! Let's wrestle!"[43]

The words sent chills through Rickman. He whispered to his roommate, "Just tell him I'm not here." The roommate obliged, but Hobbs refused to leave.[44]

"I know you're in there, Rickman!"[45]

Rickman refused to answer. Moments later, he heard a loud crack above the room's large, thick door. Hobbs busted through the window above the transom and was dropping into the tiny room. Rickman bolted for the window and was climbing through it when Hobbs grabbed him, tossed him back into the room, and subjected him to various wrestling moves.

Rickman's room was located on the second floor.

"I was trying to get out that window," Rickman recalled with a laugh. "I didn't care. I just wanted to escape."[46]

The most legendary story about Hobbs off the football field occurred his senior year while attending a February 18, 1969 basketball game at G. Rollie White Coliseum. Texas A&M hosted conference rival Baylor that memorable night before a packed crowd. Two weeks earlier, the Aggies had lost a controversial 66–65 game to Baylor in Waco, and tensions were high for the "Battle of the Brazos" rematch. As usual, many of the Aggie football players occupied the seats directly behind the north backboard, where they reveled in the timeless tradition of spirited, raucous cheering.

News reports document what unfolded next. At some point late in the game, A&M forward Ronnie Peret was driving for a layup, when Baylor's Tom Fried man tackled him in midair. Peret crashed to the floor in a dangerous fashion, and tempers ignited in a flash. Fellow Aggie forward Billy Bob Barnett rushed to his teammate's defense and opened a gash on Friedman's cheek with an elbow. Momentum from the blow sent Friedman sprawling to the floor behind the north backboard.[47]

Unfortunately for Friedman, he landed near Hobbs.

Stories of what happened next vary dramatically—or have even been dismissed as urban legend—but Housley was seated a few feet from Hobbs when the melee erupted. "That ain't no urban legend," said Housley, laughing. "I was watching it. . . . Let's just say Billy may have given him (Friedman) a love tap. True story."[48]

Translation: Hobbs pummeled Friedman with a rapid succession of punches to the face amid a swarm of angry and vocal Aggie football players.[49]

Hobbs, in reality, wasn't all rattlesnake. Those who knew him best saw multiple layers to his personality and a high level of intelligence, despite his reckless behavior at times. He grew up in a loving Christian home where family and friends were cherished and educational and athletic endeavors encouraged.

He also grew up poor.

The Hobbs family lived at the edge of the white section of Amarillo, at 201 North Kentucky, the last home on a paved road. The road eventually turned to gravel and led to an African American neighborhood, where Billy often found stiff competition in various sports at the nearby San Jacinto Park. He would later credit his black neighbors with a lot of his physical and competitive development as an athlete.

His brothers Gary and Joe, older by five and four years, respectively, also undoubtedly made Hobbs tough. Ottis, his father, only had a fourth-grade education and drove a truck for Dr. Pepper before using his charisma to sell insurance. Junie, his mother, worked as an attendance clerk at Tascosa High School so the family could afford "some extras." Billy was the youngest of four children, and initially the family lived in a two-bedroom house. Ottis eventually built another room onto the house, but it had no insulation and was dreadfully cold during the winter.

Billy slept in that room.

"Billy said he remembered the room would get so cold, he could scratch his name in the frost that would build up," Kristi Hobbs said. "The home had one furnace in the front of the house. Billy said he would stand by the furnace to get warm and then run quickly to the back of the house and jump into bed.

"He used to jokingly say that's why he was a champion in the hundred-yard dash."[50]

Hobbs, like other college students, discovered a streak of independence—albeit an extraordinary one—living far from home for the first time. He did so while in the spotlight as a football player but, away from notoriety's glare, he also possessed a quieter side.

Hallman is one of the few who ever witnessed Hobbs in a moment of vulnerability. Once, the Alabamian entered their dorm room, only to see Hobbs sitting on the side of his bed in tears. Hobbs held out a letter from his mother, Junie, and asked his friend to read the missive.[51]

"She was talking to him, saying 'I hope you're going to church,'" Hallman recalled. "It made Billy feel guilty, because he was raised a certain way. . . . I think he felt convicted. That's why, deep down, Billy Hobbs was a good guy.

"People used to tell me, 'Boy, your roommate is as mean as a snake.' And I'd tell them, 'No he's not. He's just got a lot of wasted energy.'"[52]

On the football field, very little of that renowned energy ever went to waste. By 1966, Hobbs helped play a leading role in A&M's marked improvement, with a 4–3 record in the Southwest Conference and a 4–5–1 slate overall. The four victories were modest at best but still a dramatic upgrade from the dreadful 1–6 finish in conference a year earlier. The season also signified the arrival of the 1965 recruiting class—Stallings's first as a head coach.

Hargett, who missed his entire freshman season due to knee surgery, rebounded by the second week of the 1966 season to win the job of starting quarterback against Tulane. Despite a 21–13 loss in that game, he completed a school-record 21 passes for 229 yards. He finished the season with 1,532 yards passing.[53]

Housley also earned All-Southwest Conference honors as tailback, with 548 yards and three touchdowns rushing.

Maurice Moorman, a 6-foot-5, 250-pound tackle, reached national prominence with the Aggies as an All-American selection. The Kentucky transfer's performance was so dominant at times that professional scouts were already raving about him in private circles.[54]

Stallings and his staff also moved Bob Long to wide receiver, where he became an increasingly steady hand and one of Hargett's favorite targets. Long caught the second most passes on the team with 23 receptions—Maxwell grabbed 27 passes—while averaging 10.9 yards per catch.[55]

Each development proved significant.

The Texas A&M Board of Directors was certainly encouraged enough after the season to offer Stallings a new six-year contract with a "substantial increase" in salary.[56] Stallings had clearly earned the board's confidence with his coaching decisions, but his greatest contribution to the 1966 campaign might have been his salesmanship.

Prior to the season, Stallings had landed a highly coveted recruit in Larry Stegent, a tough, slashing runner with great hands and blocking techniques. In fact, there wasn't much Stegent couldn't do on the football field. He earned All-State honors at the all-male St. Thomas High School in Houston and also became his alma mater's first representative in the esteemed Big 33 Football Classic in Pennsylvania.[57]

Stegent appeared destined to sign with Louisiana State University. Then he met Stallings.

"This was the last place I wanted to come," an amused Stegent said at the time of Texas A&M. "After all, I'd already been to one school that didn't have any girls.

"Then I talked to Coach Stallings. He told me he was going to get a winning tradition started at A&M again and that he wanted me to be a part of it. I told him, 'So do I.'"[58]

Stegent wasn't alone. As the 1967 season approached, he joined a varsity team filled with players who shared the same goal—restore Texas A&M to football glory. They were talented, improving, and determined to succeed.

Most importantly, they believed in the mission and each other.

NOTES

1. Rick Rickman, interview with author, September 5, 2018.
2. *Bryan (TX) Daily Eagle*, July 4, 1965.
3. Stallings, interview with author, July 8, 2015.
4. Rickman, interview with author, September 5, 2018.

The Bryant family outside their Moro Bottom, Arkansas, home when Paul was a child. (Courtesy of the Tuscaloosa News*)*

Main Street of Fordyce, Arkansas, circa 1927, and the Lyric Theatre (second building on the left), where Paul W. Bryant wrestled a circus bear and earned his famous nickname. (Author's collection)

The Fordyce High School Redbugs captured a state championship with an undefeated record in 1930. Paul "Bear" Bryant (second from the right) helped anchor the line at left tackle. (Author's collection)

A hungry Paul "Bear" Bryant played end for the University of Alabama and helped the Crimson Tide to a national championship in 1934. (Author's collection)

Rob Roy Spiller, now chairman of the Junction National Bank, worked at the local Texaco gas station and bus depot in 1954. He sold "a lot" of tickets to Aggie players wanting to escape Bryant's hellish training camp. (Author's collection)

Wanda Teel of Junction, Texas, proudly displays the only known film of the "Junction Boys" in action in 1954. Elmer Parrott, Teel's father and then the facility manager of the Junction Adjunct, filmed the historic footage with his new Bell & Howell 8-millimeter movie camera. (Author's collection)

Elmer Smith—another Arkansan—served Bryant as a loyal assistant coach at Texas A&M and then Alabama and earned a reputation as a fierce taskmaster. (Author's collection)

Coach Bryant once called Alabama quarterback Joe Namath "the best" athlete he had ever seen. (Author's collection)

Coach Bryant instructs his star quarterback Joe Namath, whose off-field troubles led to a suspension in 1963 and may have saved his career. (Author's collection)

BOBBY JOHNS   ALABAMA

Bobby Johns rose from obscurity to become a two-time All-American defensive back for the Crimson Tide. (Author's collection)

DENNIS HOMAN   ALABAMA

Dennis Homan earned legendary status at Alabama as an All-American receiver and Kenny "Snake" Stabler's favorite target and roommate. (Author's collection)

Coach Bryant considered the talented—and wayward—Kenny "Snake" Stabler the best downfield passer he had ever coached in 1967. (Author's collection)

EDD HARGETT   TEXAS A&M UNIVERSITY

Quarterback Edd Hargett proved to be a cool customer and dangerous passer under pressure for the Aggies in 1967. (Author's collection)

BOB LONG

TEXAS A&M UNIVERSITY

Two-sport standout Bob Long became a receiving threat for the Aggies, catching 24
passes and a team-high eight touchdowns in 1967. (Author's collection)

BILL HOBBS   TEXAS A&M UNIVERSITY

Billy Hobbs gained folklore status at Texas A&M as a wild man off the field. On the field, Hobbs harnessed his restless energy to become an All-American linebacker and collegiate Defensive Player of the Year in 1967. (Author's collection)

ROLF KRUEGER   TEXAS A&M UNIVERSITY

The 6-foot-4, 225-pound Rolf Krueger arrived at Texas A&M with little fanfare but became a dominant force on the Aggie offensive line before embarking on a career in the National Football League. (Author's collection)

LARRY STEGENT   TEXAS A&M UNIVERSITY

Running back Larry Stegent was a human highlight reel as a sophomore, making a number of circus catches, key runs, and one vicious block of note in 1967. (Author's collection)

WENDELL HOUSLEY   TEXAS A&M UNIVERSITY

Wendell Housley emerged from Dallas County as a highly recruited running back who earned All-Southwestern honors as a sophomore and then heroic status in the 1968 Cotton Bowl Classic. (Author's collection)

Alabama quarterback Kenny "Snake" Stabler listens to Coach Bryant's instructions during the 1968 Cotton Bowl Classic against the Texas A&M Aggies. (Author's collection)

Ken Stabler 1968 Cotton Bowl

Kenny "Snake" Stabler prepares to unleash a pass during the 1968 Cotton Bowl Classic against Texas A&M's ferocious defense. (Author's collection)

TEXAS AGGIES

1967 FOOTBALL PRESS BOOK $1.00

The 1967 Texas A&M game program featured standout quarterback Edd Hargett and two dominant lineman charged with protecting him—All-American Maurice Moorman and Bryan's own Rolf Krueger. (Author's collection)

Joe Namath at gravesite

Former Alabama quarterback Joe Namath appears somber and in deep thought as he stands graveside at Coach Bryant's funeral in 1983. (Author's collection)

Rick Rickman served Coach Stallings as a student manager during A&M's miraculous 1967 season. (Courtesy of Rick Rickman)

Gene "Bebes" Stallings was a lightly recruited player from Paris, Texas, who scratched and clawed his way into the Aggie starting lineup as an end and eventually into Coach Bryant's esteem. (Author's collection)

Kenny "Snake" Stabler sloshes his way into Alabama history during his fabled "Run in the Mud" against rival Auburn in December 1967. (Courtesy of Paul W. Bryant Museum)

Billy Hobbs (left), Edd Hargett (second from left), Shirley Hargett, Houston Post *sports editor Clark Nealon (third from right), and Coach Gene Stallings (right) pose at an awards presentation hosted by the newspaper in December 1967. Hobbs won defensive MVP of the Southwest Conference, while Hargett won offensive MVP. (Courtesy of Kristi Hobbs)*

Aggie linebacker Billy Hobbs makes a sensational play for an interception against Texas. (Courtesy of Kristi Hobbs)

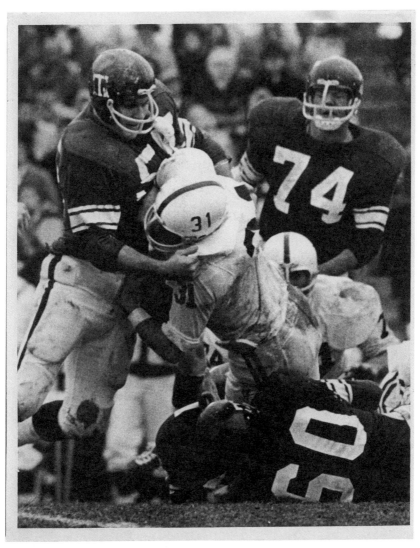

Aggie linebacker Billy Hobbs manhandles Alabama fullback David Chatwood during the 1968 Cotton Bowl Classic in Dallas. (Courtesy of Kristi Hobbs)

Pastor Billy Hobbs proudly poses with Kenyan children during a mission trip to Kenya in 2003. (Courtesy of Kristi Hobbs)

Coach Bryant shortly after his arrival at Texas A&M in 1954. (Courtesy of Texas A&M University Athletics)

Quarterback Edd Hargett and fullback Wendell Housley (#27) roll to the right in a thrilling battle against Texas Tech on the road. (Courtesy of Cushing Memorial Library and Archives)

Gene Stallings returned to his alma mater at Texas A&M in December 1964 to become the new Aggie head coach and the youngest head coach in the nation at age 29. (Courtesy of Texas A&M University Athletics)

The 1956 Texas A&M Southwest Conference Championship team photo.
Stallings—a captain—was one of 10 Junction survivors on the squad. (Courtesy of
Texas A&M Yearbook Collection, Cushing Memorial Library and Archives)

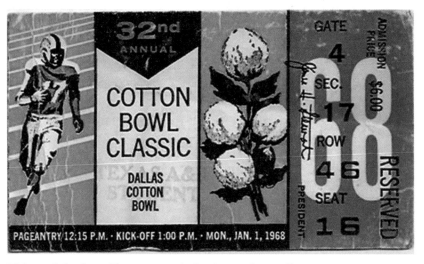

Ticket stub for the 1968 Cotton Bowl Classic. (Author's collection)

5. Long, interview with author, August 23, 2018; Rickman, interview with author, September 5, 2018; Housley, interview with author, August 28, 2018; Hallman, interview with author, September 14, 2018.

6. Hallman, interview with author, September 14, 2018.

7. Hargett, interview with author, March 22, 2018.

8. Herskowitz, interview with author, August 20, 2018.

9. Ibid.

10. Hallman, interview with author, September 14, 2018.

11. Bryant and Underwood, *Bear*, 165.

12. *Houston Chronicle*, May 9, 1965.

13. Hargett, interview with author, March 22, 2018.

14. Rickman, interview with author, September 5, 2018.

15. Hallman, interview with author, September 14, 2018.

16. Long, interview with author, August 23, 2018.

17. Housley, interview with author, August 28, 2018.

18. Ibid.

19. Hallman, interview with author, September 14, 2018.

20. Ibid.

21. Housley, interview with author, August 28, 2018.

22. Ibid.

23. Rickman, interview with author, September 5, 2018.

24. Long, interview with author, August 23, 2018.

25. Hallman, interview with author, September 14, 2018.

26. Ibid.

27. Ibid.

28. Ibid.

29. Rickman, interview with author, September 5, 2018.

30. Ibid.

31. Hallman, interview with author, October 9, 2018.

32. Hallman, interview with author, September 24, 2018.

33. Hargett, interview with author, March 22, 2018; Hallman, interview with author, September 14, 2018; Housley, interview with author, August 28, 2018.

34. Housley, interview with author, August 28, 2018.

35. Hargett, interview with author, March 22, 2018.

36. Ibid.

37. Krueger, interview with author, September 5, 2018.

38. *Houston Post*, October 26, 1967.

39. Ibid.

40. Hallman, interview with author, September 14, 2018.

41. Hargett, interview with author, March 22, 2018.

42. Ibid.

43. Rickman, interview with author, September 5, 2018.

44. Ibid.

45. Ibid.

46. Ibid.

47. *Battalion*, January 23, 1970.

48. Housley, interview with author, August 28, 2018.

49. Ibid.

50. Hobbs, interview with author, February 5, 2019.

51. Hallman, interview with author, September 14, 2018; *San Antonio Express-News*, August 24, 2004.

52. Hallman, interview with author, September 14, 2018.

53. Hargett, interview with author, March 22, 2018.

54. *Houston Post*, September 11, 1967.

55. Long, interview with author, August 23, 2018.

56. Stallings vertical file, Cushing Memorial Library and Archives, Texas A&M University.

57. *Houston Post*, September 29, 1967; Hargett, interview with author, March 22, 2018.

58. *Houston Post*, September 29, 1967.

CHAPTER 10

"Poor Aggies!"

They were ringing those damn cowbells out there and driving us crazy, and then those cowbells went silent.

—Larry Stegent, Aggie running back, on the Texas Tech game in Lubbock

Paul W. "Bear" Bryant's shadow covered every corner of College Station in the late summer of 1967. His legacy lingered like the East Texas heat, powered anew by the optimism and promise of the present A&M football team.

High expectations were once again the order of the day, and those expectations extended beyond Texas and onto the national stage, where the talents of Edd Hargett, Wendell Housley, and Maurice Moorman were among those being touted in the press. Naturally, any hint of an A&M reemergence invoked memories of Bryant's storied four-year run on the Brazos River. A writer for *Sports Illustrated* penned what everyone was thinking: "For the first time since Bear Bryant left College Station for Alabama in 1957, the old military school has enough determined, rugged players to rate among the top contenders not only in the Southwest Conference, but in the nation."[1]

Renewed talk of "the Bear" signaled hope in Aggie nation.

Sports editor Clark Nealon of the *Houston Post* echoed the national magazine's words when he declared the Aggies were "probably the best since Bear Paul Bryant honored the shores of the Brazos . . ."[2] Nealon's claim can hardly be defined as bold, but in the decade since Bryant's departure, Aggie fans had found little to cheer about until the return of Gene Stallings. Now, with hope on their side, fans welcomed the chance to again revel in the same glory as that of Bryant's 1956 Southwest Conference championship squad.

"There were a lot of people who were always talking about Bear Bryant," Krueger recalled, "He was held in high esteem by a lot of people in Texas."[3]

The invocation of Bryant's name boded well for the new Aggies, even if it meant crawling out from beneath a giant shadow. In truth, these Aggies were unfazed by anyone else's expectations. They had their own dreams to chase. They signed with Texas A&M to engage in highly competitive, meaningful football games under Stallings and to restore a winning tradition. Lofty expectations were not only part of the deal but something they wholeheartedly embraced.

"We can be as good as we want to be," Moorman told a reporter matter-of-factly while chewing on a few blades of grass. "And we want to be national champions."[4]

Moorman's bravado underscored the football program's changing culture. The Aggies expected to win, and while Stallings wouldn't have spoken those words publicly, he surely smiled at them privately. Stallings didn't return to College Station simply to work hard or put on a good show. He returned to produce a winner, and for the first time since his arrival, he strongly believed his roster amounted to a bona fide contender.

The potential for success left Stallings admittedly "scared to death"—not of winning, but of a missed opportunity. Second chances are rare. "That's why I'm here every morning at five a.m.," he told a reporter.[5]

Stallings downplayed his team's prospects whenever possible with the press. He told one local reporter, "There's just no way we can be considered contenders."[6] And when *Sports Illustrated* came calling for its annual college football preview issue, he seized the underdog role. At one point during the interview, the writer pointed to a maroon helmet on the coach's desk. The helmet belonged to Aggie senior linebacker Robert Cortez and showed the signs of football combat from the 1966 season—a "smudge of burnt orange for Texas, a pinch of green for Baylor . . ." Stallings assumed his role, adding in a sorrowful drawl, "When I'm feeling low, I just take a good look at that helmet. It reminds me that I know where I can find at least one contact football player."[7]

The writer dubbed Stallings "a pessimist." He should have called the Aggie coach a showman, perhaps the best in college football since, well, Bear Bryant. Stallings knew the tough, fearless players who filled his roster. Billy Hobbs, Rolf Krueger, Wendell Housley, Maurice Moorman, Edd Hargett . . . the list went on. Stallings wasn't fooling anyone else either. Bill Beall, a Louisiana

State University assistant, had scouted A&M's spring game earlier in the year. Afterward, Beall declared, "That's going to be the surprise team in this part of the country . . ."[8]

Stallings shunned the praise.

In the company of friends and boosters, Stallings occasionally let down his guard when speaking of his team's prospects. One such occasion took place a month before the September 16 season opener with Southern Methodist University, at an event in Houston to welcome a new club of Aggie patriots. The nationally televised game against SMU—the Southwest Conference defending champion—had generated a lot of excitement among the Aggie faithful. During a question-and-answer period, one man cleared his throat and asked, "Coach, I don't want to put you on the spot, but where do you think the Aggies will finish this year?"[9]

Stallings bypassed a safe answer in lieu of a bold proposition.

"You come see us play SMU," the coach replied, "and if you don't feel you were well represented, you just write me a little ol' letter and I'll mail you five dollars for your ticket."[10]

Stallings's confidence sprang from his team's well of talent and growing experience. On August 31, he opened camp with 21 returning lettermen, 12 of whom were returning starters. Hargett led the charge at quarterback, now two years removed from the operation on his left knee. A bulky, metal-hinged brace would remain affixed to his knee, however. While the brace never affected his ability to pass (since he planted with his right foot), it was just bulky and long enough to impede his mobility while running. Still, a number of sports scribes were still impressed with the junior's ability to cut and run.[11]

Stallings, of course, claimed "tape and a prayer" were all that held Hargett's knee together.[12]

As for Hargett's passing, no one questioned his arm or accuracy. University of Arkansas head coach Frank Broyles called Hargett "one of the best passers we've seen."[13] Hargett was also expected to have a number of good targets to choose from, including fellow juniors Tommy Maxwell and Bob Long.[14]

The Aggies were also expected to deliver a punishing ground game. Preseason prognosticators raved about their backfield tandem of Ross Brupbacher (6-foot-2, 200 pounds) and Wendell Housley (6-foot-2, 219 pounds), the latter of whom had received All-Southwest Conference honors a year earlier as a sophomore tailback. Both were big, punishing runners, and some were already comparing Housley to Aggie legend John David Crow—fairly or otherwise.[15]

By all accounts, one of A&M's greatest strengths could be found on the right side of its offensive line. Stallings moved Moorman (6-foot-5, 242 pounds) to guard and Krueger (6-foot-4, 225 pounds) to tackle and had Tom Buckman (6-foot-3, 212 pounds) returning at the end. *Sports Illustrated* predicted the Aggies "may return to the big time on one play alone—a power slash to the strong side . . ." led by Moorman, Krueger, and Buckman. Sportswriter Bill van Fleet of the *Fort Worth Morning Star-Telegram* called the power slash "an automatic four yards, even when the defense knows that it's coming."[16]

In addition, Aggie punter Steve O'Neal received increasing praise as the season opener drew nearer. One report noted how the junior had "looked exceptionally good performing his punting chores, continuously sending them high and long."[17]

Stallings originally approached O'Neal about trying out as a punter during the second semester of his freshman year. At the time, the Hearne, Texas, native was already attending A&M on a track and field scholarship. One persistent local legend about O'Neal told how he first came to the attention of Stallings. As the story goes, Stallings pulled into a Hearne gas station while on the road in 1965. Stallings and the owner began talking Aggie football, and while pumping gas and checking under the hood, the man casually informed the coach that the best punter in the state was already enrolled at A&M.[18]

"I'm not so certain that's actually how it happened," O'Neal said years later. "There are actually several versions of the story, but the gas station version does make for a much better story."[19]

In 1967, O'Neal found himself part of another kind of story, one worthy of remembrance as a legend—yet a legend featuring all the twists and turns and high drama of a talented Aggie team on the brink of obscurity.

· · ·

Thirty-four thousand raucous fans and a national television audience of six million greeted the Texas A&M Aggies in their season opener against SMU at Kyle Field. The Mustangs were expected to test the Aggies immediately, despite only one of its nine All-Southwest Conference players from its championship team returning.

The electrifying Jerry Levias carried the bulk of SMU's hopes as the lone All-Southwest Conference returner, and some argued that might be enough. Levias—the second African American scholarship athlete in the conference—had led the Mustangs with seven touchdown receptions during their championship run a year earlier.[20]

SMU coach Hayden Fry opted to feature Levias out of the backfield as the Mustangs opened their conference-title defense against A&M. Levias, listed at 5-foot-9 and 177 pounds, played much larger on the field. He also possessed an enormous heart, succeeding despite a constant barrage of racial slurs and physical abuse by opponents. At the urging of his grandmother, Levias wore jersey number 23 to remind him of Psalm 23: "Yea, though I walk through the valley of the shadow of death, I will fear no evil: for thou art with me."[21]

Each game tested his faith in one fashion or another. The matchup against A&M proved no different.

The game lived up to its advance billing as a showdown of conference contenders. Levias and his teammates were engaged in a hard-fought battle when SMU quarterback Mike Livingston injured a knee on a 3-yard touchdown run with 18 seconds left in the first half. Livingston's touchdown gave SMU a 10–7 halftime lead, but his injury cast a pall over the team when it learned he could not return.[22]

SMU's backup quarterback Ines Perez—himself all of 5-foot-4—played valiantly in Livingston's absence. He completed six of his first eight passes as the Mustangs clung to a 13–10 lead, with 3:29 left in the game and A&M backed to its own 17-yard line.

The situation presented the first opportunity for the Aggies to show their moxie.

Hargett and the Aggie offense refused to disappoint. The junior guided the Aggies to the SMU 29-yard line with little more than a minute left on the clock. Earlier in the drive, on a fourth-and-seven, Hargett calmly connected with Tommy Maxwell for what was likely a game-saving first down. He then completed consecutive passes to Maxwell (17 yards), Jimmy Adams (16 yards), and Ross Brupbacher (15 yards) before the Mustangs dropped him for a loss at the 29.[23]

Finally, with two A&M kickers awaiting orders on the sideline, Hargett rendered any discussion of a game-tying field goal moot. He tossed a perfectly placed pass toward the end zone and into the hands of Bob Long for a 29-yard touchdown.[24]

Thunderous cheers rained on the Aggies as they took a 17–13 lead with 43 seconds left in the game. Hargett masterfully engineered what appeared to be a game-winning, 83-yard scoring drive. Stallings and his players were now four downs from their first victory of the new season.

A year earlier, Fry called his Mustangs "miracle workers" after they won three games by scoring in the final seconds of each, effectively pulling out the wins in a combined total of 42 seconds. Yet questions remained whether this SMU team could produce similar magic. If they could, the answer likely rested in the extraordinarily athletic hands and feet of SMU's star.

Levias, like his Aggie adversaries, refused to disappoint.

On the ensuing kickoff, Levias—SMU's lone return man—caught the ball at the 18-yard line and returned it 24 yards to the Mustang 42 with 36 seconds remaining. The play ended with Levias being flung into a sideline bench. He arose groggily but immediately.

"The last thing I remember was being thrown into the bench after the kickoff," Levias later told reporters.[25]

Moments later, Levias caught a 29-yard pass from Perez at A&M's 29-yard line. The Mustangs moved the ball forward to the 6-yard line when Coach Fry called for a curl pattern to Levias with 12 seconds on the clock.

Pandemonium spread throughout Kyle Field as Perez took the snap. The diminutive quarterback from Corpus Christi then found his primary target in Levias, who made a twisting, leaping catch in the back of the end zone. Aggie defender Jack Whitmore corralled Levias by the ankles, and the two fell to the turf together—just as a referee signaled a touchdown with 4 seconds on the clock.

SMU trainer Eddie Lane and Dr. Sam Morgan, the team physician, rushed to aid the incoherent Levias, who asked, "Did we score?"[26]

The Mustangs had pulled off a miraculous 20–17 victory, marching 54 yards in 36 seconds, and Levias had no recollection of how it happened. He undoubtedly suffered a concussion, likely when he crashed into the bench on the kickoff.

"The next thing I remember was trying to straighten out my legs in the end zone," he said afterward in the locker room. "I guess I was playing on instinct."[27]

In the A&M locker room, players were overwhelmed by the shock.

Hobbs repeatedly cried, "No! No! No!" Another Aggie banged his maroon helmet against a wall and cursed under his breath. Nearby, the usually talkative Moorman was in no mood for questions. "If you don't mind," Moorman said politely to one reporter, "I'd rather not talk about it."[28]

Maxwell, who had played brilliantly in the clutch, also wasn't in the mood to talk.

"We just slacked up when we shouldn't have," Maxwell said. "We slacked up there at the last. You'll have to excuse me if I don't feel like talking."[29]

Housley tried to offer the press something quotable when he said, "We knew they'd be tough." He knew it was a lie and defiantly retracted his statement: "No, they weren't tough. It was just Levias. He made 'em go."[30]

Nearby, Stallings stood before the media with his head bowed. His answers were short and devoid of the usual wit and snappy one-liners. He was a man choked by the stunning reality of the moment.

"I don't know what happened in the last minute," he stated candidly. "I'll have to see the film first. All I saw was that we missed some tackles and we missed several opportunities. We got some penalties a good team wouldn't have got."[31]

Whatever happened, Stallings knew it was unacceptable. Position changes would be made, mistakes would be eliminated, and practices would be tougher. Two of the numerous changes Stallings would make involved his two behemoths on the offensive line, Moorman and Krueger—both of whom would now also be used on goal-line stands. Stallings said both linemen would now probably play more on both sides of the ball.[32]

True to his word, Stallings worked the Aggies overtime the next week in preparation for a September 23 date with Purdue University at the Cotton Bowl in Dallas. Stallings wasn't pleased with his team's punt coverage against SMU. So the Aggies worked extensively on punt coverage drills deep into the hot, humid nights of East Texas. They also ran their usual set of 25 sprints, 100 yards each. Upon completion of the sprints, Stallings yelled, "All right, the first quarter's over!"[33]

"C-man," Stegent said to Hallman, "is four times 25 still 100?"

"Ain't no way we're gonna do that many," Hallman incredulously answered.

Stegent soberly replied, "You watch."[34]

Stallings proved Stegent correct. The Aggies ran a hundred 100-yard sprints until they were battered by exhaustion and drenched in sweat. "We just kept running and running and running without a drink of water," Hargett recalled. "Well, something had to give."[35]

Teammate Jim Piper became that "something." The sophomore tight end passed out at one point from heat exhaustion. Staff rushed Piper to the hospital, where he reportedly awoke three hours later. The 6-foot, 200-pounder remained in the hospital for 11 days. His weight had dropped 20 pounds by the time he rejoined his teammates, who had lost their second straight game during his absence.[36]

Again, Hargett appeared to be on the verge of orchestrating another come-back against Purdue. Trailing 24–14 in the fourth quarter, Hargett hit Bob Long with a 60-yard touchdown pass, with the receiver dashing the final 22 yards after the catch. The touchdown trimmed Purdue's lead to 24–20, a score that remained after Hargett and Housley failed to connect on a two-point pass with 6:39 left in the game.

Hargett later marched the Aggies down to Purdue's 35-yard line with a minute remaining. The comeback, however, fell short when A&M's pass protection collapsed on its final drive, and Purdue dropped Hargett back to the 45.[37]

Purdue's standout tailback Leroy Keyes led the Boilermakers by running for one touchdown and passing for another. Keyes later told Hobbs at a postseason function that he had never been hit so often as he had been in that game, comparing the Aggie defense to "a bunch of dang bees."[38]

One positive development for A&M did emerge from the loss. Fullback Larry Stegent shone when given the opportunity. He gained 43 yards on four carries and caught five passes for another 61 yards, undoubtedly earning the confidence of Stallings.[39]

In the process, Stegent broke a bone in his left hand, but he would remain in the mix the next week against LSU in Baton Rouge.[40]

The third week of the season ushered in more heartbreak for the Aggies. This time, they were handed a 17–6 loss by the Tigers, although the score wasn't indicative of LSU's dominance in front of 66,000 frenzied Louisiana fans. The Aggies' lone touchdown came with 1:17 left in the game against LSU reserves. Charlie Riggs, A&M's kicker and backup quarterback, tossed the ball to Long for a 2-yard touchdown. Riggs's ensuing pass for the two-point conversion was intercepted, a play symbolic of A&M's 0–3 starting record.[41]

By the final gun, the critics were circling.

Questions were asked about A&M's punt coverage, pass protection, defensive backfield, and ability to score points. The questions—many asked by Stallings himself—were fair, although some carried their critical analysis too far. *Houston Post* columnist Jack Gallagher wrote a column in which he crossed the threshold from legitimate analyst to snarky hitman. Four days prior to Florida State University's arrival to College Station, Gallagher let loose his acid pen in the opening lines of his column when he wrote:

> Texas A&M's 5,200-acre campus is the nation's largest. Everywhere there is room to grow along the Brazos bottomlands, and 11,000-student A&M is prepared for a 20,000 enrollment in 1976.
>
> Sad to say, A&M's football team has not kept pace with the growth. While Kyle Field's scoreboard is prepared to register any score up to 99–99, the electronic marvel has had to settle for figures that resemble softball no-hitters.[42]

Gallagher's poor attempt at humor was still but a blip in the gathering storm of consternation that swirled around the Aggie football team. Each loss added another layer of pressure for Stallings and his assistants, who tried to do everything possible to prevent the season from slipping away.

Frustrated by the losses, Stallings often received a spirited lift from an old friend. Bryant called him frequently during this period, and the young Aggie coach came to expect a call from his mentor after a loss. "Bebes," Bryant would say, "you don't need any friends when you're winning."[43]

Stallings never heard any truer words.

Fans and media alike wondered aloud if A&M's season could get any worse. Week four gave them the answer. Maybe the relentless rain that pelted Kyle Field that day against Florida State should have been the first clue. "It was raining so hard at times," Rickman recalled, "you couldn't even see across the field."[44]

"Raining and wet," said Hargett, who played the game with bruised ribs. "I don't remember much about that game."[45]

For the Aggies, there was much to forget. An interception by Aggie defensive back Tom Sooy on a goal-line stand appeared to seal an 18–13 victory for A&M in the final minutes of the game. Yet the Florida Seminoles recovered a fumble by Stegent at A&M's 27-yard line on the ensuing possession. The turnover came with a cruel irony. Stegent, playing with a cast on his broken left hand, had been moved from fullback to tailback in place of Housley, who was nursing two dislocated shoulders. Stegent responded by scoring both Aggie touchdowns. He scored on a 45-yard pass from Hargett in the second quarter and then gave the Aggies an 18–13 lead on a 6-yard touchdown run with 8:33 left in the game. On the 45-yard touchdown pass from Hargett, Stegent even drew up the play beforehand on the sideline. Stallings liked the idea and told his sophomore tailback, "Go in and call it."[46]

Florida State's Bill Moorman made a later fumble by Stegent sting when he promptly scored on a 27-yard run, giving his team a 19–18 lead with 3 minutes on the clock. The score held.[47]

The Aggies were suddenly staring at a 0–4 record. Three of those losses were decided by a total of eight points.

By now, the smell of pressure hung thick in the air around College Station. Sports editors had already relegated A&M game stories to the back pages of their sports sections, surely convinced that the promise of the 1967 Aggies must have been a mirage.

"For the Aggies, it was the same song, fourth verse," Gallagher wrote in a post-mortem of A&M's one-point loss to Florida State. "Breakdowns in the offensive and defensive lines again led to the downfall."[48]

Gallagher brought up a valid point, although other factors contributed to A&M's losing streak. Still, Florida State defenders dropped Hargett and a sub-stituting Riggs for losses on five attempted passes for a total of 35 yards. On the field, the reason for the breakdowns on the line was obvious. Krueger and Moorman—two of the biggest men on the field—were playing both ways.

"That was the most foolish thing, having us play both ways," Krueger said. "We were just gassed midway through the second quarter."[49]

Changes were made, although not under stress. Stallings and his staff con-tinued to move personnel in hopes of plugging players into positions that would ultimately give the team the best chance to succeed. No one showed signs of panic. In fact, the calmest place in Aggieland might have been the A&M locker room.

Stallings led by example.

Hargett noted how Stallings maintained his usual "mean and nasty" demeanor after the 0–4 start, adding, "In fact, he might have been a little more relaxed."[50] If Stallings felt any added pressure, he didn't show it around his players. He contin-ued to buoy spirits whenever possible, sometimes with an inspirational story at team meetings or through instruction on the field. He also fostered the timeless psychological coaching tactic of us-against-the-world at all times.[51]

In the isolation of College Station, the bunker mentality took root.

"We just hung in there," Stegent said. "There was no finger-pointing."[52]

Several factors prevented panic, such as common sense. "No one was running us off the field," Stegent said.[53] He was right. Only LSU manhandled the Aggies, who lost three games in the closing minutes of each game—one on a final play by a great player.

"In my mind, we were 3–1," Long said. "Or could have been."[54]

Hargett echoed Long's viewpoint, adding that the Aggies were still only 0–1 in the Southwest Conference, with a conference title and trip to the Cotton Bowl still in play. "We knew we could play with anybody because we had played four pretty good teams," Hargett said. "I don't think anyone was saying, 'Well, it's gonna be another bad year for the Aggies.'"[55]

Krueger tried to find some humor in the slump, quipping, "We always figured we never lost any games. We just ran out of time."[56]

Yet losing, however, was no longer an option. In that sense, every coaching move and play became critical.

Stallings continued to shuffle players prior to his team's next game with Texas Tech in Lubbock. He started by announcing Krueger would solely play defensive tackle, admitting that was where he could be a great player. He also moved Maxwell and Brupbacher—both outstanding athletes—to safety and cornerback, respectively. Second-year starter Curley Hallman slid over to the other cornerback spot to make room for Maxwell, who would continue to play both ways.[57]

"We were just getting beat deep so much," Stallings said of the position changes. "They were catching the long pass and we needed speed in the secondary."[58]

Stallings tried to maintain an environment of normalcy. He never stopped grinding, pushing, and demanding. Although there were no signs of panic, everyone moved with a sense of purpose and urgency. Some decisions were made abruptly. Brupbacher, for instance, learned of his switch to defense on the team bulletin board on Monday—five days before the Texas Tech game.[59]

The time for normal protocols had passed. The hourglass on the Aggie season was draining quickly, but inside the locker room, players remained confident. They found strength in a bond Rickman saw forged during the "physical and psychological" hell of offseason workouts and practices. Through a common journey marked by a trail of sweat and blood, Hargett watched his team evolve into "a really, really close group."[60]

The Aggies were essentially built for the lonely road ahead, even if no one believed in them. They soon discovered they weren't alone.

On Thursday, as the team prepared to depart Henderson Hall for Lubbock, the Fightin' Texas Aggie Band and 1,000 cheering students appeared in a rainstorm for an impromptu rally. For the next hour, fans shouted support, the yell squad hollered until they were hoarse, and the band serenaded the Aggie players with the school's spirited fight song—the Aggie War Hymn—as the rain left them all drenched.

The players stood amazed and inspired.

"They kept it up for an hour," marveled Hobbs, who once jokingly questioned why he played in such a remote outpost as College Station. "An hour in the rain for a losing team. You respond to that. You find a love, a special feeling, for the place."[61]

And the people.

The Aggies left College Station that day with a strong sense of determination and pride. In the hostile environment of Lubbock, they would need both.

· · ·

The Aggies weren't alone when they pulled into Lubbock.

In addition to the stream of A&M alumni and students, relatives of the players drove great distances to cheer their loved ones to victory. Moody Hallman, Curley's elder brother, punched his timecard at the B.F. Goodrich Tire Company plant in Tuscaloosa and drove all night to reach Lubbock—a grueling, 935-mile drive. Moody worked an 11 p.m.–7 a.m. shift at the plant for years, and in Curley's three years on varsity, he missed only one game. Moody wasn't about to miss this one with the season on the line.[62]

Junie Hobbs and her two eldest sons, Gary and Joe, drove most of the 121 miles south on Interstate 27 from Amarillo to see Billy hit somebody, and Robert Housley traveled more than six hours from downtown Richardson to watch his son, Wendell, level his own form of punishment out of the backfield. They were just a handful of loved ones, those who stood in Texas A&M's corner that night when the Aggies took the field at Jones Stadium.

A din of clanging cowbells from a record crowd of 48,240 fans greeted the winless Aggies and their faithful followers. Texas Tech entered the game with a 2–1 record, including an impressive 19–13 victory over the University of Texas in its lone conference game. A week earlier, Mississippi State had upset the Red Raiders 7–3, and critics accused them of "looking ahead" to A&M.[63]

The Aggies entered the game calm yet determined to "make something happen." The night before, Stallings and his entire team had enjoyed some downtime at a local theater—a pregame tradition he inherited from Bryant. The Aggies watched *Water Hole #3*, a western comedy starring James Coburn, Bruce Dern, and Carroll O'Connor, among others.[64]

Few would remember the movie or its plot. They had Texas Tech on their minds.

The next day, the battle for field position consumed the first quarter, until Texas Tech finally broke the deadlock. Kicker Ken Vinyard gave the Red Raiders a 3–0 lead at the 10:39 mark of the second quarter with a 45-yard field goal.[65]

Vinyard tried to increase Texas Tech's lead with a 55-yard field attempt in the closing minutes of the first half, only to be denied. To the delight of Stallings, the Aggies made something happen. Hobbs busted up the middle with arms outstretched and blocked Vinyard's kick through what appeared to be sheer will.[66]

Hobbs provided the spark. Moments later, the Aggies crossed midfield for the first time. Hargett then hit a wide-open Long in the middle of the end zone on a 14-yard scoring pass. Riggs booted the extra point, and A&M suddenly held a 7–3 lead.[67]

The momentum continued a few moments later when Brupbacher—in his first game on defense—intercepted a pass from John Scovell and returned it to the Texas Tech 28-yard line. Hargett rolled to his right three plays later before planting and throwing the ball across his body. Hargett's pass sailed into the far left corner of the end zone, where the 6-foot-2 Barney Harris pulled down the ball for a 15-yard touchdown with 49 seconds left in the half.[68]

Yet there would be no quitting on this night.

Texas Tech answered back on its first two possessions of the third quarter. Running back Mike Leinert scored on short bursts of 3 and 5 yards to give the Red Raiders a 17–14 lead to enter the final quarter. The Aggies responded with a nine-play, 80-yard scoring drive to open the fourth quarter, reclaiming the lead 21–17 with 13:13 on the clock. Stegent accounted for the final 13 yards when he caught a pass from Hargett over the middle and fell into the end zone.[69]

Though the slugfest didn't subside, no one could anticipate the drama that unfolded in the closing minutes. Backed to their own 17-yard line, the Red Raiders began an improbable drive with two 15-yard penalties. Officials flagged A&M for an illegal use of the hands, which prompted Stallings to unleash a verbal barrage on the referee who threw the flag. His temper cost the Aggies dearly when the same referee hit the coach with another 15-yard penalty for unsportsmanlike conduct. Suddenly, Texas Tech had moved back up to its own 48.[70]

Rickman was standing behind Stallings when the second flag landed at the coach's feet.

"I saw coach's face go pale," remembered the former student manager. "He knew. The place got quiet. He was stone silent."[71]

Stallings would later recall thinking at that moment, with the season hanging in the balance, "What have I done?"[72]

Scovell converted a fourth-and-nine moments later to running back Roger Freeman with a pass to the A&M 14-yard line. Two plays later, Scovell faked a handoff and pitched to his left, to Baker, who sprinted the final 4 yards untouched into the end zone. Hobbs, the closest Aggie defender, ripped his chin strap off in frustration as Texas Tech took a 24–21 lead with 53 seconds left in the game.[73]

Jones Stadium reverberated with cheers, clanging cowbells, and chants of "Poor Aggies! Poor Aggies! Poor Aggies!" Somewhere in the madness of those stands, Junie Hobbs and her two eldest sons were being forced to listen to Texas Tech fans seated immediately behind them loudly ridicule the Aggies and their fans.[74]

A&M's chances appeared dire.

"There was a feeling of unbelief," Krueger said. "Just unbelief."[75]

Texas Tech coach J. T. King then ordered a squib kick to prevent a long return.

King's decision to play it safe on the kickoff likely stemmed from what happened in 1962 at Kyle Field. In that game, the Red Raiders took a 3–0 lead on a field goal with 19 seconds left in the game. On the ensuing kickoff, Aggie Danny McIlhany fielded the ball 3 yards deep in the end zone and returned it 103 yards for a game-winning touchdown. That stinging loss probably haunted King, who now tried to prevent another miracle finish by the Aggies.

The odds were stacked heavily in King's favor.

But King had handed the Aggies a dash of hope; Brupbacher smothered the ball at A&M's own 41-yard line with 51 seconds remaining.

Edd Hargett and his teammates didn't flinch. Hargett immediately hit an open Stegent down the sideline for a 21-yard gain into Texas Tech territory. Three incompletions later, on a fourth-and-15, Hargett dropped back with the season on the line. Off his back foot, he heaved a ball 28 yards down the middle of the field in the direction of Long, who was surrounded by three defenders. Long leapt high with outstretched arms while on the run, to make a circus catch at the 15-yard line while sandwiched between two defenders. The game film would later show five Red Raiders in Long's vicinity at the time of the catch—three of whom were within an arm's length.[76]

A&M promptly called a timeout with 3 seconds on the clock.

During the timeout, Gallagher saw Stallings wrap his arm around Riggs's shoulders while the Aggies talked. The sportswriter assumed they were discussing whether to go for the tie or victory.

"I think Stallings had already made up his mind," Hargett said. "We had already lost a conference game. If we tie a game, it's not gonna help us. We were gonna go for the win."[77]

Hargett called for a "Pass 62"—the same play that accounted for A&M's three touchdowns that night. The play called for Housley to slip out to the flat, Buckman to cut across the middle, and Long to run a curl route—all on the left side of the field. Stegent, meanwhile, was supposed to sell the play-action, hold for a block if needed, and release downfield to the right corner of the end zone.[78]

The Aggies would win or lose on a throw into the end zone. Or so they thought.

As Hargett took the snap, he noticed a referee toss a flag out of the corner of his eyes. A Texas Tech lineman—one of only three sent on the rush—had jumped offside. Hargett knew the Aggies had a free play, although he may have been one of only a few who did. He dropped back and, when he saw his receivers covered downfield, tucked the ball and took off running.[79]

"I said, 'Oh, no!'" Housley recalled. "I thought, *You've gotta be kiddin'! You've gotta be kiddin'!*"[80]

Amazingly, Hargett found an open field as he scrambled for the pylon with a brace fastened to his left knee. Then as Hargett reached the 10-yard line, Texas Tech's defensive lineman George Cox closed in on the Aggie quarterback. The footrace became a blur.

"I was five to eight yards from the sideline," recalled Cox in a 2011 interview with the *Lubbock Avalanche-Journal*. "The only way he (Hargett) could go was through me or out of bounds. The next thing I know, the lights went out."[81]

Stegent delivered an explosive blindside block on the 6-foot-2 Cox, and the 215-pounder toppled like a tree. Hargett dashed into the corner of the end zone untouched as the final gun sounded. He didn't stop until he reached the locker room.[82]

"I've always said I was clipped," said Cox, who underwent reconstructive knee surgery the next day, from the result of what turned out to be a career-ending play. "I didn't have any proof of it. The only way the guy (Stegent) could have blocked me was coming from the side."[83]

Long defended his teammate's block.

"Back in those days, if you got your helmet in back, it was a clip," Long said. "And if you got your helmet in front, it wasn't a clip. And Stegent definitely got his helmet in front."[84]

Clip or no clip, Texas A&M would have received another play due to the off-side penalty. But one more play was not needed. No one threw a flag on Stegent's block.

"They were ringing those damn cowbells out there and driving us crazy, and then those cowbells went silent on that last play," Stegent recalled. "It was a great feeling."[85]

Boos replaced the cowbells in protest of Stegent's block. Outraged Texas Tech fans spilled onto the fringes of the field. The mood had clearly intensified, but officials still required A&M to kick the extra point despite no time on the clock. Hallman, the Aggie holder, told Riggs, "Just kick the ball and let's get out of here."[86]

As soon as Riggs booted the ball through the uprights, Hallman grabbed the kicking tee and started to sprint off the field for the safety of the locker room. Riggs hesitated for a moment and, fearing he might be left to the mob, shouted, "Curley, wait up! Curley, wait up!"[87]

Aggie fans, meanwhile, rejoiced in triumph. Robert Housley would later tell his son, "You know, I turned around and I tried to find the one person who was singing, 'Poor Aggies!' And he had already snuck out of the stadium."[88]

Gary and Joe Hobbs lost track of their mother in the crowd as dejected Texas Tech fans rushed for the exits. They searched and found her a few moments later, chastising a large man in Texas Tech garb. Hargett would later retell the story, musing, "There she was—this little ol' woman pointing her finger right in some guy's chest, just lettin' him have it."[89]

The Southwest Conference was now on notice.

"When we were in the huddle to kick the extra point, we were real excited," Stegent recalled. "We knew we had finally broken the ice."[90]

NOTES

1. "If They Charge," *Sports Illustrated*.
2. *Houston Post*, September 10, 1967.
3. Krueger, interview with author, September 5, 2018.
4. *Houston Post*, September 11, 1967.

5. Ibid., September 13, 1967.

6. Ibid., September 9, 1967.

7. "If They Charge," *Sports Illustrated*.

8. *Houston Post*, September 9, 1967.

9. Ibid., August 18, 1967.

10. Ibid.

11. Hargett, interview with author, October 11, 2018; *Houston Post*, August 31, 1967, and September 1, 1967.

12. "If They Charge," *Sports Illustrated*.

13. Ibid.

14. *Houston Post*, September 11, 1967.

15. "If They Charge," *Sports Illustrated*.

16. Ibid.

17. *Houston Post*, September 4, 1967.

18. Rusty Burson, *Texas A&M Where Have You Gone?* (New York: Sports Publishing, 2004), 42.

19. Ibid., 42–44.

20. John Hill Westbrook broke the Southwest Conference color barrier with Baylor University September 10, 1966, against Syracuse. Westbrook had earned a scholarship a year earlier when he tried out for Baylor's freshman team.

21. *Houston Chronicle*, August 21, 2013.

22. *Houston Post*, September 17, 1967.

23. Ibid.

24. Ibid.

25. Ibid.

26. Ibid.

27. Ibid.

28. Ibid.

29. Ibid.

30. Ibid.

31. Ibid.

32. *Houston Post*, September 20, 1967.

33. Hallman, interview with author, September 14, 2018.

34. Ibid.

35. Hargett, interview with author, October 11, 2018.

36. *Houston Post*, December 13, 1967.

37. Ibid., September 24, 1967.

38. Hargett, interview with author, March 22, 2018.

39. *Houston Post*, September 24, 1967.

40. Ibid., September 27, 1967.

41. Ibid., October 1, 1967.

42. Ibid., October 4, 1967.

43. Stallings and Cook, *Another Season*, 87.

44. Rickman, interview with author, September 5, 2018.

45. Hargett, interview with author, March 22, 2018.

46. *Houston Post*, October 8, 1967; *Houston Post*, October 9, 1967; *Houston Post*, November 1, 1967.

47. Ibid.

48. *Houston Post*, October 9, 1967.

49. Krueger, interview with author, September 5, 2018.

50. Hargett, interview with author, March 22, 2018.

51. Rickman, interview with author, September 5, 2018.

52. Larry Stegent, interview with author, August 29, 2018.

53. Ibid.

54. Long, interview with author, August 23, 2018.

55. Hargett, interview with author, March 22, 2018.

56. Krueger, interview with author, September 5, 2018.

57. *Houston Post*, November 1, 1967; Hallman, interview with author, September 14, 2018.

58. *Houston Post*, October 30, 1967.

59. Ibid., November 1, 1967.

60. Rickman, interview with author, September 5, 2018; Hargett, interview with author, March 22, 2018.

61. "The Hilarious Aggies Offer Raucous Doings in the Land of Nothing to Do," *Sports Illustrated*, September 8, 1968.

62. Hallman, interview with author, October 9, 2018.

63. *Houston Post*, October 14, 1967.

64. Herskowitz, interview with author, August 20, 1967.

65. *Houston Post*, October 15, 1967.

66. Ibid., October 18, 1967.

67. Ibid., October 15, 1967.

68. Ibid.

69. Ibid.

70. Ibid.

71. Rickman, interview with author, September 5, 2018.

72. Stallings, interview with author, July 8, 2015.

73. *Houston Post*, October 15, 1967.

74. Zwerneman, *Game of My Life*, 64.

75. Krueger, interview with author, September 5, 2018.

76. *Houston Post*, October 15, 1967.

77. Hargett, interview with author, March 22 2018.

78. Zwerneman, *Game of My Life*, 68.

79. Hargett, interview with author, March 22, 2018.

80. Housley, interview with author, August 28, 2018.

81. *Lubbock (TX) Avalanche-Journal*, October 7, 2011.

82. Hargett, interview with author, March 22, 2018; Stegent, interview with author, August 29, 2018.

83. *Lubbock (TX) Avalanche-Journal*, October 7, 2011.

84. Long, interview with author, August 23, 2018.

85. Stegent, interview with author, August 29, 2018.

86. Hallman, interview with author, October 9, 2018.

87. Ibid.

88. Housley, interview with author, August 28, 2018.

89. Zwerneman, *Game of My Life*, 64.

90. Stegent, interview with author, August 29, 2018.

CHAPTER 11

The Streak

Boy, when we beat Arkansas, I remember flying back on the plane, and all of a sudden we felt this could be a team of destiny.

—Rick Rickman, Aggie student manager

Winning is contagious.

The Aggies certainly enjoyed the taste of victory in the aftermath of their miraculous comeback against Texas Tech, and they provided a triumphant encore the next week. This time, A&M thrashed Texas Christian University 20–0 in College Station, improving its conference record to 2–1. Stallings was enjoying his postgame banter with the press when a young autograph hunter approached. The boy politely asked Stallings if he would sign his game program.

"Be glad to, son," said Stallings, flattered by the young fan's attention. "But you ought to get some of these players first. I'm just an old has-been."[1]

The boy nodded and sympathetically replied, "Yeah, but that's all right, coach, you're getting better."[2]

The humor—and humility—of the moment added a perfect postscript to A&M's second straight victory of the season. In truth, Stallings and his Aggies were getting better, or at least it appeared that way as the big plays started to fall their way.

Big plays again played a role against TCU.

Linebacker Billy Hobbs accounted for the most defining play of the game in the fourth quarter. A&M clung to a 7–0 lead at the time, and TCU drove to the Aggie 7-yard line in hopes of tying the game. TCU quarterback Dan Carter (who had replaced starter P. D. Shabay) then tried to toss the ball to receiver Bill Ferguson in the end zone, when Hobbs ruined their plans.

Hobbs swooped in to intercept Carter's soft pass, returning it a Southwest Conference–record 102 yards for a touchdown. Along the way, Grady Allen provided a key block on TCU tailback Ross Montgomery, perhaps the only player capable of catching the speedy Aggie defender.

The score gave A&M a commanding 14–0 lead.

"I'll never be able to figure out what made them throw then," Hobbs said afterward. "It was first down and I for one just wasn't expecting it."[3]

Hobbs, who snagged a second TCU pass during the game, now had five interceptions in six games.

Winning began to shine a spotlight on other Aggies who were posting impressive numbers. Bob Long gave the Aggies a 7–0 lead against TCU with a 28-yard scoring pass from Hargett—the fifth time the two connected for a touchdown.[4]

Punter Steve O'Neal, meanwhile, entered the TCU game with a national-best 45.2-yard average per punt.[5]

Of course, the individual statistics were indicative of the overall talent A&M possessed all along. Yet adversity continued to shadow this team. A bombshell of a different sort hit the Aggies two days before a home game with Baylor University. Stallings strode into the meeting room, his heels clicking loudly as he walked. He lectured his players on the importance of attending classes and then announced, "There's two guys in here who will never wear the maroon and white jersey again."[6]

The two players were being kicked off the team for missing too many classes. Rolf Krueger and his roommate, Jack Whitmore—a sophomore halfback from Houston—immediately looked at each other.

"Jack," Krueger said.[7]

"Rolf," Whitmore replied. "I'll see ya next year."[8]

Not everyone knew who the two players were, but Krueger would later confess "it could have been a lot of people."[9] After the team meeting had ended, Krueger and his teammates soon learned the names of the two banished players— All-American lineman Maurice Moorman and Max Clark, a redshirt sophomore fullback from Tyler. News of Moorman's dismissal hit Krueger hard.

"Mo was a good guy," Krueger said. "He was tough."[10]

The two were friends and fellow linemen who had bonded during hellish offseason workouts and regular-season practices. Each day, the two powerful young men would get fully dressed in their gear 45 minutes before practice and sit under the shade of a tree.

"I would sit out there before practice and go, 'Jesus Christ, man,'" recalled Krueger, as if transported back to those afternoons. "We'd just be sitting there, kind of getting our guts together."[11]

Word of Moorman's removal from A&M sparked the newswires statewide, and the telephone at the senior's off-campus apartment started to ring nonstop. Moorman refused to answer. He stopped by the apartment to inform his wife, Trish, that he had been kicked off the team for missing classes. A review of the records in the registrar's office revealed Moorman had cut as many as 15 classes in one course alone. Moorman would later admit he knew what was coming; earlier in the day, he'd met with Stallings in his office and learned of his fate.

For Stallings, there was a flashback to the episode with Joe Namath.

"I told Maurice I didn't have a choice," Stallings remembered. "He said he understood."[12]

Stallings added somberly, "Then he cried . . . and I cried."[13]

The decision brought Stallings no comfort. Dutifully, he released a short statement to the press later that day:

> Texas A&M University is an educational institution that is represented in intercollegiate football by student-athletes. These two young men were not attending classes regularly and they have been dismissed from the squad. The dismissal is immediate and definite and there will be no further comment on it from me.[14]

Curley Hallman first learned of Moorman's fate at Sarge's, a joint adjacent to campus where he shot pool regularly with Larry Stegent and the teammate affectionately known as "Mighty Mo." He found Moorman alone, doing something he loved more than school—shooting pool.

"Mo, you want to play a game before we go to practice?" asked Hallman, oblivious of Moorman's dismissal.[15]

Moorman looked up with reddened eyes. He had obviously been crying, and Hallman knew then without asking. The two friends shot around for a little bit before parting ways.

"I was sad because Mo was one of my pool-shootin' buddies," Hallman said. "And he was a great football player. Then I went to practice to try to get better."[16]

Later that day, Moorman sat down at his apartment with *Houston Post* sportswriter Joe Heiling to address his removal from the team. The 6-foot-5, 241-pounder barely squeezed into a brown recliner in the living room as he answered questions. To his credit, Moorman took responsibility for his punishment with class.

"It was my fault," Moorman said in a voice that was barely audible. "What happened to me . . . well, I don't have anybody else to blame but myself . . . I just missed too many classes. There's nothing else coach Stallings could do. He makes the rules and you have to abide by them. I've got the highest regard in the world for coach and his staff. He did what he thought was best—and it hurt me. But I know he was right."[17]

Moorman's voice fell silent before speaking of his teammates.

"The loss of one person won't hurt this team," Moorman concluded. "It's like coach Stallings said, 'When we win, it's a team effort. When we lose, it's a team defeat.' I feel I let them down because I was part of that team."[18]

The Aggies responded to the loss of their All-American lineman just as they had with their 0–4 start. They kept fighting.

Big plays were once again the trademark of another A&M victory, its first without Moorman. The Aggies picked off six Baylor passes en route to a 21–3 triumph. Cornerback Ross Brupbacher accounted for two of those interceptions. Ivan Jones also picked off two passes, while Tommy Maxwell and Hallman each grabbed one.

"We just kept making big play after big play, and not all on defense, either," Brupbacher said after the game. "Our offense made some big ones, too."[19]

Bob Long hauled in two more touchdown passes, including a shoe-top snag with 40 seconds to go in the first half to give A&M a 14–0 lead. The scoring strike gave Hargett nine in the season, seven of which were caught by Long. Hargett also received help from Moorman's replacement, the unheralded sophomore Carl Gough of College Station.

Stegent, meanwhile, continued to perform well out of the backfield. He gained 138 yards and a touchdown on 29 carries (behind some key blocking from fullback Wendell Housley) and moved, in the words of Mickey Herskowitz, "like a line of poetry."[20]

By Sunday morning, the Aggies were suddenly in first place with a 3–1 conference record. Krueger noted there was nothing "magical" about what the Aggies were doing.

"I don't know if you call it a culture or whatever," Krueger said. "As football players, you're just conditioned to keep moving ahead. . . . It's about getting up each day and getting after it again. And never quit. Never give up. We'd be very, very tired, but we never gave up."[21]

Few outside of College Station were sold on A&M's resurgence, though. Believers would have been especially hard to find in Fayetteville, Arkansas, where the Aggies were scheduled as homecoming fodder for University of Arkansas coach Frank Broyles and his squad. The historic record didn't bode well for A&M's chances. The Aggies had last defeated Arkansas in 1957—Bryant's final season at A&M. The month of November also appeared ominous for the Aggies 10 years later, in 1967. Broyles had won nine consecutive homecomings and amassed a combined 28–3 record during the month of November at Arkansas.[22]

Only these Aggies were a different breed. Unfavorable odds didn't faze them, and good teams didn't intimidate them. Housley echoed the sentiments of his teammates when he said, "By then, we knew we could play with anybody."[23]

The Aggies obliterated the odds in Fayetteville with a come-from-behind 33–21 victory over Arkansas in blustery conditions. Hargett threw a 14-yard scoring strike to Maxwell with 12 minutes left for a 26–21 lead that the Aggies never relinquished, recording their fourth straight win.[24]

Stegent, still playing with a heavily bandaged left hand, punched the ball across the goal line from 1 yard out for A&M's final score. A quarter earlier, Stegent had returned to the huddle limping on one knee, but he showed no ill-effects of the pain on the final drive. He grabbed a short pass from a scrambling Hargett and turned it into a 35-yard pass play with a twisting, squirming run to the Arkansas 16. A few moments later, he plunged into the end zone to secure the victory.[25]

Stegent's toughness impressed everyone, especially those who counted most. Hargett called his teammate "probably the toughest guy I ever played with." The Aggie quarterback described Stegent as "tough, physical, and about half-mean on the football field."[26]

Hargett, meanwhile, completed 13 of 23 passes, for 180 yards and three touchdowns in the face of "a fierce Arkansas rush." He ran for another touchdown from 1 yard out for A&M's first score in the first quarter.[27]

"His improvising rattled us," Broyles said of Hargett. "He forced us to make alterations and we left our game plan to do it. But we had no choice. If we'd stayed in our game plan we would have been in just as bad shape. In other words, Hargett had us one way or the other."[28]

Housley opened the fourth quarter for the Aggies with a 12-yard scoring strike from Hargett. Housley's touchdown capped an 11-play, 68-yard drive for A&M and, at the time, trimmed the Razorbacks' lead to 21–20.

Housley, however, had to be carried to the bench after teammate Carl Gough stepped on his left foot. Housley suspected his foot was broken. His suspicions were confirmed when the team returned to College Station. X-rays showed one bone lying on top of another. The injury would prevent Housley from playing the next week against Rice University in Houston.[29]

"Nobody really thought we could beat Arkansas," Rickman recalled. "Boy, when we beat Arkansas, I remember flying back on the plane, and all of a sudden we felt this could be a team of destiny."[30]

One Aggie supporter didn't need to wait until the return trip home for such a revelation. The fan hugged A&M tackle Harvey Aschenbeck—a junior from Bellville who had partially blocked a punt in the fourth quarter—and yelled, "Great game, Harvey!"[31]

"We're gonna get Bear in the Cotton Bowl!" the fan then screamed. "We're gonna beat the hell out of the Bear!"[32]

Stallings, of course, entertained no such talk.

"Bryant?" Stallings coyly responded to one reporter when asked about a potential showdown with his former mentor. "Bryant? Does he coach at Rice? If he doesn't coach at Rice I'm not thinking about him."[33]

Stallings wanted his players only thinking about Rice—a team that had won two conference games in the previous two seasons. Paranoia closed in on Stallings, with rival Texas looming the week after Rice. On Thursday, he loaded his players on two buses bound for Houston, where he checked them into the Shamrock Hilton Hotel 52 hours in advance of Saturday's kickoff with Rice.[34]

The unusual move prompted a comical exchange between Stallings and Herskowitz.

"What are you doing in town?" Herskowitz asked the coach.

"I came down to play a football game," Stallings replied.

"Who's coaching the team while you're gone?"

"I brought them with me."

"This early? Why? So they can get acclimated to the weather?" Herskowitz asked sarcastically.

"That's part of it."

"You're kidding. I mean, Houston isn't exactly at the other end of the continent."

"No, but it's humid here," Stallings said with a straight face. "We don't get to work out at home until four or five in the afternoon. Yesterday, I wore a sweat-shirt and a jacket. I don't expect to be wearing them Saturday at two p.m., and I wanted our kids to work out in the weather they'll be playing in."[35]

Herskowitz and Stallings had known each other for 13 years, far too long for either to ditch the playful banter. By now, the two friends enjoyed the sarcastic give-and-take too much.

But Stallings eventually gave Herskowitz the straight scoop.

"We couldn't turn around without all those people in College Station asking about Texas and, shoot, we have to play Rice," Stallings explained. "I just needed to get them away from it, from the bonfire and the ticket requests and all that. They may get distracted down here, but at least they'll be thinking about Rice."[36]

As it turned out, the Aggies dispatched Rice 18–3 on the strength of two fourth-quarter touchdowns by a pair of Houston natives—Maxwell and Stegent. Maxwell accounted for the first of those touchdowns, on a 7-yard pass from Hargett. Stegent later delivered the knockout blow with a 23-yard scoring run, after fullback Bill Sallee sprang him at the line of scrimmage with a stout block.[37]

A&M's Southwest Conference record improved to 5–1 with one game remain-ing against Texas.

Ironically, the final gun signaled the real drama. Most of the 58,000 fans in attendance at Rice Stadium remained in their seats long after the two teams left the field. They held transistor radios snugly against their ears, listening to the Texas–TCU game 165 miles away in Austin. A Texas victory meant a winner-take-all game for the conference championship on Thanksgiving Day; a Longhorn loss ensured A&M at least a share of the crown.

Beneath the stands, in the Aggie locker room, players sat at their cubicles or moved about the room in the usual postgame manner.

A thunderous roar suddenly erupted outside in the stands. TCU scored in the final 61 seconds of the game to upset Texas 24–17, handing the Longhorns their second conference defeat. The Fightin' Texas Aggie Band launched into the Aggie War Hymn as fans cheered and sang and hugged. A decade of losing left the Aggie fan base starved for success—any success. Why, even a piece of a title provided reason enough for celebration. But the Aggie players weren't so easy to please.

Linebacker Ivan Jones probably spoke for many of his teammates when he shrugged at the news of TCU's upset victory and said, "It doesn't matter." He continued, "We've got to beat Texas anyway. We aren't settling for no ties."[38]

NOTES

1. *Houston Post*, October 27, 1967.

2. Ibid.

3. Ibid. Hobbs's interception officially went into the record book as a 100-yard touchdown return and tied a mark set by SMU's Charley Jackson in 1957. Hobbs also broke a 25-year-old A&M record held by Cullen Rogers. In 1942, Rogers returned an interception 99 yards for a touchdown (*Houston Post*, October 26, 1967).

4. *Houston Post*, October 22, 1967.

5. Ibid.

6. Hallman, interview with author, September 14, 2018.

7. Krueger, interview with author, September 5, 2018.

8. Ibid.

9. Ibid.

10. Ibid.

11. Ibid.

12. Stallings, interview with author, July 8, 2015.

13. Ibid.

14. *Houston Post*, October 27, 1967.

15. Hallman, interview with author, September 14, 2018.

16. Ibid.

17. *Houston Post*, October 27, 1967.

18. Ibid.

19. *Houston Post*, October 29, 1967.

20. Ibid.

21. Krueger, interview with author, September 5, 2018.

22. *Houston Post*, November 5, 1967.

23. Housley, interview with author, August 28, 2018.

24. Ibid.

25. Ibid.

26. Hargett, interview with author, October 11, 2018.

27. Ibid.

28. *Houston Post*, November 6, 1967.

29. Housley, interview with author, August 28, 2018; *Dallas Morning News*, January 2, 1968.

30. Rickman, interview with author, September 5, 2018.

31. *Houston Post*, November 5, 1967.

32. Ibid.

33. Ibid., November 17, 1967.

34. Ibid.

35 Ibid.

36. Ibid.

37. *Houston Post*, November 19, 1967.

38. Ibid.

CHAPTER 12
High Tide

Basically, we thought they stole it from us.
—Bobby Johns, Alabama defensive back, on being denied
the 1966 national championship

Winning.

Quarterback Kenny "Snake" Stabler, defensive back Bobby Johns, and receiver Dennis Homan knew little else after their arrival to Alabama in 1964. As freshmen, they watched the varsity team win a national championship and helped lead the Crimson Tide to their second consecutive national title the next season.

The winning continued in 1966 when, as juniors, the dynamic threesome led Alabama to an 11–0 record. The season developed into a masterpiece for the two-time defending national champions. Alabama began with a preseason number one ranking and finished with a 34–7 demolition of previously unbeaten and heavily favored Nebraska in the Sugar Bowl.

The Crimson Tide held claim as the only unbeaten and untied team in the nation. They also walked away from their storied season uncrowned.

Curiously, pollsters had voted instead to split the national championship between the University of Notre Dame and Michigan State University. Notre Dame and Michigan State had each finished 9–0–1, after a highly publicized matchup of unbeaten teams ended in an uneventful 10–10 tie. Naturally, Alabamians protested until they were hoarse; the slight struck a nerve. Others beyond the Cotton State also expressed dismay by the obvious oversight. *Sports*

Illustrated's Dan Jenkins dealt some critical analysis of the newly crowned co-champs the week after Alabama's snub.

"Be truthful now, Notre Dame and Michigan State," Jenkins wrote pointedly. "Would you really want to play Alabama? Would you honestly care to spend an afternoon trying to swat those gnats who call themselves linemen and swirl around your ankles all day? Why, Heavens to Bear Bryant, nobody ought to want to play Alabama unless it enjoys going to football clinics. Which is exactly what last week's Sugar Bowl was—a clinic, with Bear Bryant instructing the nation on what a top-ranked team is supposed to look like."[1]

Nothing eased the pain for Alabama's football players, though. They felt the sting of injustice.

"I'm just thinking that most of the sportswriters and newspapers didn't like Alabama anyway," Homan said. "I guess because we were winning all the time. All those teams up North and out West, they just didn't want to see us win it. But I think that was the main reason. That should have been our third year in a row. In fact, that was the best team we had.

"But hey, we knew in our hearts we were the number one team."[2]

A year before, following the 1965 season, Bryant had ordered a telegram to be posted in the dorm: "Congratulations on winning the national championship. Let's get started Monday on making it three in a row." Players had swelled with pride, inspired to accomplish what no other college football team ever had. No major college team had ever won three consecutive national titles. The Crimson Tide responded by defeating every team placed in their path, shutting out 6 of 11 opponents along the way. They then toppled a gigantic Nebraska team so soundly in the Sugar Bowl that Bryant afterward told reporters he lacked the vocabulary to properly praise his team. Such giant-slaying victories by diminutive Alabama had led *Sports Illustrated* to later remark: "It was embarrassing, like getting mugged by a kindergarten class."[3]

Bobby Johns, who had risen from obscurity to the status of two-time All-American, left everything on the field during the 1966 campaign and on New Year's Day against Nebraska. He played the game of his life against the Cornhuskers, picking off a Sugar Bowl–record three interceptions to help preserve Alabama's perfect season. Then the shocking news of the final polls arrived—a stinging rebuke of everything Alabama had bled and sweated for on the field.

In the end, people wondered if the polls were punishment for the plague of segregation. Or were the polls actually about something as trivial as jealousy?

Were the polls even about football anymore?

"It was a shocker," said Johns, recalling his raw feelings. "It was awful. We couldn't believe it. We were national champions two years in a row—and then to not win it. We couldn't figure out what had happened. We just figured they didn't want a southern team to win three in a row. Nobody had ever won three in a row before.

"Basically, we thought they stole it from us."[4]

Against this backdrop, Bryant and his Crimson Tide entered the 1967 season. The Associated Press ranked Alabama number two before the season, although by then no one associated with the program trusted polls anymore. If anything, the lessons of 1966 planted seeds of doubt in the Alabama locker room—not toward one another but toward the system.

Bryant's greatest challenge as he entered the new season appeared obvious. He had to prevent any hangover from the disappointment of 1966. He needed his players to focus on the only thing they could control: football.

On paper, Alabama presented all the trappings of another national title contender. Stabler, Homan, Johns, and a stellar defense unquestionably provided the pillars for another prospective championship run. From a defense that allowed an average of four points per game, 8 of 11 starters returned, including Johns—a newly minted All-American.

Stabler led the Southeastern Conference in passing accuracy, completing 74 of 114 passes (64.9 percent) for 956 yards and nine touchdowns. He also led Alabama in rushing with 397 yards. Stabler's all-around athleticism had long reminded Bryant of Namath, as did his smooth release and quick footwork. By the time Alabama arrived in New Orleans for the Sugar Bowl, Bryant was even saying his left-handed quarterback possessed "the best touch for long passing I've ever seen."[5]

The usually fearless Stabler lived up to the hype in the Sugar Bowl, completing 12 of 18 passes for 218 yards and one touchdown in the blowout of Nebraska. He also ran for another touchdown in the game and was named its most valuable player.

Dennis Homan entered the 1967 season as Stabler's main target with the loss of All-American Ray Perkins, who had led the Crimson Tide in catches (33), receiving yards (490), and touchdown receptions (7). Homan finished second in each team category, with 23 catches for 377 yards and five touchdowns, but he first caught Bryant's attention as a running back on the freshman team.

From atop his tower, Bryant often watched the freshman team run plays in practice. He noticed Homan's ability to catch Stabler's passes out of the backfield.

One day prior to his sophomore season, Bryant called Homan into his office and said, "Dennis, I'm gonna make a wide receiver out of you."[6]

"Yes, sir," Homan replied.

Decades later, Homan would laughingly confess, "Of course, I would have said 'Yes, sir' if he would have said he was gonna move me to tackle."[7]

Homan, Stabler, and Johns shared a lot in common. All three were raised in Alabama—which is to say, they were all raised on the legend of Paul W. "Bear" Bryant. If Bryant's giant shadow didn't blot out the sun where they lived, it was only a matter of time before it would.

In Birmingham, Bobby Johns attended Banks High School and took over the starting quarterback position his senior year. Johns first encountered Bryant that season at a Birmingham country club where alumni gathered to hear the coach speak. Each Sunday during the season, Bryant traveled to Birmingham to film the *Bear Bryant Show*, and after the hour-long production, he stopped by the country club to address the crowd.

Johns remembered watching the show with the Alabama boosters that day, prior to Bryant's arrival. Naturally, he knew of Bryant's reputation as an outstanding football coach. In Alabama, Bryant's coaching accomplishments were hard to miss. What the 18-year-old quarterback didn't comprehend, however, was the magnitude of Bryant's presence.

During the televised show, Johns listened to those around him chuckle and laugh aloud at Bryant's entertaining country wit. He observed how comfortable the coach made those in attendance feel with his humor as if they were listening to a neighbor or a favorite uncle. The room buzzed with lively banter and conversations even after the show.

Twenty minutes later, the mood in the room changed dramatically.

Bryant walked into the room, and all eyes honed in on his lumbering 6-foot-4 frame. The room—filled with many of Birmingham's most prominent citizens—fell silent.

"Talk about respect," Johns recalled. "It was almost fearful. They were in awe of him. And he was bigger than life. He was a John Wayne-type personality. It was kind of interesting. I thought, *Well, maybe this guy is a big deal.*

"At that point, I realized this is somebody special."[8]

A few years later, Bryant would ironically think the same of Johns, who almost missed his chance to play for the Crimson Tide. College recruiters were hardly hounding the 6-foot-1, 155-pound Johns as he entered his senior year, even in an era when scholarships were doled out in unlimited numbers. Alabama and

Samford University—a well-respected private school in Birmingham—were the only two colleges to offer Johns a scholarship. No other colleges were even calling.

"For some stupid reason, I put Alabama off," Johns remembered. "I said, 'Let me think about it.'"[9]

Banks High School head coach George "Shorty" White urged his lightweight quarterback to wait for an offer from Auburn University. Then one day, Alabama assistant coach Sam Bailey called Johns with a direct question: "Well, are you gonna take the scholarship?"[10]

"Well, coach," Johns said. "I don't know. I'm still thinking about it."[11]

Losing patience, Bailey replied, "If you're not gonna take this scholarship, let us know so we can give it to somebody else."[12]

Clarity hit Johns like a blindside blitz. As quick as he could spit out the words, the teenager blurted, "Coach, I'm coming to Alabama."[13]

In Muscle Shoals, some 113 miles northwest of Birmingham, Bryant's reputation alone changed Dennis Homan's fate. Homan grew up determined to play football at the University of Mississippi, in a state where his family roots were deeply entrenched.

Plans changed when Gene Stallings visited Homan's home in Muscle Shoals, a small town on banks of the Tennessee River. Stallings, then Bryant's assistant, strode into the home with one simple message: "Coach Bryant would like to see you go to Alabama."[14]

The legend wanted Dennis Homan to wear an Alabama jersey.

Homan looked up at Stallings and replied, "You tell coach I'm comin'."[15]

Kenny "Snake" Stabler, then the most coveted prize of the 1964 recruiting class, also fell under of the spell of the charismatic Bryant. Like a lot of Alabama boys, he grew up listening to the games of Bryant's Crimson Tide on the radio with his father. The Stabler family lived in Foley, a small town in the far southwestern corner of the state, where Leroy "Slim" Stabler worked as a mechanic, and his athletically talented son explored his rebellious streak.

The elder Stabler constantly encouraged Kenny to play football, and despite a strained relationship with his son, frequently watched Foley High School's practices while still dressed in his greasy work clothes. At 6-foot-5, he too was hard to miss. By most accounts, Slim Stabler was a hard-drinking, hard-working man who battled demons from his combat in World War II, trauma particularly associated with the Allied invasion of Anzio, Italy.

Slim Stabler realized a football scholarship could carry his son far in life, although his boy was also coveted many Major League Baseball scouts. The New York Yankees reportedly offered the 6-foot-2, 190-pounder $50,000 to sign a minor league contract—a ton of money in 1964 and, as Kenny later added, "especially in our house."[16] But Stabler dreamed of playing football at Alabama and following in the legendary footsteps of idols such as Pat Trammell, Billy Neighbors, Billy Richardson, and Joe Namath.[17]

Young Stabler did his part on the field. In three seasons at Foley, he led his team to a combined 29–1 record and three consecutive state titles. He also represented his school in Alabama's annual high school all-star game the summer after graduation. Along the way, he picked up a catchy nickname. The story of his nickname features a coach named Denzil Hollis, who watched Stabler return a punt 60 yards for a touchdown in a junior varsity game. Stabler zigged and zagged between and around defenders all the way to the end zone, prompting Hollis to declare, "Damn, that boy runs like a snake."[18]

The nickname stuck like pine tar.

So did Stabler's love of the University of Alabama and its famous football coach. Stabler recalled the moment Bryant personally entered his home on a recruiting visit, one memorable day in Foley. As it turned out, the sight of Bryant's face proved enough to seal the deal.

"That was it," Stabler remembered. "He was so big and had that face that looked like it should have been carved in Mount Rushmore."[19]

Stabler, Homan, and Johns would in time form the foundation on which Alabama's hopes rested. By 1967, their journey had prepared them well, with each having endured a variety of trials and tribulations under Bryant. All of which helped transform them into Alabama legends in their own right.

Johns arrived in Tuscaloosa like a lot of Alabama recruits and discovered he would eventually be playing another position. "I figured Snake was the guy to beat," Johns said. "But when I got down there, I saw the handwriting on the wall. Snake was a better prospect than I was. I tell people now, 'I don't know what those coaches were thinking?'"[20]

Of course, Johns knew the game. In those days, college teams hoarded as many of the best athletes as they could sign and then assigned them to positions where they could produce the best results for the team. Bryant switched players around all the time, as he did with Homan and then Johns before their sophomore seasons. Johns moved to the defensive backfield. Both Homan and

Johns would earn All-American honors in their respective positions by the end of their Alabama careers.

Johns intercepted his first pass as a starter in the 1965 season opener against Georgia, a game Alabama lost 18–17 in heartbreaking fashion.

"Georgia threw a flea-flicker pass play," Johns recalled. "That was the worse feeling in the world because I felt like I had contributed to us getting beat. Coach Bryant kept telling us we still had a chance to win the national championship. We thought he was crazy. But it went down just like he said it would."[21]

Johns started every game for the next three seasons.

Homan made his fateful debut six weeks later in Jackson, Mississippi, against Mississippi State University. In the first quarter, Homan became so involved in the action on the field, he failed to realize he was standing next to Bryant on the sideline. After one play, Homan said aloud to himself, "That corner can be beat on the post route. He's playing too far outside."[22]

A deep, gravel voice behind him asked, "What did you say?"[23]

Homan turned and saw Bryant. He swallowed hard and replied, "The post looked open to me."[24]

Bryant grabbed Homan by the shoulders with his big hands and pushed him onto the field, barking, "Well, get your butt in there and run it."[25]

Homan informed quarterback Steve Sloan of the next play. Sloan promptly connected with Homan on a 65-yard touchdown pass on a post route to give the Crimson Tide a 7–0 lead. Alabama eventually defeated Mississippi that day 10–7.

"I was so wide open on that play, and it seemed like an eternity for that ball to get to me," Homan recalled. "You think all kinds of things when you run these routes. I was thinking, *Boy, if you miss this pass you better keep on running.* And thank goodness I did catch it.

"I never came out after that."[26]

Bryant's intensity shadowed their every move at Alabama, whether it through the brutal regimen of offseason training or his unyielding demands on the football field. There were certain rites of passage every Alabama player experienced, from puking in one of the barrels during offseason gym class to hearing the thunderous footsteps of Bryant descending from his tower. Players observed three ways in which Bryant climbed down from his tower. He walked, trotted, and ran.

"And if he was runnin' down those steps, you were just prayin' to the Lord that he wasn't comin' to your group," Homan said. "Cause that meant he saw something he didn't like at all."[27]

Bryant's assistant coaches could be nearly as brutal, and none more than Stallings prior to his departure for Texas A&M in the winter of 1964. Homan remembered Stallings as a strict, unyielding taskmaster.

"Stallings was probably one of the toughest, toughest coaches I ever played for," Homan said. "It was his way or the highway. He was sort of a clone of Coach Bryant, and he was tough. And a play had to be right, or you would run it over and over until you got it right. He probably worked harder than any coach or player on the field."[28]

Players and coaches feared Bryant's wrath most of all.

One memorable incident defined Bryant's temper as much as any other at Alabama, and it took place October 16, 1965, at Birmingham's Legion Field after a game with Tennessee. The Crimson Tide struggled that day, despite outgaining Tennessee 361 yards to 195, mostly due to three second-half fumbles. Despite the mishaps and lost opportunities, Alabama drove to the Tennessee 4-yard line with Stabler—then a backup—behind center on the final drive. With seconds left in the game, Stabler glanced up at the scoreboard and saw it was third down. He quickly took the snap and threw out of bounds to stop the clock so kicker David Ray could attempt a game-winning field goal. But the yardage marker on the field showed fourth down.

Tennessee took over on downs, escaping with a 7–7 tie in front of 70,000 stunned fans.

Johns remembered running to the locker room after the game to discover the door padlocked. He and his teammates crowded around the door, waiting for a manager to let them in so they could await their explosive coach. Suddenly, Bryant bullishly pushed his way to the front of the pack, angrily asking, "What the hell's goin' on?"[29]

Chief Joe Smelley, an Alabama state trooper assigned to protect Bryant, stood by the coach's side. He was a middle-aged, rotund man of nearly 300 pounds, who loved sipping whiskey and the notoriety of being Bryant's bodyguard. The job required him to carry a pistol, although no one was sure he knew how to use it properly.

Bryant looked at the padlock and then at Smelley.

"Smelley, shoot the damn lock off," Bryant ordered.[30]

"Well, Coach, I can't do that," Smelley protested. "The bullet might ricochet and hit one of these players."[31]

"Well, then get the hell out of the way," bristled Bryant, pushing the hefty patrolman aside. Bryant dropped his shoulder and rammed the door with one, violent thrust. He knocked the padlock hinges from the doorframe. The players and coaches filed nervously into the locker room one by one.

"There were probably a hundred people in that locker room," Johns recalled. "And you couldn't hear anything. Nothing."[32]

Bryant surprised his players during the postgame talk. He took the blame for the confusion at the end of the game, hoping to ease the pressure of a tie. "But you can still win a national championship if you think you can," Bryant said. "Unless I've misjudged you . . ."[33]

Stabler loved Bryant for those moments, although their relationship was far from ideal. Tensions frequently overwhelmed the love. The notoriously wayward Stabler angered Bryant often with episodes of smoking, drinking, breaking curfew, and cutting classes—all rebellious traits seemingly engrained in his DNA. *Sports Illustrated* once compared Stabler to Huckleberry Finn, noting with some irony how "he even looks like Huckleberry Finn."[34]

But Stabler's relationship with Bryant reached a breaking point in the spring of 1967.

Trouble began when Stabler tore cartilage in his knee while running through a drill at a spring practice. Bryant ordered his quarterback to stay off the knee until it healed. Stabler obeyed but became "bored" with his extra idle time.[35]

"So I started going to visit my girlfriend down in Mobile," Stabler said. "We had study hall from 7:30 to 9:00 [p.m.]. I would skip study hall, jump in the car and drive four hours to Pritchard, Alabama, hang out with this girl I was seeing down there for four hours, jump back in the car and drive four hours back to try to make a 7:00 [a.m.] class. But I didn't make many of those."[36]

Teammates frequently tried to cover for Stabler—not because of his talents but because he was so damn likeable. Players often crowded around him at Bryant Hall, where he held court with a variety of hilarious stories. Running back Ed Morgan said decades later, "Snake probably kept me from getting a B rather than a C a few times because it was a lot more interesting to listen to his stories than study."[37]

No one tried to protect Stabler more from himself than Homan, his roommate and close friend. Although Homan dutifully noted that he wasn't a saint in college either, adding with a laugh, "So it didn't help that I was rooming with him."[38]

Yet Stabler's level of mischief seemed to supersede that of everyone around him. Homan remembered countless mornings when he had to drag his buddy out of bed so he could attend a class—that is, if Stabler were even in his bed.

"A lot of nights, I knew Stabler wasn't gonna be in for bed check," Homan explained. "I'd always put these pillows in his bed, and I had 'em lookin' pretty good, too. We even had an old, cutoff mop we put up there for his head."[39]

The ruse lasted only so long. One night, the coaches entered the room to inspect Stabler's bed. Homan rolled over and pretended to be asleep when they discovered the pillows and mop. One of the coaches punched Homan in the shoulder, hollering, "Where's Snake?"[40]

"Well, heck," Homan replied coyly, "isn't he in bed?"[41]

"No, he's not in bed. We got pillows over here."[42]

Homan shrugged and said, "I don't know anything about that."[43]

Stabler's behavior continued to spiral out of control. His final rebellious act that spring—the one that sent Bryant into a rage—might have been when a girlfriend accidentally drove his Corvette through the front window of a downtown business in Tuscaloosa. She was driving for Stabler because he had been drinking beer. After the crash, Stabler proceeded to climb behind the wheel, back his car away from the wreckage, and drive away.

Morgan tracked down Stabler later that night in town at Smith's Motel. Morgan knocked on the door to Stabler's room and informed his teammate that the police wanted to talk to him.

"Whatever it is," Stabler replied, "it's going to have to wait."[44]

Then one day while at his parents' home in Foley, Stabler received a telegram that read, "You have been indefinitely suspended.—Coach Paul W. Bryant."[45]

Stabler received another telegram the next day from "Broadway" Joe Namath: "He means it."[46]

Stabler had officially landed in Bryant's doghouse for what the coach described as "a combination of things." The suspension arrived at a time when Bryant fretted over his team's morale as it prepared to enter the 1967 season. "They just kept piling up and I couldn't overlook them," Bryant said of Stabler's offenses and his decision to discipline the player. "I finally suspended him for the team."[47]

Stabler soon enrolled in summer classes at his own expense. He also reported to Bryant weekly until his summer courses ended. He then marched into Bryant's office and plopped into the lumpy couch in front of Bryant's desk.

Bryant seemed to tower above everyone who sat there, like a king on his throne.

"Coach, I have done everything necessary to become eligible by SEC standards," Stabler said. "My grade point is back up and I want to come back out for the team."[48]

Spitting a mouthful of tobacco juice, Bryant leaned forward and looked down at Stabler menacingly.

"You don't deserve to be on this team," he said. "Get your ass out of here."[49]

For a moment, Stabler sat silently as the words sank in. He then stubbornly replied, "Well, I am going to come back out anyway, coach."[50]

Bryant finally said, "We'll see."[51]

On August 17, 1967, Bryant issued a brief statement to the press: "Kenny Stabler will be permitted to rejoin the football squad for all practices beginning Sept. 1. Ken has assured me he will adhere to the academic regulations of the university and will pursue his degree until he graduates. I feel he is deserving of another chance."[52]

Stabler celebrated by buying a case of beer and driving home to Foley, "throwing away the empties at every stop sign."[53]

NOTES

1. Dan Jenkins, "Best and Worst of the Bowls," *Sports Illustrated*, January 9, 1967.
2. Dennis Homan, interview with author, September 26, 2018.
3. Pat Putman, "Pride in the Red Jersey," *Sports Illustrated*, October 11, 1971.
4. Bobby Johns, interview with author, October 3, 2018.
5. "As the Snake Can Testify, Beware the Wrath of the Bear," *Sports Illustrated*, September 10, 1967; Bryant and Underwood, *Bear*, 274.
6. Homan, interview with author, September 26, 2018.
7. Ibid.
8. Johns, interview with author, October 3, 2018.
9. Ibid.
10. Ibid.
11. Ibid.
12. Ibid.
13. Ibid.
14. Homan, interview with author, September 26, 2018.
15. Ibid.
16. Gold, *Bear's Boys*, 218–19.
17. Ibid., 219.
18. William Browning, "One Last Smile with the Snake: Remembering Kenny Stabler," *SBNation.com*, December 9, 2015 (accessed October 1, 2017).
19. Gold, *Bear's Boys*, 219.
20. Johns, interview with author, October 3, 2018.

21. Tommy Hicks, *Game of My Life: Alabama* (Champaign, IL: Sports Publishing, 2006), 70.

22. Homan, interview with author, September 26, 2018.

23. Forney and Townsend, *Talk of the Tide*, 102.

24. Ibid.

25. Ibid.

26. Homan, interview with author, September 26, 2018.

27. Ibid.

28. Ibid.

29. Johns, interview with author, October 3, 2018.

30. Ibid.

31. Ibid.

32. Ibid.

33. Keith Dunnavant, *The Missing Ring: How Bear Bryant and the 1966 Alabama Crimson Tide Were Denied College Football's Most Elusive Prize* (New York: St. Martin's, 2006), 70.

34. "As the Snake Can Testify," *Sports Illustrated.*

35. Gold, *Bear's Boys*, 220.

36. Ibid.

37. Browning, "One Last Smile."

38. Homan, interview with author, September 26, 2018.

39. Ibid.

40. Ibid.

41. Ibid.

42. Ibid.

43. Ibid.

44. Browning, "One Last Smile."

45. Gold, *Bear's Boys*, 220.

46. Ibid.

47. Bryant and Underwood, *Bear*, 276.

48. Gold, *Bear's Boys*, 221.

49. Ibid.

50. Herskowitz, *Legend*, 167; Gold, *Bear's Boys*, 221.

51. Gold, *Bear's Boys*, 221.

52. *Houston Post*, August 18, 1967.

53. Herskowitz, *Legend*, 167.

CHAPTER 13

The Aggie War Hymn

So goodbye to Texas University
So long to the orange and the white
Good luck to dear old Texas Aggies
They are the boys who show the real old fight

—the Aggie War Hymn

Twenty-eight sportswriters across the Lone Star State predicted the Thanksgiving Day showdown between Texas University and Texas A&M. Only one picked the Aggies to win.[1]

The sole dissenter among the Texas sporting scribes was Louis Cox, a veteran of the *Dallas Times-Herald* and either a genius or fool, depending on where your loyalty rested. If nothing else, the predictions of the state's sportswriting fraternity reflected the rivalry's history. The Longhorns led the series 51–17–5 and had won the last 10 annual Thanksgiving Day clashes against the Aggies. In fact, A&M's last victory over Texas occurred when Gene Stallings was a senior captain for Bryant's Aggies in 1956.[2]

As for Bryant, he won only one of four meetings with Texas while at the helm of A&M. A sportswriter once asked if Bryant could explain why Texas dominated the series, and he famously replied, "I guess they hate us a lot worse than we hate them."[3]

The series produced plenty of near-misses and hard-fought losses by A&M through the years. Only a year earlier, Texas had defeated A&M 22–14, and in 1965—Stallings's maiden season—the Longhorns edged a game Aggie squad

21–17 at College Station. But as one diehard Aggie booster stated after A&M's victory over Rice, "I've had enough of those moral victories. Now I'd like a few immoral ones."[4]

The rivalry's lopsided history also cultivated a cottage industry of humor, often at the expense of the Aggies. Columnist Jack Gallagher recalled how his late colleague Homer Norton usually summarized the big game by writing, "A&M won the halftime show but Texas won the football game." Gallagher's punchline: "His observation was almost always followed by a dissenting letter from Vincent DiNino, the Longhorn band director."[5] Of course, the Fightin' Texas Aggie Band deserved praise for its great tradition and performances. Former Texas All-American Maurice Doke once said of the songs played by the famed Aggie band, "Listen, those songs are so great they even fire us up."[6]

The Aggies wanted to attain a similar success on the football field—punchlines and odds be damned.

Then again, those paying attention to the 1967 season clearly understood this chapter of the rivalry would be anything but a laugher. The Aggies carried a quiet confidence that had grown since their miraculous victory in Lubbock. They had won their last five games, fueled by a swarming defense that created 15 turnovers during the streak. Overall, A&M entered the Texas game with a defense that had amassed a total of 33 total turnovers in nine games—15 more than it gave opponents.

"You were demanded to follow your technique and sprint to the football," Hallman said of the Aggie defense. "And once that confidence level started growing, and we created turnovers, the opportunity is there to make something happen. When confidence grows and you see the fruits of your hard work, good things happen. Then that chemistry is developed."[7]

By now, the Aggies knew who they were and what they were capable of doing under pressure. "We knew we could play with anybody," Housley said.[8] Texas included. The tradition of the Longhorns was something A&M respected, but Krueger made it clear he and his teammates were "not intimidated by them."[9]

Hallman explained the matchup in more diplomatic terms.

"They had earned their position as one of the great programs in the history of college football," he said. "We were trying to get where they had been."[10]

Three potent players stood in A&M's path—quarterback Bill Bradley and backfield mates Chris Gilbert and Ted Koy.

Bradley presented a dual threat as a passer and runner. He even returned punts and alone averaged 160 all-purpose yards per game. Three years earlier, he led Palestine High School to a state championship with a 24–15 victory over San Marcos. Legend has it, Bradley saved the day that game by switching the ball from his typical right hand to his left to throw the touchdown pass.

Gilbert, a bit undersized at 5-foot-11 and 180 pounds, brought a similar level of gravitas to the Texas offense. The Houston native ran for 1,080 yards in 1966 and was 32 yards shy of reaching another 1,000-yard season. A week earlier, in the loss to TCU, Gilbert broke loose for a 96-yard touchdown run—his ninth in as many games.

Aggie linebacker Ivan Jones had played against Gilbert in high school and recalled that meeting for members of the media. "I know there were times in that game when I misjudged his speed," Jones said. "There were several times when I would have an angle on him and miss the tackle. His speed was deceptive, even then."[11]

Koy, meanwhile, didn't have the eye-catching statistics of Gilbert. But at 6-foot-2, 210 pounds, he earned his keep as a bullish blocker.

"Koy was like a lineman in the backfield," Krueger said. "Hell, he was bigger than me."[12]

Almost.

Bradley, Gilbert, and Koy presented the Aggies with a great challenge as much as A&M's defense presented them with the three Texas standouts. "We're real proud of our pursuit," Jones said. "If any of 'em get loose, we'll have people after 'em. We don't think that breaking one tackle will get it. They'll have to break eleven."[13]

The matchups excited Stallings, who told the press, "Anybody who doesn't want to get ready for this one is dead and don't know it."[14]

Reports of a potential A&M-Alabama showdown in the Cotton Bowl had first hit the newspapers a few days earlier. Sportswriters were eager to cover a Stallings-Bryant matchup, and one of them asked the Aggie coach his thoughts about potentially facing his mentor as he prepared for Texas. Stallings incredulously replied, "How can you think about anything beyond?"[15]

Stallings wasn't in the mood to talk about the Cotton Bowl. Not everyone shied away from the topic, though. Jones—arguably A&M's most entertaining quote—said what was on everyone's mind in College Station.

"There's no doubt about it," Jones said. "This is the biggest game around here in ten years. We want to go to the Cotton Bowl and we know there's only one way to get there—over Texas' body."[16]

Game day ushered in an unusual amount of energy and excitement around Kyle Field. Scalpers made a killing with ticket sales, and all those who held a ticket promised that their team would be the big winner. Everyone expected an entertaining battle, perhaps even one for the ages.

The promise alone proved worth the price of admission.

In the A&M locker room, Wendell Housley asked team physician Dr. Henry McQuaide to give him a shot to numb the pain in the foot he had broken 19 days earlier in Arkansas. The fullback had been forced to miss the Rice game but wasn't about to sit out against Texas with a championship on the line. Dr. McQuaide obliged with a cortisone shot.[17]

Receiver Bob Long suited up for the big game, armed with confidence and resolve.

"We were expecting to win," Long later said. "Texas had been beat. We knew they were not indestructible."[18]

As usual, Hargett quietly battled his nerves prior to the opening kickoff. The nerves always vanished after the first snap from center when, in his mind, it then became "just another game." Only Hargett knew this time it wasn't just another game. This game had to be won.[19]

If anything, Hargett and his Aggie teammates might have entered the game with a motivational edge. Whether real or perceived, they thought Texas players, coaches, and fans carried themselves with an air of superiority.

"I think we thought that, but I don't know it was true," Hargett said. "But I think we thought that. . . . It was just a feeling they thought we were just a bunch of ol' farm boys. . . . I guess we always felt they thought they were better than us."[20]

The psychological dynamics of the rivalry soon took center stage on the field. As the captains for both teams met at midfield for the pregame coin flip, players for both teams simultaneously lined up on their respective hash marks and glared across the field in a staredown worthy of a heavyweight title fight.[21]

Fans roared wildly. A classic defensive slugfest then followed.

Hobbs, fittingly, drew first blood. With the game scoreless, Hobbs picked off a pass from Bradley late in the second quarter at the Texas 11-yard line. Moments later, Stallings called on Charlie Riggs to attempt a 32-yard field goal. Riggs missed a 33-yard attempt in the first quarter when his kick sailed wide to the left.

Now Riggs tried to gauge the swirling wind at Kyle Field. He couldn't. Flags on both ends of the field pointed toward the 50-yard line.

Riggs proceeded to kick the ball high into the air as if hitting a wedge shot on a golf course. At first, his kick looked woefully short but then continued to gain altitude in the tricky wind. "It started out straight, and I thought it would be true," said Hallman, the kicker's trusty holder. "But then it started hooking."[22]

The ball finally struck the left upright a few feet above the crossbar and squirted through the uprights to give the Aggies a 3–0 lead with 5:36 left in the half. The score held at halftime, although the damage by A&M should have been much greater. The Aggies moved the ball to the Texas 30-, 13-, and 9-yard lines in the first half and had only produced three points for their efforts.

The second half started ominously for the Longhorns.

Gilbert returned the opening kick of the second half to the Texas 24-yard line before he encountered Aggies Tommy Maxwell and Leroy Hauerland. One of Gilbert's blockers clashed with Maxwell, who first got a hand on the hard-nosed Texas runner. Then Hauerland—a junior safety from Sealy, Texas—halted Gilbert by plunging a helmet into his ribs.[23]

Initially, Gilbert thought he had the air knocked out of him. Coach Royal asked his star running back if he was all right, and Gilbert replied, "Yes." He ran into the huddle for the next play with a bruised hip but said he had "no power, no push off." Gilbert returned to the sideline, where the team doctor informed him he had a hip pointer—a debilitating pelvic contusion caused by a direct blow.[24]

"I got a cortisone shot," Gilbert later said, "and it didn't deaden my leg at all."[25]

Gilbert didn't play another down the rest of the game.

The Longhorns and Aggies continued to slug it out in the middle of the field for the rest of the third quarter. The intensity mounted as A&M clung to a 3–0 lead. Finally, Texas struck pay dirt with 11:11 left in the game. Bradley capped a seven-play, 55-yard drive when he crossed the goal line from 2 yards out to give Texas a 7–3 lead.

Yet the mood at Kyle Field quickly changed.

The Aggies took possession of the ball on their own 20-yard line when the ensuing kickoff sailed into the end zone without a return. Hargett called for a bootleg where his first option was to tight end Tom Buckman on a crossing pattern. The play called for Long to run a deep route to clear the safeties, but Hargett threw an incomplete pass to Buckman.

Long returned to the huddle with a message for his quarterback.

"Their safety is cheating up," Long declared. "I can get behind him."[26]

Hargett called the same play. Texas safety Ronnie Ehrig nudged forward, just as Long had observed. Ehrig then made the critical mistake of letting the Aggie receiver pull even with him at full speed. Hargett saw the opening. He unleashed a perfect pass 30 yards downfield into the hands of Long, who never broke stride and left a diving Ehrig in his wake.

Long outraced defensive back Pat Harkins the final 50 yards to complete the 80-yard scoring strike. Riggs booted the extra point, and A&M regained the lead at 10–7 with 10:55 remaining in the game.[27]

"We just tried to get ahead so the defense could hold 'em off," Long said. "We knew the game wasn't over. There was a lot of fightin' left to go."[28]

Bradley desperately tried to rally the Longhorns on their remaining four possessions. Two of those possessions ended with Aggie interceptions—a second one to Hobbs and one to Buster Adami, a sophomore linebacker from Freer, Texas. Adami's interception proved especially painful for the Texas faithful.

The Longhorns faced a third-and-five at the Aggie 15-yard line when Bradley threw a pass to tight end Ed Small, who appeared open at the 7. But Adami whirled at the last second and dove to catch Bradley's pass, dropping immediately at the 7 before leaping to his feet in celebration.[29]

Bradley gallantly drove Texas down to the Aggie 38-yard line with 6 seconds to play. Then, on the fourth-and-one, Bradley connected with tight end Tom Higgins, who caught the pass out of bounds. The Aggies took over on downs, and the only act that remained was a clean snap and drop. In the words of *Houston Post* columnist Mickey Herskowitz, "Hargett fell down like a soldier throwing himself upon a hand grenade" as the clock expired.[30]

Bedlam erupted among the 50,000 fans in attendance. On the field, Aggie players jumped excitedly and embraced one another in a state of euphoria. Somehow, against all odds, they had ensured their place in A&M history as undisputed champions of the Southwest Conference.

Aggie student manager Rick Rickman soaked in the scene with wonderment. He gazed into the stands where men and women, young and old, hugged and wept joyfully. At first, he thought, *Wow, this is great. But good grief . . .*[31]

Then it dawned on Rickman that 26 years had passed since Texas A&M last appeared in a Cotton Bowl. In 1942, ninth-ranked A&M had lost to 20th-ranked Alabama 29–21. Rickman suddenly understood the depth of the love Aggie fans had for their team.[32]

"So many had tears in their eyes and crying," Rickman said. "I remember thinking, *Man, I am watching a piece of history here.*"[33]

Helmets could be heard ricocheting off the floor behind the closed doors of the Texas University locker room. Inside, players wept quietly and consoled one another. Royal sat slumped in a chair in an equipment room full of litter.

"It's just the kind of loss that tears the guts out of you for a week or two," said Royal, barely audible. "Go back and look at the films and see all those near plays and near misses. But I'm proud of our defense, except for one play, and that one was for the whole load of watermelons."[34]

Gilbert, meanwhile, sat dejected with his head bowed. He still wore his uniform despite having missed the entire second half with a hip-pointer. "I even hollered out there and it hurt," he explained in disbelief. "Sure, I feel all right now. But what the heck . . ."[35]

The Longhorn star threw his hands up in frustration. He realized the moment had slipped away.

Emotions were far different in another part of Kyle Field, where the doors to the Aggie locker room remain locked. Pandemonium reigned inside as the players sang the Aggie War Hymn.

Frank Scovell, chairman of the Cotton Bowl's selection committee, waited outside the locker room with members of the press and some influential alumni. Scovell—father of Texas Tech quarterback John Scovell—looked around at the waiting crowd and quipped, "I came to invite them. Do you think they'll accept?"[36]

Laughs broke out. Somewhere in the crowd, Eugene Stallings Sr.—Gene's father—also prompted smiles when he was overheard saying, "I've lived seventy years, and I just now realized today what Thanksgiving really means."[37]

Emotions were naturally running high inside the Aggie locker room.

"It was just euphoria," recalled Housley, whose inability to play at 100 percent due to his foot injury had rendered him ineffective. "Not only had we beat Texas on Kyle field—in our house—but we also won the Southwest Conference championship. We achieved two big goals at the end of the day. What's not to be happy about?"[38]

Housley would now have time to heal his foot before the Cotton Bowl Classic on New Year's Day. He wasn't the only Aggie who needed rest in the aftermath of the Texas game. By all accounts, the savage clash took a physical toll on everyone. A quick glance at Hargett told the unvarnished story of the 74th edition of the Texas University–Texas A&M rivalry. One reporter noted his cut lip, blackening beneath the eyes, and face ringed by sweat.

Victory surely numbed the pain. Afterward, the battered but elated Hargett signed programs for a number of young Aggie fans and declared, "This is the happiest moment of my life."[39]

Stallings expressed a similar sentiment.

"I won't take anything away from Texas," Stallings told reporters. "They came from behind and fought all the way." He then reflected on his team's journey, adding, "But I've never been prouder of a team in all my life. They showed a lot of class. The kids were zero and four and came back to win six straight. This is the happiest moment of my athletic career."[40]

Hobbs savored the moment, comparing A&M's unlikely rise from winless team to conference champions to a "fairy tale."[41] If so, Hobbs often played the role of hero. He accounted for two of A&M's five turnovers against Texas with two interceptions—his sixth and seventh picks of the season. He also amassed a season total of 162 yards on interception returns, including his record-setting, 100-yard return for a touchdown against TCU four weeks earlier.

Stallings respected Hobbs's smashmouth style of play so much that he compared him to Alabama's legendary linebacker Lee Roy Jordan on the record with the *Houston Chronicle*. Hobbs deserved the praise.[42]

So did all the Aggies who were now officially slated to play Bryant's Crimson Tide in the Cotton Bowl. Questions about the New Year's Day showdown hit Stallings before he could even catch his breath in the locker room.

"Right now, I just want to enjoy the victory over Texas," Stallings said candidly.

Later, in the postgame press conference, Stallings allowed himself to speak of the upcoming Cotton Bowl matchup with Alabama. "There's nobody I'd rather play than Alabama," he said. "I know their people and I have a lot of friends in Alabama. And I think it will be a lot of fun preparing my team to play Coach Bryant's team."[43]

The storyline sounded almost too good to be true. Center stage at the Cotton Bowl: the master versus the protégé. The pregame hype alone promised to produce a media circus.

A headline in the *Houston Chronicle* the next day summed up the mood in Aggieland: "Aggies ARE Back, In Tall Cotton."[44] Then again, if that headline failed to evoke passions, senior lineman Robert Cortez surely did so when he yelled across the locker room, "Beat the Bear!"[45]

NOTES

1. *Houston Post*, November 25, 1967.
2. Ibid.; *Houston Post*, November 22, 1967.
3. Ibid.; *Houston Post*, November 23, 1967.
4. *Houston Post*, November 23, 1967.
5. Ibid.
6. Ibid.
7. Hallman, interview with author, October 9, 2018.
8. Housley, interview with author, August 28, 2018.
9. Krueger, interview with author, September 5, 2018.
10. Hallman, interview with author, October 9, 2018.
11. *Houston Post*, November 22, 1967.
12. Krueger, interview with author, September 5, 2018.
13. *Houston Post*, November 22, 1967.
14. Ibid.; *Houston Post*, November 23, 1967.
15. Ibid.; *Houston Post*, November 21, 1967.
16. Ibid.; *Houston Post*, November 22, 1967.
17. Housley, interview with author, August 28, 2018.
18. Long, interview with author, August 23, 2018.
19. Hargett, interview with author, October 11, 2018.
20. Ibid.
21. *Houston Post*, November 24, 1967.
22. Ibid.
23. *Houston Chronicle*, November 24, 1967.
24. *Houston Post*, November 24, 1967.
25. Ibid.
26. Zwerneman, *Game of My Life*, 70.
27. Ibid.; *Houston Chronicle*, November 24, 1967; Long, interview with author, August 23, 2018.
28. Long, interview with author, August 23, 2018.
29. *Houston Post*, November 24, 1967.
30. Ibid.
31. Rickman, interview with author, September 5, 2018.
32. Ibid.
33. Ibid.
34. *Houston Post*, November 24, 1967.
35. Ibid.
36. Ibid.
37. Ibid.
38. Housley, interview with author, August 28, 2018.
39. *Bryan (TX) Daily Eagle*, November 24, 1967.

40. *Bryan (TX) Daily Eagle*, November 24, 1967.

41. *Houston Post*, November 24, 1967.

42. *Houston Chronicle*, November 24, 1967.

43. *Bryan (TX) Daily Eagle*, November 24, 1967.

44. *Houston Chronicle*, November 24, 1967.

45. *Bryan (TX) Daily Eagle*, November 24, 1967.

CHAPTER 14
Run in the Mud

Some players want to win for God and country. . . . Then some players just want to kick your ass. That was Kenny Stabler.

—Charles H. Land, *Tuscaloosa News* sports editor

Tornadoes were reportedly spotted near Legion Field on the night of December 2, 1967, as bitter rivals Alabama and Auburn prepared to play the annual Iron Bowl. No one would have been surprised to hear about the twisters given the hurricane-like storm that engulfed Birmingham.[1]

The wind whipped so intensely the rain fell sideways.

Umbrellas were turned upside down or simply blown from the hands of their owners. And yet 71,200 fans packed the stands, in what can only be interpreted as the true measure of Alabamians' love for football. In fact, some fans might have been less shocked by weather than by the presence of Texas A&M coach Gene Stallings strolling the muddy field before the game with his former mentor. Stallings told reporters he and his wife were in town "just to visit some old friends and root for Bama, not to scout."[2]

A week earlier, Stallings and his Aggies had punched their ticket to the Cotton Bowl Classic in Dallas with a thrilling 10–7 victory over rival Texas. Four days before A&M's historic victory, Bryant had formally accepted the Cotton Bowl's invitation on behalf of Alabama—a 7–1–1 team that had stumbled in a season-opening 37–37 tie to Florida State and a 24–13 loss to Tennessee.[3]

"I am highly honored that the Cotton Bowl feels our team is worthy of bowl consideration," Bryant said diplomatically at the time of the announcement. "We hope we can prove deserving."[4]

As for the Alabama players, the Cotton Bowl didn't impress them much, and Bryant knew it wouldn't even before he accepted the invitation. Alabama's back-to-back national titles of 1964 and 1965 were still fresh in everyone's minds, as fresh as the pain of the missing championship ring of 1966. Now, for the first time in four years, the Crimson Tide sat outside the national championship picture. In the words of Bobby Johns, everything else—the prestigious Cotton Bowl included—sounded like "a real letdown."[5]

The psychologist in Bryant clearly had work to do before New Year's Day. Of course, thoughts of the Cotton Bowl had to wait. In Alabama, most sins could be forgiven with a victory in the Iron Bowl.

So as the wind howled and the rain pelted the flesh, Bryant inspected a chilly Legion Field with Stallings by his side. Frankly, there wasn't much information to gain. Local high schools and colleges used Legion Field so frequently during the season that even on a sunny day a blade of grass would be hard to find. The grounds crew had therefore scattered hay about the field and painted it green to look like grass for the spectators. They painted nothing more than hay on a dirt field, which on this night turned into a giant mud puddle.

Bryant returned to the locker room to inform Stabler that passing would be "stupid" under the conditions. He determined the game would be won or lost at the line of scrimmage in the slosh and in a tug-of-war for field position.[6]

At least one player thought a little psychological warfare might set the tone.

Auburn linebacker Gusty Yearout—a 5-foot-11, 205-pound scrapper who earned a scholarship as a walk-on—worked himself into a frenzy as he strode to midfield with the other captains. Alabama's repeated success caused the Tigers (6–3) to despise their rivals, and Yearout wanted to make it clear from the start he wasn't going to be intimidated. The senior gnashed his teeth and spit as the officials introduced the captains.

Yearout plunged into such a trance that he didn't hear a word. Suddenly, a friendly voice snapped Yearout to attention.

"Gusty, what are y'all doin' after the game?" Stabler casually asked as the officials were still giving instructions. "Why don't y'all come down to the Bankhead Hotel afterward? We got a suite, and we're gonna have a lot of beer and girls."[7]

Stunned by Stabler's cool demeanor, Yearout stammered and replied, "What time does it start?"[8]

Pressure meant nothing to Stabler—even in a torrential downpour with 71,200 people watching his every move. Yearout discovered then what Stabler's teammates had witnessed on countless occasions on and off the field: nothing ever rattled Stabler.

"Snake was a free spirit," Dennis Homan said. "Snake could be out all night, come back and get an hour of sleep, wake up and play like he'd slept for a week. He was the only player I ever knew who could do that. He was just an athlete, and he was a heady ballplayer."

Stabler's reputed steely nerves sometimes overshadowed his competitiveness.

"Some players want to win for God and country," explained Charles Land, the *Tuscaloosa News* sports editor who covered the game. "Some players want to beat certain schools. Then some players just want to kick your ass. That was Kenny Stabler."[9]

In other words, Stabler shared a lot in common with his coach.

As Bryant predicted, Alabama and Auburn traded blows throughout the game for field position. At times, Johns remembered digging in for the next play, struggling to see the Auburn quarterback through the sheets of rain. As the game progressed, players became mired in some six inches of mud and water.[10]

The chain gang struggled at times to identify yardage markers.

By halftime, nothing had been settled. The first half ended in a scoreless standstill.

"We went into halftime and changed uniforms," Yearout said. "When we came out for the second half, we were completely soaked within thirty seconds."[11]

Auburn finally broke the deadlock in the third quarter on a 38-yard field goal from John Riley, a walk-on kicker from Abbeville, Alabama. The Tigers penetrated Alabama's 10-yard line on four occasions, only to be turned away each time. Riley's miraculous kick seemed almost insurmountable given the unyielding rain and wind.

Then, late in the fourth quarter, Alabama caught a break. Auburn fumbled the snap on a punt at Alabama's 46-yard line. Two plays later, on a third down, Stabler called for a rollout option at Auburn's 47-yard line. He never intended to pass.

Stabler took the snap and rolled to his right, nearly avoiding a diving Yearout at midfield. Alabama tight end Dennis Dixon toppled Yearout at the ankles. Stabler then slid back inside and cut behind Homan, who leveled a knee-capping block of defensive back Buddy McClinton.

Homan's perfectly executed block sprang Stabler loose down the sideline.

Scott Hunter, a backup quarterback, stood next to Bryant with a drenched clipboard as Stabler slithered down the sideline. He peeked around Bryant's large frame, hoping to see the play unfold.

"He (Stabler) just keeps running and running and running, and the thing must have gone on for twenty seconds," Hunter said, "and I start thinking, *Hey, he might score.*"[12]

Stabler outraced every Auburn defender in pursuit, including talented defensive back Jimmy Carter, who made a desperate lunge at the goal line. Carter rode Stabler to the ground as the two players slid across the muddy end zone, spraying puddles of water and sending Alabama fans into a frenzy.

Conditions were so bad on the field that Stabler would later say, "Once I started running, I just went straight for the chain-linked fence."[13] The 47-yard touchdown run—immortalized as the "Run in the Mud"—resulted in an unforgettable 7–3 Alabama victory and forever entrenched Stabler in Alabama lore.

Homan would later joke with his roommate that the famous game should have been dubbed the "Block in the Mud."[14]

"I'd remind him that I wasn't there to block," Homan laughed. "I was there to catch passes. That was the only block I ever made. Snake would just laugh and say, 'Yeah, but it was a good one.' Hey, Snake was a heck of a runner."[15]

Decades later, Yearout still claims Dixon tackled him as he was about to take down Stabler in the Alabama backfield.

"Every time Bama ran an option play I knew it because they would take the tight end (Dixon) and move him outside five to ten yards from the tackle," Yearout said. "So on this play, I knew it was coming and I'm yelling. When the ball was snapped, I just cut inside. I had a clear path to Stabler, who veered into the backfield.

"That's when Dixon grabbed me by the ankles and I went down. I would have gotten Stabler."[16]

No official tossed a flag.

Furor over the holding debate has never died. Guy Rhodes, then a 20-year-old sports editor of Auburn's student newspaper the *Auburn Plainsman*, still contends Yearout and the Tigers were the victims of some "home-cooking" stewed by the ringmaster, Bryant.

"Dennis Dixon tackled Gusty Yearout," Rhodes said emphatically. "Why didn't they call it? We were playing Alabama in Legion Field. Although it was supposed to be a neutral site, it wasn't. The people taking your tickets wore Alabama hats.

The people working the concessions wore Alabama hats. That was basically a home game for Alabama."[17]

Johns may have offered the best comeback to Auburn's complaints.

"My answer to that is if it hadn't rained, we would have beat the hell out of 'em," said Johns, the two-time All-American. "It wouldn't have been close."[18]

The loss cut deep for Auburn. Sportswriter Jimmy Bryan of the *Birmingham News* would describe players in the Auburn locker room as "muddy, bloody boys—men who wept openly and unashamed."[19]

A soaked Bryant rejoiced with his team in the aftermath, praising the leadership of Stabler "on and off the field." One reporter asked him about the weather, and he said, "I think those were the worst conditions I've ever seen a football game played in."[20]

No one could think of one worse.

Eventually, the conversation turned to the Cotton Bowl. Bryant sidestepped any talk of the upcoming New Year's Day bowl game with Texas A&M, saying he preferred to "enjoy this one for a while."[21]

Land finally asked Bryant and Stallings what they talked about on the field. The mentor and his onetime protégé gave Land a preview of the show soon to follow in Dallas.

"He wanted to talk about the Texas game and I wanted to talk about Auburn," Bryant said. "We didn't have a meeting of the minds."

As if on cue, Stallings grinned wryly and added, "He said I ought to talk about the Texas game. He said that was the last one I was going to win for a while."[22]

NOTES

1. Forney and Townsend, *Talk of the Tide*, 109. For the 1993 book, Dennis Homan told the authors, "I remember tornadoes were hitting all around the stadium, and the playing surface was six inches of mud."

2. *Tuscaloosa (AL) News*, December 3, 1967.

3. *Houston Post*, November 21, 1967.

4. Ibid.

5. Johns, interview with author, October 3, 2018.

6. *Tuscaloosa (AL) News*, December 3, 1967; Gold, *Bear's Boys*, 222.

7. Gusty Yearout, interview with author, September 14, 2018.

8. Ibid.

9. Land, interview with author, March 30, 2018.

10. Johns, interview with author, October 3, 2018; Forney and Townsend, *Talk of the Tide*, 109.

11. Yearout, interview with author, September 14, 2018.

12. *Montgomery Advertiser*, July 9, 2015.

13. Gold, *Bear's Boys*, 222.

14. Homan, interview with author, September 26, 2018.

15. Ibid.

16. Yearout, interview with author, September 14, 2018.

17. Guy Rhodes, interview with author, September 13, 2018.

18. Johns, interview with author, October 3, 2018.

19. *Birmingham News*, December 3, 1967.

20. *Tuscaloosa (AL) News*, December 3, 1967.

21. Ibid.

22. Ibid.

CHAPTER 15
Show Bear

Stallings and Bryant was the show. The game was secondary to that.
—Edd Hargett, Texas A&M's quarterback

Paul W. Bryant learned the value of showmanship decades before he arrived in Dallas on the eve of the 1968 Cotton Bowl Classic. Perhaps it was a gift from God or maybe the learned behavior of an impoverished country boy desperate to survive.

Or both.

Wherever the talent sprang from, throughout his lifetime Bryant had perfected the ability to entertain a crowd. He did so as a barefoot youngster racing against the clock from the Fordyce railroad station to Smith Chapel, on the football field, and obviously when he climbed onto the Lyric Theatre stage to wrestle a circus bear. Years later, at the Grove in College Station, Bryant had generated thunderous cheers from 6,000 cadets when he stomped on his coat.

And in Alabama, where his act produced a perennial powerhouse and three national championships, he walked on water. Few outside Tuscaloosa probably understood this more than Aggie cornerback and Alabamian Curley Hallman, who said that in his home state they make jokes about Bryant "feeding ten thousand people with a Coke and a bag of potato chips."[1]

Now the man who once wrestled the circus bear had, in many respects, evolved into the show bear. Whether in front of a microphone or television camera, Bryant could be expected to entertain with his quick wit, blunt verbiage, and plainspoken wisdom. And he rarely disappointed his audience.

Bryant turned again to his charm offensive for the media horde that descended upon Dallas to cover the 32nd edition of the Cotton Bowl Classic, although no one had to dig for a storyline. Gene Stallings coaching against his beloved mentor offered enough interest to keep reporters busy. Sportswriter Mickey Herskowitz, who knew both men personally, called the Cotton Bowl week "one of the great experiences" of his storied career—one that has spanned more than six decades. Herskowitz fondly recalled how there were "so many great lines and great moments and memories to write about."[2]

The storylines were ripe for the picking about the relationship of the two men, each with deep ties to A&M and Alabama.

The warm-up to the Bryant-Stallings act began behind the scenes in a short meeting with Cotton Bowl officials to discuss ground rules for the game. The meeting occurred on a Thursday morning—four days before kickoff—to decide some technical matters, such as what type of football would be used, since each conference used different brands.

Bryant sipped on a cup of coffee as the men talked.

"I don't care which ball we use," said Stallings, restlessly tapping his spoon and fork on the table. Bryant broke into a smile as he watched his former player and assistant coach fidgeting and quipped, "By Sunday night, Bebes won't be sleeping a wink. He'll be throwing up, snapping at people and looking at his watch."[3]

Stallings offered no snappy comeback. He knew Bryant was right.

Punchlines flew fast and furious at the daily press conferences, which under normal circumstances would have been conducted separately. But due to their unusually close relationship, everyone wanted the two coaches to appear together—Bryant and Stallings included.

For the national press, the genuine affection between the two men became immediately evident. Bryant referred to Stallings by his childhood nickname, "Bebes," or simply "that skinny ol' boy." Stallings, meanwhile, always addressed Bryant respectfully as "Coach."[4]

The first joint press conference spoke to the power of Bryant's charisma and growing legend. Stallings sat amused when the two coaches first began to field questions from reporters.

"Coach Bryant" . . . "Coach Bryant" . . . "Coach Bryant" . . . Finally, Bryant said, "Why don't someone ask Bebes a question?"[5]

"So some reporter asked me a question," Stallings recalled. "Then it went back to 'Coach Bryant,' 'Coach Bryant.'"[6]

If the spotlight didn't naturally fall on Bryant, he usually found a way to make sure it did. The daily press conferences were held in the afternoon. Since Alabama practiced in the mornings, Bryant could leisurely shower and dress before meeting reporters. Stallings's schedule didn't offer such a luxury. He hustled straight from practice to the press conference and appeared one afternoon in a maroon windbreaker, muddy khakis and work boots, and a soiled A&M baseball cap set low on his forehead. He arrived to find members of the media surrounding Bryant, dressed in a classic Hickey Freeman suit and polished alligator shoes.

Bryant noticed Stallings enter the room and playfully told the media, "I refuse to have my picture taken with anybody that looks that bad."[7]

Laughter erupted.

"You taught me to work," Stallings replied. "I can party after the game."[8]

The next day, Stallings tried to upstage Bryant by dressing in a tuxedo fit for the Oscars. As soon as A&M's practice ended, he hurried to clean and dress and was "feeling sharp" when he arrived for the press conference.[9]

Yet once again, he found the media buzzing around Bryant. The Alabama coach sported a cowboy hat and suit and, when he sat down, exposed a pair of leather boots with embroidered letters that read "TEXAS AGGIES." Cameras popped and clicked as Bryant caressed the boots and proclaimed, "I'm rather proud of them. Some Aggie ex gave 'em to me after we won the title in fifty-six. Stallings and those fellows earned these boots for me."[10]

Stallings sat with his arm draped around Bryant's neck and smiled.

"All the photographers were taking pictures of Coach Bryant," Stallings said with a laugh. "No one even noticed my tux.

"Coach Bryant always had a knack for stealing the spotlight."[11]

Stallings and Bryant also spent a lot of time trying to out-poormouth one another. Bryant playfully offered the opening salvo with a scene-setter for the media: picture a team that hasn't won in a decade, last played in the Cotton Bowl 26 years ago, and is now playing against a coach who jilted your university. Bryant concluded that the end result was "probably the greatest, most one-sided psychological advantage any team ever had."[12]

Stallings later told reporters he thought he and his coaching staff had a good recruiting year, adding, "Of course, we recruited a bunch of kids who couldn't play for Alabama."[13]

Ever ready with a witty counter-punch, Bryant cracked without hesitation, "Well, hell, Bebes, we still have some you recruited and they can't play for Alabama, either."[14]

Some members of the regional and national media grew weary of the mentor-versus-pupil angle after a while, mostly because the two were so similar. Stallings mimicked nearly everything his former coach did and said, and Alabama and A&M mirrored one another on the field. Herskowitz even joked in one column that the game should be called the "Xerox Bowl" because "the teams are identical copies."[15]

One reporter asked Stallings about his team's game day routine. Stallings dutifully ran through a typical agenda, listing a team prayer among other things. The reporter flippantly asked, "Well, do you have Coach Bryant's prayer?"[16]

"Yes, we do," Stallings replied. "It's called the Lord's Prayer."[17]

The reporter asked no more questions.

Behind the scenes, A&M's players paid no attention to the media circus. "They loved it," Edd Hargett said of Stallings and Bryant. "All they had to do was show up. We really weren't even involved in it. When they were together, we weren't around."[18] Teammate Wendell Housley added that Stallings and Bryant simply "played their part."[19]

The Aggies, meanwhile, focused on the task at hand—Alabama. No one else seemed interested.

"Stallings and Bryant was the show," Hargett said. "The game was secondary to that."[20]

The truth is, both Bryant and Stallings desperately wanted to win the game, if for no other reason than bragging rights. Bryant and his team actually landed in Dallas on Christmas Eve, eight days before the game. The Crimson Tide held its first practice the next day. The Aggies reported to Dallas a day later and practiced in full gear. In the 32-year history of the Cotton Bowl, no teams had arrived earlier.[21]

Stallings was certainly antsy to gain an edge.

J. T. Reynolds—one of A&M's two African American walk-ons—claimed Stallings required his players to sit in a darkened room to meditate on "hating" Alabama players prior to the Cotton Bowl.[22]

Curley Hallman also remembered the meditation room. He recalled the room being the brainchild of assistant coach Elmer Smith, and the defensive back entered the darkened quarters one day before practice with his pool-playing buddy, Larry Stegent. A lone candle sat in the middle of the table, intended to create a mood of solitude for mental preparation.

As Hallman remembered, Stegent made the most of the moment. He pulled out a cigarette, lit it on the candle, and propped his feet up on a chair as he puffed away. "Larry probably smoked two packs a day," Hallman said. "But he could run all day."[23]

Stegent finished his cigarette and snuffed it out on the floor. He and Hallman then left to dress for practice. Yet neither player realized Smith was sitting in a darkened corner of the room the entire time. Alarmed by Stegent's smoke break, Smith later reported to Stallings, "Coach, we got a problem."[24]

So ended the meditation room.

"It was short-lived," Hargett recalled with a chuckle. "I don't even know if I ever made it in there before they shut it down. I don't think I ever went in the meditation room because Stegent shut it down so quick. I don't know who I was gonna whip, I guess; who I was gonna meditate on."[25]

Stallings spent the weeks prior to the Cotton Bowl attending the usual postseason awards banquets and holding workouts before the holiday break. He attended one festive banquet in which he shared an honor with USC coach John McKay, who hosted several A&M assistant coaches for a week to watch the Trojans' spring practices.

"I've been expecting a check," McKay joked with his A&M counterpart.

"After our first four games," Stallings quickly replied, "I started to send you a bill."[26]

Stallings wasn't the only Texan in a good mood. Fans and local businesses throughout the Bryan-College Station area expressed their support of their bowl-bound Aggies in various ways. Marquees along State Highway 6 between Bryan and College Station were emblazoned with slogans. One read "Kill the Bear." A sandwich shop advertised "Bear Burgers for New Year's," and yet another declared, "Stallings for President."

General Rudder reportedly asked in jest if his job was in jeopardy.[27]

Naturally, the support followed Stallings and his Aggies to Dallas. The neon-lighted message board atop the Blue Cross Building downtown blinked on and off with two rapid proclamations: "The Aggies Are Back" and "Gig 'em Aggies."[28]

Snow also greeted the Aggies upon their arrival to Dallas. Stallings outfitted his team with tennis shoes on the first day and then held a 45-minute workout inside the automobile building at the State Fairgrounds. Alabama, meanwhile, braved the freezing elements at Bryant's insistence to prepare for the potential bad conditions on game day.[29]

Reporters naturally wanted each coach's thoughts on the prospects of playing in bad weather.

"You can't predict weather any more than you can predict how a football game with turn out," Bryant drawled. "We played in the Sugar Bowl one year and it rained every day for a week. Then just five minutes before kickoff the rain stopped and the skies cleared away."[30]

Stallings nodded and chimed in, "I was there and I remember actually what happened. Just as they introduced coach Bryant on television the rain stopped and the sun came out and the crowd went wild."[31]

Fans pointed at Bryant as he walked the field and gazed skyward in disbelief.[32]

The event only enhanced Bryant's legend. Of course, many stories about him increasingly blurred the line between myth and reality. The tall tales grew taller with each retelling, although Bryant offered a charismatic persona that seemed to render some tales plausible. By December 1967, Bryant's face showed signs of aging, but his legend hadn't lost any of its luster. If anything, the wrinkles and graying hair added to his image as a football sage.

And no one could dispute Bryant's resume. Sports editor Benny Marshall of the *Birmingham News* beautifully wrote of Bryant at this time, "An ordinary guy couldn't have crammed into 100 years of Bryant at Alabama all the things that have happened since he came to rejoin his heart at Tuscaloosa where he'd left it many autumns ago."[33]

If Marshall's words sounded sappy and sentimental, that's because they were. The words were also true.

Bryant was indeed no "ordinary guy." Stallings recognized something special about Bryant the first time he saw him step onto the stage at the Grove so long ago and in the many football battles they shared together after that magical day. Bryant's wisdom meant something to Stallings, enough to meticulously jot down the coach's words in notebooks he carried and preserved.

Stallings unabashedly idolized his former coach and mentor. No fewer than six pictures of Bryant hung on the paneled walls of his College Station office, and for those who knew both men, they often heard echoes of Bryant in the young coach's sayings and speech.

"I think in his lifetime a boy should be four points behind with four minutes to play and he should win a few," Stallings would say. "He should be four up with four to go and lose a few. But the most important thing is that he should compete."[34]

Stallings inherited those exact philosophical words from Bryant.

As a result, Bryant shadowed the A&M program daily. "Coach Stallings would mention Coach Bryant regularly," Housley recalled. "Daily."[35]

Through inspirational stories, drills, and philosophies, Stallings shared cherished pieces of Bryant with his coaching staff and players.

Playing Alabama therefore offered Stallings a rare opportunity.

"Yes, I wanted to win the game," Stallings said in retrospect. "But more importantly, I wanted my players to be exposed to Coach Bryant. In those days, both teams spent time together at various functions and dinners and such. My team heard me talk so much about Coach Bryant, I thought it was really special that they were finally going to meet him."[36]

For most of the Aggies, it would be their first encounter with the man who had shadowed their program in story and legend. If nothing else, Bryant's physical appearance certainly left an impression.

"Coach Bryant in particular just kind of filled up a room," Hargett remembered. "He was a big guy—a big, rawboned guy. Whatever it is, he had it. Stallings also had it to some degree, but not as much as Coach Bryant."[37]

Aggie student manager Rick Rickman also remembered Bryant's overpowering aura.

"Bear Bryant—a big man—would walk into a ballroom," Rickman recalled. "There might be four hundred people, a lot of noise and talking, and he would just mumble and he would command a room. He had that look, too.

"I think he and Coach Stallings used to practice it—that big stare."[38]

Aside from the Bear-versus-Bebes hype, oddsmakers generally favored Alabama by six or seven points. On paper, the bookies were probably right. Twenty-three Alabama seniors were playing in their third major bowl game in as many seasons. During that period, the Crimson Tide had amassed a combined 28–2–2 overall record, with one national championship and victories in the Orange Bowl and Sugar Bowl.[39]

"We didn't know what losing was," said Dennis Homan, who earned All-American honors in 1967 with 54 receptions for 820 yards and nine touchdowns. In the process, Homan set a school record with 18 total touchdown receptions in three seasons.[40]

Stabler, meanwhile, completed 103 of 178 passes, for 1,214 yards and nine touchdowns during the 1967 campaign. All nine of Stabler's touchdowns were thrown into Homan's steady hands.[41]

Homan and Stabler developed a special kind of chemistry, dating back to their days together as freshmen. The precise timing of Homan's routes and placement of Stabler's passes came only after countless hours of practice, often long after teammates had left the field.

"Snake and I got it down so good, he knew where I was gonna be before I got there," Homan said. "He's reading the backs and linebackers, and he knows what I'm gonna do. The ball would be thrown before I even made my last cut."[42]

The thunderstorm that engulfed the Alabama-Auburn game prevented Stallings from gleaning anything of value for him and his coaching staff to utilize for the Cotton Bowl. Yet stopping Stabler and Homan was a top priority for the Aggies as well as a no-brainer.[43]

Newly proclaimed All-American, linebacker Billy Hobbs promised to play a major role one way or another with that mission. Hobbs averaged a surreal 20.1 tackles a game and entered the bowl with a team high of seven interceptions, for a total of 162 yards returned.[44]

Hobbs didn't stand alone on a defense that produced 39 turnovers during the regular season—a total that gave the Aggies plus-19 in takeaways. Running back-turned-cornerback Ross Brupbacher did his part with five interceptions in six games since making the switch to defense.[45]

On film, the Alabama–A&M matchup appeared to be a toss-up. At least that was the overwhelming consensus of the Aggie players, who by then were far more concerned with their assignments than what their opponents could do.

The Crimson Tide still presented something unique.

"We didn't have to do anything to get ready for Alabama," said Hargett, who had completed 99 of 208 passes, for 1,526 yards and 14 touchdowns. "We watched the films and thought, *Wow. Is that us or them?* It was just like watching our defense."[46]

Receiver Bob Long—Hargett's favorite target—likened the matchup to preparing for an "inner-squad game." Both teams were small, quick, and tough and basically ran the same offense and defense. An amused Long added, "So it was like playing ourselves."[47]

If the Aggies owned one clear advantage, it might have been motivation. Playing in the Cotton Bowl was a dream come true for most of the Aggies. Stallings never had to question whether his team would play hard.

The stage was too big and historic.

"Being a Texas kid and growing up here," explained Stegent, "the Cotton Bowl meant everything."[48]

Aggie defensive lineman Rolf Krueger sensed an entirely different mood with the Alabama players. He described them as "aloof, like they weren't worried about [the Aggies]."[49]

Sportswriter Charles Land of the *Tuscaloosa News* admittedly felt the same way, adding, "The Alabama contingent—certainly the Alabama media contingent—all thought Alabama would win the game."[50]

Alabama's air of confidence should have come as no surprise to a team that had lost twice in three seasons. The Crimson Tide earned the right to be confident, but Bryant worried his team would be complacent.

Psychologically, Bryant tried to spark motivation in his players through the press. Shortly after his team's arrival to Dallas, Bryant pointed out how Alabama could become the first team to win the Orange Bowl, Sugar Bowl, and Cotton Bowl in successive years.

Whether his players cared was another matter.

Perhaps there were other signs. Alabama's two-time All-American defensive back Bobby Johns shocked several sportswriters during an impromptu interview in the lobby of the Marriott Motor Motel. By then, his rise to prominence under Bryant made for good copy. His reputation as a tall, rangy defender with great instincts had grown to such heights, he only had one interception during the regular season; no one threw in his direction.

Then Johns casually remarked that he had yet to see film of Hargett. Reporters pressed for an explanation.

"When we broke practice for the holidays the A&M game films hadn't arrived yet," Johns politely explained. "So I haven't yet seen him play."[51]

Johns grinned and surveyed the spacious lobby, adding, "Now that we're settled down here I expect I'll see a few reels of Hargett."[52]

Bryant's instincts were correct.

"For us, the Cotton Bowl was a big downer," Homan admitted. "Most of us didn't even want to go out there and play the game."[53]

The Aggies couldn't wait to play the game.

Quietly, the Aggies counted down the days to the Cotton Bowl—a nationally televised game that would be played before 75,500 fans. No one wanted to play the game more than Housley, whose junior campaign had been plagued by injuries. The bruising fullback had dislocated his shoulders in back-to-back weeks against Purdue and LSU before breaking his left foot in A&M's comeback victory over Arkansas. The broken foot prevented him from playing against Rice and then limited his duty against Texas.

By New Year's Eve, Housley and his teammates had waited 36 days to take the field at the famed Cotton Bowl. The rest did Housley wonders. Stallings first reported Housley was running at full speed December 16, and the Richardson native expressed an eagerness to make up for lost time.[54]

One other thing gnawed at Housley.

"We read the newspapers a lot," Housley said. "It was hyped as this dream game with the old master going against the former player and assistant coach. Everything was Coach Bryant this and Coach Bryant that. Frankly, we were tired of hearing about Coach Bryant.

"I think a lot of the guys . . . were just ready to blaze our own trail."[55]

NOTES

1. Herskowitz, *Legend*, 165.
2. Herskowitz, interview with author, August 20, 2018.
3. *Houston Post*, December 29, 1967.
4. Ibid.
5. Stallings, interview with author, July 8, 2015.
6. Ibid.
7. Stallings and Cook, *Another Season*, 87.
8. Herskowitz, *Legend*, 164.
9. Stallings, interview with author, July 8, 2015.
10. Herskowitz, *Legend*, 164; Stallings and Cook, *Another Season*, 88.
11. Stallings, interview with author, July 8, 2015.
12. *Houston Post*, December 29, 1967.
13. Herskowitz, *Legend*, 163.
14. Ibid.
15. *Houston Post*, December 29, 1967.
16. Herskowitz, interview with author, August 20, 2018.
17. Ibid.
18. Hargett, interview with author, March 22, 2018.
19. Housley, interview with author, August 28, 2018.
20. Hargett, interview with author, March 22, 2018.
21. *Daily Oklahoman* (Oklahoma City), December 24, 1967.
22. J. T. Reynolds, interview with author, April 10, 2016.
23. Hallman, interview with author, September 14, 2018.
24. Ibid.
25. Hargett, interview with author, October 11, 2018.
26. *Houston Post*, December 8, 1967.
27. Ibid., December 13, 1967.
28. Ibid., December 31, 1967.
29. Ibid., December 28, 1967.

30. Ibid., December 29, 1967.

31. Ibid.

32. Ibid.

33. *Cotton Bowl Classic*, program for January 1, 1968.

34. Ibid.

35. Housley, interview with author, August 28, 2018.

36. Stallings, interview with author, July 9, 2015. In a December 25, 2005, interview with the *Gadsden (AL) Times*, Stallings said, "I wanted my players to see him, hear him, feel him if they could. I wanted them to get that chance because, in my opinion, he was the greatest college coach ever, and I still feel that way."

37. Hargett, interview with author, March 22, 2018.

38. Rickman, interview with author, September 5, 2018.

39. *Houston Post*, December 20, 1967; *Houston Post*, December 13, 1967.

40. Homan, interview with author, September 26, 2018.

41. *Houston Post*, December 28, 1967. Like for a lot of things about Texas A&M and Alabama, the fingerprints of both coaching staffs could be found in Tuscaloosa and College Station. For instance, Aggie assistant coach Dee Powell initially recruited Stabler (*Houston Post*, December 27, 1967).

42. Homan, interview with author, September 26, 2018.

43. *Houston Post*, December 8, 1967.

44. Ibid., January 1, 1968.

45. Ibid., December 13, 1967.

46. Hargett, interview with author, March 22, 2018; *Houston Post*, December 27, 1967.

47. Long, interview with author, August 23, 2018.

48. Stegent, interview with author, August 29, 2018.

49. Krueger, interview with author, September 5, 2018. Several Alabama players battled the flu in the days leading to the Cotton Bowl, including Stabler. All were declared healthy by kickoff (*Daily Oklahoman* [Oklahoma City], December 31, 1967).

50. Land, interview with author, March 30, 2018.

51. *Houston Post*, December 27, 1967.

52. Ibid.

53. Homan, interview with author, September 26, 2018.

54. *Houston Post*, December 17, 1967; *Houston Post*, December 24, 1967; Housley, interview with author, August 28, 2018.

55. Housley, interview with author, August 28, 2018.

CHAPTER 16
Cotton Bowl Classic

You're gonna have to come with your best to beat the Bear.

—Gene Stallings

Freezing temperatures rang in the New Year throughout the Dallas metropolitan area.

Gene Stallings awoke at 6:30 a.m. on game day with his usual restless energy. He opened the curtains to his room at the Hilton Hotel on Mockingbird Lane and stared out the window at the parking lot below. Freezing rain and sleet beat steadily against the glass.

The skies were dark and ominous.

Still, the gloomy weather failed to dampen his excitement. The Cotton Bowl Classic marked his first as a head coach. He cinched his maroon tie neatly, slid on a gray jacket, and laced his work boots before descending into the hotel lobby well ahead of his players.

Stallings anxiously sipped coffee from a Styrofoam cup and again stared out a window. He killed time by watching the wind sweep puddles from one spot to another on the blacktop, while his mind drifted to the countless moments that had led to this day. He felt an "unusual tension" about the game due to all the personal storylines and the intensity of the media spotlight.

"Plenty had been written about teacher versus pupil," Stallings would write decades later, "and I certainly didn't want to look bad—especially with all the media hype."[1]

A few hours later at the team breakfast, the coach's steak and eggs sat mostly untouched. He walked among his players and noticed they weren't eating much either. By 10:30 a.m., Stallings and his team had departed for the Cotton Bowl on what was normally a 15-minute drive. Despite a police escort, Stallings worried about traffic given the foul weather and amount of people in town for the game. He wanted to reach the stadium two hours before the 1 p.m. kickoff.[2]

Stallings worried about a lot that morning. He fretted over the traffic, the weather, and the game's outcome given all the words that had been spoken beforehand. Mostly, he seemed to worry about Bryant. Or, more precisely, he worried about living up to his former coach's high standards. He carried the mantle of Bryant coaching disciple with great pride, and he now faced the day of reckoning.

Would he pass the test? Could he indeed defeat the master?

Bryant's philosophies on football and life became Stallings's philosophies on football and life in many respects. At the core of those teachings existed one fundamental concept: "Never confuse activities with accomplishments."[3]

"People will always say how hard they work, or how long they work," said Stallings, echoing his mentor's words. "I'm not interested in how hard you worked on something. Or how long it took you. I just want to know if you got results. We live in a results-driven society. Period.

"A lot of people don't understand that concept."[4]

Stallings did because Bryant did.

Bryant also taught Stallings to meticulously take note of every minute detail. Upon arrival to the Cotton Bowl, Stallings weathered the freezing temperatures to inspect the field. The grounds crew removed a tarp scarred with holes, exposing a field of mostly dead grass that was somewhere between "spongy and hard turf" from a week of rain, sleet, and snow. Workers had painted the field for the television audience. Countless chugholes filled with water also littered the field.[5]

Stallings ordered his head equipment manager to gather all the team managers and sop the water from the holes with towels. Immediately.

"I don't want Edd Hargett slipping in 'em," Stallings said sternly.[6]

Moments later, Aggie managers were combing the field for every chughole as the players dressed in the locker room. The players embraced their game-day routines. Some discussed the weather and how to best stay warm. Others talked about various topics, if they talked at all.

At some point, someone mentioned the anticipated crowd of 75,000 fans.

"I know one damn thing," Stegent chimed in, "we could be playing in China and there's one guy who will be at our game, and that's Curley's brother, Moody Hallman."[7]

Hallman laughed. Stegent spoke the truth.

Hallman—the "Alabama Aggie"—harbored no ill-will toward Bryant for not recruiting him. He instead felt overwhelmed by the excitement of fulfilling a childhood dream in a Texas A&M uniform. Stallings gave him a once-in-a-lifetime opportunity to play college football, and now he was about the take the field on a grand stage to play against "a great team." In fact, he still held Bryant in high esteem.[8]

"In Coach Bryant, you were playing against a true living legend," Hallman said. "A lot of people become legends after they pass away. We were playing against a coach who is a living legend. We were excited, but we were very confident."[9]

During the Christmas break, Hallman had returned home to Northport, Alabama, and was interviewed by *Tuscaloosa News* sports editor Charles Land for a feature. Hallman expressed that confidence by predicting, "It will be a long trip back for all the Alabama fans."[10]

Now minutes before running onto the field, Hallman double-checked the laces on his shoes and quietly prayed.

Hargett, meanwhile, battled his typical pregame nerves as he quietly suited up. Outside in the stands, his wife, Shirley, chipped ice off her seat. Shirley had been sick the night before, prompting Edd to sleep in Stegent's room on the eve of the big game. Stegent normally roomed with tight end Barney Harris, but Harris had returned home to San Antonio to attend his father's funeral. Ben B. Harris had died on Christmas Day, and Stallings advised Barney to stay with his family and not worry about playing in the game.

Harris instead gathered his emotions after the funeral and caught a flight back to Dallas to join his teammates for the Cotton Bowl. He privately told Hargett, "That's what Dad wanted [me] to do."[11]

Other stories played out behind the scenes.

Fullback Wendell Housley felt healthy for the first time since the September 16 season opener against SMU. He had dislocated his left and right shoulders in successive weeks against Purdue and LSU. The injuries were never made public, and he continued to play by injecting cortisone into the shoulders and having them heavily taped. But the tape left him further restricted, and once the cortisone wore off, the excruciating pain returned.

Finally, after realizing Housley had "a defective pair of shoulder pads," the team special ordered a new set. "The new shoulder pads were bigger and had more padding," Housley recalled. "They set up off my shoulders and put the pressure on the chest and back instead. When I went to the new shoulder pads, it totally eliminated my shoulder problems as far as taking a blow."[12]

Housley's frustrations mounted when he suffered a broken left foot in the road victory over Arkansas—an injury that had since had time to heal. During warm-ups, he ran and cut across the brown turf of the Cotton Bowl free of pain. He felt good, but Stallings had other plans.

"You know, you've been hurt," Stallings told Housley before the game in his deep drawl. "And I'm just not gonna start you."[13]

"OK," Housley replied. "You're the coach."[14]

Bill Sallee would instead start at fullback, joining tailback Larry Stegent in the Aggie backfield. Only a year earlier, Housley earned All-Southwest Conference honors as a tailback. Stallings approached Housley about moving to fullback once Stegent emerged on the scene with impressive performances.

"Coach," Housley said at the time, "I'll do anything I need to do to help the team."[15]

Despite the frustration, Housley maintained a quiet confidence he would eventually be called upon to contribute against Alabama. Housley recalled those times on a third-and-one when Stallings would call timeout, grab him forcefully by the facemask, and say through clenched teeth, "Look, you better make it."[16]

Housley usually did.

"I knew if it was gonna get to the point where we needed to do something, I was gonna get to play," Housley said.[17]

If anyone doubted Bryant's influence with Stallings, they were surely convinced once and for all during pregame warm-ups. Alabama and A&M mirrored each other with the precision of the Fightin' Texas Aggie Band or a synchronized swimming team. From stretching exercises to drills to offensive and defensive plays, each team shadowed the other as if rehearsed. Each new whistle brought a new level of wonderment for fans and players alike.

"The whistle blew, and we changed and they changed," Housley remembered. "We did the same thing. . . . We'd start going through our offensive plays and they'd start going through their offensive plays. I mean, it was amazing."[18]

Afterward, in the locker room, Stallings offered a few final words as kickoff neared. He reminded his team to "show your class" and "make something

happen"—by now, his signature mantras. He told them the game would ultimately be a reflection of how they played and then imparted one final thought
when he said, "You're gonna have to come with your best to beat the Bear."[19]

The Aggies then ran onto the field to meet their destiny. A number of notable
Aggie alumni and former teammates of Stallings from the 1956 championship
squad crowded their sideline—John David Crow, Jack Pardee, Loyd Taylor, Bobby
Marks, Dennis Goehring, and Charlie Krueger, Rolf's elder brother. For the first
time in their lives, they found themselves rooting against Bryant.[20]

The lines were drawn in this festive family feud.

A national television audience of millions settled in to watch the game. On
the field, hype over both coaches finally fell silent to the roar of 75,500 fans. Now
ironically, the players were largely left to determine the game's outcome.

For Bryant and Stallings, the moment marked a historic milestone in their
long journey together. In the seconds before kickoff, the legend and protégé were
left to pace the sidelines alone with their thoughts.

• • •

Aggie Bob Long booted the opening kickoff into the arms of Tommy Wade,
who caught the ball a few feet into the end zone and then broke loose down the
Alabama sideline. Hallman finally rode Wade to the turf at the Alabama 35-yard
line, perhaps saving a touchdown return.

As Hallman raised his head, he saw a familiar face.

"I looked up at Coach Bryant and he looked like he was ten-foot tall," Hallman
recalled. "I remember I jumped up in the air. Coach was looking at me, and I
turned my fanny and started running off."[21]

The adrenaline flowed.

On Alabama's first play from scrimmage, Stabler rolled to his right only to see
the 6-foot-4, 227-pound Krueger closing in on him. Stabler rushed the pitch to
his tailback, but because of the din of the crowd, no one heard his audible. The
ball fell loose on the turf, and a diving Krueger recovered the ball at Alabama's
28-yard line.

While the Aggie defenders jumped up and down, someone grabbed Hallman
by the arm. He turned and saw another familiar face.

"Hey Curley, what are doing after the game?" Stabler said in a squeaky voice
amid the pandemonium. "You goin' home to Northport? If you do, come on over
and I'll buy you a beer."[22]

To Hallman's amazement, Stabler looked and sounded as calm as if they were at a social gathering back home in Alabama. The Aggies failed to convert the turnover into points, but Krueger's power and agility put Alabama on notice. "For the rest of the game," Krueger recalled, "they never really came in my direction at all."[23]

Stabler did more than talk on Alabama's next possession. He dazzled with his arm and legs on a 10-play, 80-yard scoring drive that he punctuated with a dive across the goal line from 3 yards out. He flipped the ball to an official, looked at Hallman standing nearby, and said, "Curley, how ya like that shit?"[24]

By the time Steve Davis booted the ensuing point-after-attempt through the uprights, Stabler's cool hand had put the Aggies equally on notice.

Aggie safety Tommy Maxwell responded on Alabama's next possession. Maxwell—A&M's two-way marvel—intercepted a Stabler pass and returned it to A&M's 18-yard line. But a clipping penalty moved the Aggies back to the 43.

Hargett promptly hit Harris on a 28-yard pass to the Aggie 15-yard line. Two plays later, Hargett rolled to his right as Stegent swung left out of the backfield. Hargett then planted and threw across the field to Stegent, who caught the pass and spun to avoid defensive back Bobby Johns. In the same motion, Stegent stepped on and over Johns, planted his right hand on the turf to keep from falling, and catapulted himself into the end zone from 2 yards away.

"I grabbed him [Stegent], and I had him but I let him get away," Johns said afterward in disbelief. "I let him get away."[25]

Stegent's acrobatic touchdown catch covered 13 yards, and the PAT by Charlie Riggs tied the game 7–7. The score held through the end of the first quarter.

Spectators were watching a potential classic unfold.

Davis opened the second quarter with a 36-yard field goal to give the Crimson Tide a 10–7 lead. But Alabama's lead wouldn't last thanks to A&M's big-play defense. In the final minute of the first half, Stabler connected on a 12-yard pass with Perry Willis, who fumbled at A&M's 44-yard line as Billy Hobbs closed in for the tackle. Defensive end Jim Piper, who suffered a heat stroke in the first week of the season, recovered the fumble at Willis's feet.

Hargett and the Aggie offense again went to work with 30 seconds on the clock. On the third-and-10, Hargett lofted a 17-yard pass along the Aggie sideline to move the ball to the Alabama 39-yard line. He then found open tight end Tommy Buckman on a 21-yard completion down to the 18. Moments later, Stegent made another circus catch on an underthrown pass by Hargett. This time,

Stegent reached back and batted the ball in the air with his left hand as he spun toward the end zone. He again batted the ball upward while spinning and hauled it in just as defensive back Eddie Propst tackled him at the seven.

Twenty-one seconds remained on the clock.

Hargett faded back on the next play and threw a scoring strike over the middle to Maxwell, who secured an inside angle on Johns as he swept across the end zone. Johns hit him hard, but Maxwell hung on for the touchdown. Riggs missed the ensuing PAT, and the Aggies retreated to the warmth of the locker room at halftime with a 13–10 lead.

The Aggies emerged from the locker room with one simple plan for the offense: run. Stallings wanted to pound Alabama's defense with a ground attack, but more important, he wanted to put the game into the hands of All-American linebacker Billy Hobbs and A&M's swarming defense.[26]

For the Cotton Bowl, the Aggies ran an I formation with a twist. In a normal I formation offensive set, the fullback and tailback lined up directly behind the quarterback. A&M ran the same set but placed the fullback much closer to the quarterback—a move that allowed the fullback to hit the line quicker and shortened the defense's time to read the option. The Aggies utilized this set occasionally throughout the season, especially in the victory over Arkansas.[27]

Alabama's feisty defense rendered A&M's new formation largely ineffective throughout the first half, though.[28] Then the odds finally caught up with the Crimson Tide on A&M's second possession of the third quarter.

Back-to-back 4-yard runs by Stegent and a 10-yard pass to Harris moved the Aggies into Alabama territory at the 34. The Aggies then turned to Housley, who carried the ball only twice in the first half for 7 yards. This time, he took the ball from Hargett and crashed through the line between blocks by guard Mark Weaver and tackle Carl Gough, for a gain of 13 yards to Alabama's 21.[29]

"They weren't anticipating me running the ball," Housley recalled. "It was such a quick deal. They (the Crimson Tide) were waiting for the play to develop, and while they were waiting, I was already on the other side, running."[30]

Two plays later—at the 20-yard line—Hargett checked down the Alabama defense and again called Housley's number on a quick dive off tackle. Housley shot through the line in a blur, sprang by another key block from Weaver on Alabama guard Alvin Samples. Simultaneously, Housley slipped through the arms of linebacker Bob Childs and broke into the secondary.

The hard-hitting Johns crashed in on Housley at the 12, but he again bulled through the defender's clutches as he continued plowing forward. Just then roving linebacker David Bedwell wrapped his arms around the fullback. Housley powered past Bedwell as well, shedding him at the three. At that moment, Propst tried to corral Housley short of the goal line, but he too was dragged a few yards before the powerful Housley finally toppled to the turf.

Housley, still clutching the football tightly beneath Propst, stared through his facemask at maroon paint. He slammed the ball to the turf and yelled, "Dadgum-mit!" He thought he had fallen short of the goal line. He was wrong.[31]

"You scored!" screamed Buckman, the Aggie tight end. "You scored!"[32]

The clocked showed 8:32 left in the third quarter. Riggs kicked the PAT to give A&M a 20–10 lead, although everyone knew Stabler, Homan, and company weren't done fighting.

Stabler, who only days earlier had battled the flu, promptly marched Alabama 83 yards down the field on nine plays for another touchdown. A 22-yard pass to Homan moved the Crimson Tide to A&M's 7-yard line before Stabler covered the rest of the distance two plays later on a scoring run—his second of the game.

Fullback David Chatwood then took the handoff up the middle on a two-point conversion but was gang tackled by the Aggies short of the goal line. Bryant would later jokingly complain to Stallings, saying he always tended to defend the outside on goal-line stands. "So I knew that when you went for two, you would be slanting your guys to the outside, and that little ol' play would go right up the middle, and it would work for a two-point conversion," Bryant later said. "You've really changed!"[33]

Stallings informed his old coach of one other uncomfortable fact about that play: the Aggies only had 10 players on field.[34]

Both coaches were so focused on the chess match at hand that Stallings and his staff became baffled at one point when Bryant sent his punter into the game on a third down. Stallings shrugged and responded by sending his punt returner onto the field. Confusion reigned on the Alabama sideline. Bryant mistakenly thought it was fourth down, and his assistants were reluctant to inform him of his blunder.[35]

Finally, one of Alabama's assistants scrounged up enough nerve to inform Bryant it was only third down. Bryant immediately sent Stabler back into the game to replace the punter—then a penalty. A player who entered the game had to stay on the field for at least one play. No penalty was called. Stallings countered by replacing his punt returner only to have an official yell, "Whoa! You can't do that. He's got to stay in one play."[36]

Stallings bolted onto the field and barked at the official.[37]

"Now wait a minute, fellow," Stallings yelled. "I'm sitting right here watching Coach Bryant send his punter in, and then Coach Bryant took his punter out!"[38]

The official looked up at Stallings and replied, "You ain't Coach Bryant."[39]

And so tensions mounted.

By the start of the fourth quarter, nothing had been decided. A&M clung to a precarious 20–16 lead made even more precarious by the presence of Stabler and Homan on the other side. The fate of the game clearly rested on the strength of the Aggie defense, which had already recovered two fumbles and picked off two of Stabler's passes.

Alabama, however, remained dangerous.

The Aggie defense proved equal to the task, forcing punts on Alabama's first two possessions of the fourth quarter. Then, with only minutes remaining, Stabler began to guide the Crimson Tide down the field. A 15-yard holding penalty by the Aggies provided the spark, giving Alabama a first down at their own 44-yard line. Stabler proceeded to connect with flanker Perry Willis for 7 yards and a 14-yard pass to Homan to move the ball to the A&M 35.

By now, everyone in the Cotton Bowl knew Stabler's first option would be Homan.

On the next play, Stabler dropped back and threw a quick pass to Homan. Aggie linebacker Ivan Jones and Homan both dove for the ball as it fell incomplete. Stabler looked again for Homan on second down. This time he found Homan all alone at the 17-yard line with seemingly nothing between him and the end zone. But the ball skipped uncharacteristically off his fingertips and landed on the churned turf for another incomplete pass.

Homan clutched his helmet in anguish.

"I must have taken my eyes off the ball," Homan would later tell reporters. "I was just too anxious. There sure wasn't anybody else around."[40]

Then, on the fourth-and-10, Stabler threw a quick pass over the middle to tight end Hunter Husband, who was instantly hit by Hobbs and brought down by a swarm of Aggie defenders. Hunter was 4 yards short of the first down, and A&M took over on downs at its own 29 with 1:16 left in the game. But the Aggies failed to run out the clock, and after three failed runs, they were forced to punt one last time.

The ball sat at Alabama's 42-yard line when the dust settled. Twelve seconds remained on the clock.

Stabler returned to the field with the hopes of the Alabama faithful riding on his legendary left arm. From the shotgun, Stabler took the snap and almost instantly stepped forward to avoid an onrushing Krueger. Defensive tackle Lynn Odom followed right behind Krueger with his arms flailing as he tried to reach Stabler, who fired a spiral toward an open Willis.

The errant pass sailed over the fingertips of Willis and into the hands of Hallman—the "Alabama Aggie." Hallman, who picked off a Stabler pass late in the third quarter, returned the ball 14 yards before being tackled.

Hallman leapt from the ground and threw the ball high into the air as his teammates rejoiced around him. Fellow cornerback Ross Brupbacher maintained enough presence of mind in that dizzying moment to catch the ball upon its descent and give it to Hallman on the sideline as Hargett took the final snap to run off the clock.

"Are you crazy?" Brupbacher joyfully said to Hallman. "Keep this ball."[41]

Fans poured onto the field in jubilation. The Fightin' Texas Aggie Band, meanwhile, launched into another spirited rendition of "the Aggie War Hymn." In the middle of the field, Bryant and Stallings weaved their way through the crowd for the traditional handshake. The drama of the final quarter left Stallings drained, joyful, and overwhelmed with "a sense of relief."

Finally, through the maze of people, he and Bryant locked eyes—the legend and his protégé. Stallings noticed a labored gait in Bryant, probably from the arthritis in his hips. His heart pounded as he reached out to shake his beloved mentor's hand. A grinning Bryant suddenly hoisted the gangly Stallings up by a leg and awkwardly lifted him off the ground with a hug. Bryant's houndstooth hat nearly toppled from his head. Sportswriter Mickey Herskowitz would write how Bryant held Stallings for a moment "like a father helping his son to see a parade."[42]

"I'm gonna carry you off this field, boy," Bryant said. "Congratulations."[43]

Bryant's surprising—and classy—gesture caught Stallings off guard and prompted a beaming smile.

Newspaper photographers captured the moment on film from several different angles. Jack Beers Jr. snapped one of those classic images for the *Dallas Morning News*. (The photograph, however, would not be his most famous. Five years earlier, on November 24, 1963, Beers photographed the moment Jack Ruby shot Lee Harvey Oswald in the basement of the Dallas Police Station.[44])

In the press box, *Tuscaloosa News* sports editor Charles Land watched the Bryant hug amid the crush of people below, calling it "the perfect tribute" to Stallings.[45] Not everyone in Alabama shared Land's sentiments.

Johns, a fierce competitor, watched his coach pick up Stallings with mixed feelings.

"I don't know that it struck me very good," Johns said candidly. "I'd never seen that from Coach before. Something he always said, though, 'You're gonna win with class and you're gonna lose with class.' And he was good at that. And that's what he did with Coach Stallings after the game—class."[46]

Homan agreed.

"Coach Bryant was a classy guy," Homan said. "No doubt about that. He was a tough dude, but I guarantee he had class drippin' off him."[47]

So did Homan. The All-American receiver respectfully answered questions by the reporters after the game, including inquiries about his dropped pass at the 17-yard line. Homan offered no excuses.

"We made too many mistakes," he said. "I know I did."

Homan still caught a game-high of six passes for 90 yards.

Decades later, Homan reflected on the game.

"I think we sort of went through the motions, and the score indicated that," Homan admitted. "And I'm not taking anything away from A&M. They had a good football team. . . . I know one thing we found out pretty quick. They were tough. I mean, their defense was tough. Coach Stallings, his number one thing—defense. He had them prepared and they had great players."[48]

Reporters asked Stabler about the noise levels after the game, and he admitted it was difficult to call audibles early and at the end with the game on the line. Yet he too credited the Aggies—namely, their tenacity. The Aggies picked off three of his passes and recovered two fumbles, giving them 44 turnovers on the season—an incredible average of four turnovers a game.

"They just stayed after us," said Stabler, who completed 16 of 26 passes for 179 yards. "We knew Coach Stallings would have 'em sky high for us. If we'd been forty touchdowns ahead, they would have still got after us."[49]

In the Aggie locker room, Stallings spoke briefly to his team before giving the game ball to Harris, the sophomore end who buried his father on the eve of the game. Harris caught two passes for 38 yards but, more importantly, had inspired his teammates by his mere presence.

Stallings decided to hold an impromptu press conference in the locker room but sternly ordered his student managers to bar any other outsiders from entering. Student manager Rick Rickman and others were sent to guard the front door from intruders.

A celebration soon erupted as a herd of reporters filtered throughout the crowded room.

Housley—Dallas County's only representative on the field—savored the moment and his performance in his backyard. Housley finished with a team-high of 59 yards rushing and arguably the greatest run in Aggie history.

"Boy, it was wonderful to finally have a game like this," Housley told reporters. "Especially here in my own neighborhood. We had a real calm approach to this game. We wanted it badly but we didn't get too keyed up for it. That helped."[50]

Krueger, who harassed Stabler for four quarters, offered lofty praise for Housley.

"If we hadn't had Wendell, I think it would have been a different day that day," Krueger said. "He made the difference. He was an impact guy. He broke the game for us."[51]

In another corner of the locker room, Hargett wrapped an arm around Hallman atop a bench as the two posed for a photographer. "You see this guy here," Hargett said with a laugh. "This is the guy Alabama didn't want. We're glad they didn't."[52]

Seated below Hargett and Hallman, a drenched Hobbs spoke with reporters about facing Alabama's vaunted offense. The All-American linebacker learned he had just been named the Cotton Bowl's MVP along with teammates Hargett and Allen.

Amid the noise, Hobbs thoughtfully paid respects to Crimson Tide quarterback Kenny "Snake" Stabler.

"That Ken Stabler is a great quarterback," Hobbs said. "He's a real good faker with that football and Alabama is the best we've played all year, too."[53]

Moments later, Rickman heard a loud knock at the locker room door. He cringed. Then a louder knock. He ignored that one too. He hoped the knocking would stop, because he didn't want to confront the person on the other side.

Coach Stallings issued a stern warning: no outsiders were allowed in the locker room.

A third knock—the loudest thus far—echoed in Rickman's ears. Panic began to overtake him. His heart pounded. He could hear Coach Stallings verbally tearing into him and thought, *Boy, Coach is gonna get angry unless I shut this person down.*

Reluctantly, Rickman opened the door.

There, filling the doorway like Goliath, stood Bryant.

"To me, that was the first life-or-death decision I ever had to make," Rickman mused. "Who's gonna kill me: Coach Bryant or Coach Stallings?"[54]

Rickman decided wisely, blurting, "Come on in Coach Bryant."[55]

One of the managers—Rickman doesn't remember whom—breathlessly announced to Stallings, "Coach Bryant is coming! Coach Bryant is coming!"[56]

Stallings excused himself from the media huddled around him, quipping, "I guess I better go see him. I may need a job sometime."[57]

"Coach, are you looking for me?" Stallings asked Bryant with a smile.[58]

"No, I've seen all of you I want to see," Bryant wryly cracked. "I want to talk to the players."[59]

Stallings beamed with pride.

Bryant moved about the room, graciously offering congratulations. The roots of the moment probably dated back to 1951, when Bryant's Kentucky Wildcats upset national champion Oklahoma 13–7 in the Orange Bowl. Afterward, Sooner coach Bud Wilkinson had entered the Kentucky locker room to personally congratulate each player.[60]

Now, 27 years later, Bryant honored Stallings and his troops with the same type of sportsmanship. Bryant shook Mark Weaver's hand and joked aloud, "I'm glad to see you won in spite of Stallings."[61]

Reporters laughed.

Bryant asked Stallings to introduce him to Housley. Bryant laid eyes on Housley and firmly shook his hand, adding, "I want to meet the young man who beat me today."[62]

Housley stood speechless.

Stallings, as he had done countless times before in the presence of Bryant, stood in awe of his former coach. He would later reveal that Bryant's appearance in A&M's locker room meant more to him than Bryant's famous hug at midfield. For all he ever wanted to do was to share Bryant's wisdom—about football and life—with his players and the world.

Simply put, Stallings loved the man. And Bryant loved him.

In the end, their relationship and legacies became intertwined like the roots of a mammoth oak—strong and everlasting.

NOTES

1. Stallings and Cook, *Another Season*, 88.
2. Ibid., 88–89.
3. Stallings, interview with author, July 8, 2015.

4. Ibid.

5. Housley, interview with author, October 26, 2018; Rickman, interview with author, September 5, 2018.

6. Rickman, interview with author, September 5, 2018.

7. Hallman, interview with author, September 14, 2018.

8. Ibid.; *Houston Post*, January 2, 1968. The term "Alabama Aggie" was coined by *Houston Post* sportswriter Mickey Herskowitz.

9. Ibid.

10. Ibid.

11. Hargett, interview with author, March 22, 2018; *Dallas Morning News*, January 1, 1968; *Dallas Morning News*, January 2, 1968.

12. Housley, interview with author, October 26, 2018.

13. Ibid.

14. Ibid.

15. Ibid.

16. Ibid.

17. Ibid.

18. Housley, interview with author, August 28, 2018.

19. Ibid.

20. Herskowitz, *Legend*, 165.

21. Hallman, interview with author, September 14, 2018.

22. Ibid.

23. Krueger, interview with author, September 5, 2018.

24. Hallman, interview with author, September 14, 2018.

25. *Houston Chronicle*, January 2, 1968.

26. Stallings and Cook, *Another Season*, 89.

27. Hargett, interview with author, October 11, 2018.

28. Ibid.

29. Mark Weaver, a senior from Victoria, Texas, was one of Texas A&M's five seniors. In the January 1968 issue of *Sports Illustrated*, Weaver was one of the magazine's selections for its All-Bowl Team. Thirty-five years later, in 2003, Weaver's wife, Linda, tracked down the magazine and purchased it for $25. Linda surprised her husband, saying, "I never told him I had found it until the day it arrived in the mail to us. The look on his face was priceless when he opened it up and saw it, and he was so happy to finally have that in his hands" (*Hill Country News*, September 18, 2003).

30. Housley, interview with author, August 28, 2018.

31. Ibid.

32. Ibid.

33. Forney and Townsend, *Talk of the Tide*, 110.

34. Ibid.

35. Herskowitz, interview with author, August 20, 2018.

36. Forney and Townsend, *Talk of the Tide*, 110.

37. *Houston Post*, January 2, 1968.

38. Forney and Townsend, *Talk of the Tide*, 110.

39. Ibid.

40. *Dallas Morning News*, January 2, 1968; *Houston Post*, January 2, 1968.

41. Hallman, interview with author, September 14, 2018. Today, the ball—that of Stabler's last collegiate pass—is prominently displayed in Hallman's home in Alabama among a trove of other memorabilia from a storied playing and coaching career.

42. *Houston Post*, January 2, 1968; *Dallas Morning News*, January 2, 1968; Stallings and Cook, *Another Season*, 90.

43. *Dallas Morning News*, January 2, 1968.

44. Ibid.; *Dallas Morning News*, June 30, 2002.

45. Land, interview with author, March 30, 2018.

46. Johns, interview with author, October 3, 2018. Several Aggie players said they never saw Bryant's famous hug because Stallings didn't allow players to shake hands with their opponents.

47. Homan, interview with author, September 26, 2018.

48. Ibid.

49. *Houston Post*, January 2, 1968.

50. *Dallas Morning News*, January 2, 1968.

51. Krueger, interview with author, September 5, 2018.

52. *Houston Post*, January 2, 1968; *Dallas Morning News*, January 2, 1968.

53. *Dallas Morning News*, January 2, 1968.

54. Rickman, interview with author, September 5, 2018.

55. Ibid.

56. Stallings and Cook, *Another Season*, 90.

57. *Dallas Morning News*, January 2, 1968.

58. Stallings, interview with author, July 8, 2015; Stallings and Cook, *Another Season*, 90.

59. Stallings and Cook, *Another Season*, 90.

60. Bryant wrote in his autobiography, "And Bud Wilkinson taught me something that day. He showed me the class I wish I had. He came into our dressing room afterward and shook hands with me and as many players as he could reach. I had never done that before or seen it done. But I've done it since" (Bryant and Underwood, *Bear*, 104).

61. *Houston Chronicle*, January 2, 1968.

62. Housley, interview with author, August 28, 2018.

Epilogue

No one ever dared to call Gene "Bebes" Stallings a quitter. And no one ever will.

Not on the football field or in life.

Historians might someday consider October 7, 2017, the most symbolic moment in his career. On that day, the 82-year-old Stallings stood on Kyle Field with members of his 1967 Southwest Conference championship team to celebrate the 50th anniversary of their achievements, which had culminated with an upset victory of number seven–ranked Alabama in the Cotton Bowl. Thunderous cheers from the more than 101,000 fans in attendance rained on Stallings and his former players, who returned the love with smiles, waves, and the doffing of baseball caps.

Stallings—a man whose life had been defined by grit and determination—gingerly raised his right hand to acknowledge the Aggie faithful.

Two weeks earlier, Stallings lay in a Dallas hospital, attached to a ventilator after suffering a heart attack at his ranch outside of Paris, Texas. He had already suffered two strokes earlier in the year.

"I had a responsibility and I was going to honor it," Stallings said then. "We didn't really discuss it much with the doctors except telling them what I was going to do. We had a private jet to pick us up and carry us down. As soon as the game was over, I left and came back. It was not a struggle. It was really a joy to be able to see the players . . .

"A lot of people advised me not to do that and I just said you talk to somebody else because I'm going to go."[1]

The mere presence of Stallings stirred emotions.

"I teared up when he started talking," said Tommy Maxwell, A&M's former standout receiver and defensive back. "It all hit me. Here's a guy, by example, getting up and saying, 'Hey, I had to come here for you guys. You never quit. How am I going to quit on you? How am I going to lay on a hospital bed?'"[2]

Stallings not only willed himself to College Station, but he brought his charisma and wit in tow. Prior to the brief on-field ceremony at halftime, he waved his former quarterback Edd Hargett over as he sat in a golf cart.

"He says, 'Boy, you just forget about all those bad things I said to you. Don't let me fall,'" Hargett recalled with a grin.[3]

Hargett stood by his coach's side throughout the ceremony.

Together, Stallings and his former players had stood shoulder to shoulder in 1967, with a season on the brink of disaster. They didn't quit then either. And magical things had happened.

In the days after the Cotton Bowl victory, it became clear that expectations had been dramatically heightened for the Aggies in 1967. Experts rushed to declare Texas A&M the overwhelming favorite to repeat as Southwest Conference champion in 1968—and why not? The bulk of its returning team members featured talented and experienced players who were entering their senior season, stalwarts such as Billy Hobbs, Rolf Krueger, Tommy Maxwell, and Hargett, to name a few. As a result, the Associated Press preseason poll placed Texas A&M at number 12, but expectations in the Aggie locker room were much loftier.

Fate, however, dealt A&M a cruel blow. The Aggies were unable to recapture the magic of 1967.

Now whenever the iconic 1967 season is remembered, one question always lingers in the shadow of its glory: What happened in 1968? The Aggies finished the 1968 season 2–5 in their conference and 3–7 overall, in what marked Stallings's fourth year as head coach.

For a number of players, the disappointment of 1968 has never really vanished.

"One thing I've always been mad at Coach Stallings for," Hargett admitted. "You have twenty days of spring practice. Full pads. Full practice. And I thought, *Well, we'll go out there ten days and take a few days off, and work the young guys.* . . . Well, we went through the whole spring training full speed."[4]

Injuries followed.

Hobbs, for one, hurt his back in practice before the season opener with LSU—a nonconference game the Aggies lost 13–12. Hobbs played.

"If he (Stallings) would have left Billy home, we wouldn't have been any worse off in that game," Hargett said. "And we would have been better as the season went. But that wasn't the mind-set. You played and practiced. He got hurt, and two or three other guys got hurt. Hobbs played the whole year, but those passes he was knocking down the year before, well, he just wasn't able to get to them."[5]

Bob Long, who led the Aggies with eight touchdown receptions a year earlier, also injured himself in practice.

"I got my shoulder knocked down," Long recalled. "He (Stallings) decided to work on crack-back blocking. Well, if the guy knows you're coming, it's a different story. So I was first in line. I turned to Maxwell and said, 'Somebody's gonna get hurt.' Play started and we met shoulders. Mine went one way, and my body went the other. So I missed two and a half games.

"So I'm not a big fan of contact all week. To have a successful year, you have to be lucky with minimal injuries . . . but the law of averages caught up with us our senior year, and everybody was hurt. Hobbs had a bad back. I had one with my shoulder. Maxwell had a torn leg muscle. Edd got broken and separated ribs."[6]

Time has not tamed the fierce competitors inside of players like Long and Hargett, but it has brought the perspective of life. At least that's how both men feel today about decisions made long ago.

"At some point, you have to get over it," Hargett said of the 1968 season. "It is what it is. Can't change it. Just accept it and move forward."[7]

Stallings did.

In 1971, Texas A&M's board of directors fired Stallings after a 34–14 loss to University of Texas. Stallings finished with a combined 27–45–1 record at A&M in seven seasons, with his only winning season coming in the iconic 1967 campaign.[8]

Stallings wasn't unemployed for long. He latched on with the Dallas Cowboys in 1972, serving as Tom Landry's secondary coach.

Twenty years later, he led Alabama to a national championship. A statue of him now stands outside of Bryant-Denny Stadium on the University of Alabama campus beside other Crimson Tide luminaries, including his beloved mentor.

Bryant continued to enhance his legacy in the aftermath of the 1968 Cotton Bowl. He led Alabama to three more national titles (1973, 1978, and 1979) before he stunned the sports world by formally announcing his retirement December 15, 1982, at age 69. At the time, Bryant told reporters he loved his alma mater too much to continue, describing himself as "worn out."[9]

In typical Bryant fashion, he added moments later, "I don't have any regrets. My only real concern is for my staff. I hope none of them is out of a job."[10]

Two weeks later, Bryant led Alabama one last time as the Crimson Tide defeated Illinois 21–15 in the Liberty Bowl. Bryant retired after 38 years of coaching with an all-time record 323 wins—a record that has since been broken.

The sting of Bryant's departure hit Alabama—and the nation—much harder January 26, 1983, when the famed coach died of a heart attack. Bryant entered the Druid City Hospital in Tuscaloosa on a Thursday night, complaining of chest pains. Dr. William Hill told reporters Bryant suffered a massive heart attack at 1:24 p.m. while undergoing X-rays. The doctor restored "a weak heartbeat" for about an hour with a pacemaker before the coach was pronounced dead at 2:30 p.m.[11]

Bryant died only 37 days after he announced his retirement.

Memorials flooded into Tuscaloosa from throughout the nation. Legendary University of Oklahoma Coach Bud Wilkinson simply stated, "There will never be another like him."[12]

Frank Broyles, the former University of Arkansas coach, said, "The Bear had something beyond a knack for winning. He was a special man with a charisma that set him apart. Even his peers—his fellow coaches—never envied his success and records."[13]

Some of the commentaries on his passing were unvarnished, such as the column written by Associated Press writer Herschel Nissenson. He described Bryant's love of cigarettes and alcohol in blunt detail and related a conversation they had after Bryant had been hospitalized a few years earlier. Nissenson asked him at the time what the doctors had diagnosed.

"They said it was seventy-five percent smoking, twenty percent diet and five percent booze and other stuff," Bryant replied.[14]

"I wish," the coach added wryly, "I wish it had been seventy-five percent booze and other stuff."[15]

Bryant's legend stretched far and wide, and he received a funeral fit for a president. An estimated 250,000 people gathered along the 55-mile route on Interstate 20 from Tuscaloosa to Birmingham to pay their final respects to the Bear as his hearse passed.

Handmade signs hung from overpasses.

"We Love You, Bear."[16]

"God Needed An Offensive Coordinator."[17]

Men and women openly wept. Some women mourned with their babies in tow. One woman brought her five children, none older than 10. She remarked,

"They don't know anything about him now. I want them to know when they get big they were here to see the passing of a great man."[18]

• • •

Many of those associated with Stallings, Bryant, and the events chronicled here went on to achieve great success in their lives in one way or another. Perhaps none underwent a more profound transformation than Billy Hobbs, A&M's two-time All-American linebacker, 1968 Cotton Bowl co-MVP, and eighth-round pick by the Philadelphia Eagles in the 1969 NFL draft.

Hobbs died in 2004, but his legacy grew in the years prior to his death when he became an unlikely warrior for God. His amazing journey is the type often found in Hollywood.

As a college player, Hobbs's incredible feats on the field and wild antics off it certainly earned him folklore status among the Aggie faithful. Former teammates remember him as a talented, hard-hitting defender with speed and uncanny instincts for the football as well as a quick-tempered youngster who would fight anyone at any time—and often did.

Stallings knew it as well as anybody.

Kristi Hobbs, who married Billy in 1989, recalled the first time she met her husband's former college coach with amusement. The three were attending an event together, and Billy and Kristi drove to the airport to pick up Stallings.

"Billy said, 'Coach, this my wife, Kristi,'" Kristi said. "Gene turns and looks at me in the backseat. He says, 'Kristi, I want to tell you something. I've spent most of my life trying to keep kids in college. I spent four years trying to keep your husband out of jail.'

"That was our first meeting."[19]

Kristi laughed at the memory, adding, "Billy was a great storyteller."

One story Billy loved to tell occurred in the aftermath of the Cotton Bowl victory. He and most of his teammates wanted to party and chase girls that night in Dallas, but Stallings ordered them to instead dress in suits and ties. The coach told his players they were going to attend an alumni dinner, and the announcement landed with a thud. Players grumbled as they dressed.

As expected, the event took place in a ballroom with a big band playing dated music. Then the alumni began to greet their conquering Aggie heroes.

"One man shook Billy's hand and said, 'Great game, Billy. You really hit 'em hard,'" Kristi said. "Billy pulled his hand away and there was a hundred-dollar bill in it. So he stuck it in his pocket. Then another [alumnus] approached and said, 'Great game, Billy.' He pulled his hand away and there's a fifty-dollar bill. This happened all night long.

"Finally, as the band began to pick up, Billy's date came up to him and said, 'Billy, are we going to dance?' He said, 'Heck no, I'm gonna shake more hands.'"[20]

Hobbs never lost his sense of humor—or his mean streak—after his days at College Station. In 1969, he signed with the Philadelphia Eagles, who made him their eighth-round pick in the NFL draft. He played four seasons in the NFL with the Eagles and New Orleans Saints and another two seasons in the World Football League before retiring.

At some point during this period, he and his old teammate Wendell Housley went to a Dallas club for some drinks. In the next booth sat a man telling jokes—Aggie jokes. Each time the man finished a joke, everyone seated around him roared with laughter.

Hobbs seethed at each new joke.

"I'll be right back," Hobbs finally told Housley as he stood up.[21]

Hobbs tapped the man on the shoulder and sternly said, "Let me tell you something, buddy. I don't like Aggie jokes. If you don't shut up, I'm fixin' to shut you up."[22]

"Hey man," the jokester replied, "I'm just having fun."[23]

"Well," Hobbs responded, "your fun is over."[24]

Housley watched his fearless friend walk back to their booth and sit down. He leaned into Hobbs and said, "Billy, you're not in Amarillo, Texas, buddy. You're in Dallas man. These guys are serious. You're liable to get us shot."

Hobbs looked up at Housley and casually replied, "Well, you don't hear any more Aggie jokes, do ya?"[25]

By 29, Hobbs found himself in the same circumstance as countless other ex-professional athletes—young and unemployed. Hobbs felt adrift and reached out to Joe Richardson Jr., the Amarillo oilman who encouraged him to play at Texas A&M.

Richardson gave him a job.

Then, on November 22, 1979, while Hobbs was living in Dallas, he heard crusade evangelist James Robinson preach.

"That's where Billy first heard the Gospel," Kristi said. "He returned home and dropped on his knees and prayed. He said, 'God, if you're real, then you need to change me.' That's when Billy accepted Jesus into his heart."

Billy talked shortly thereafter to his friend and former teammate Tommy Maxwell, a devout Christian who was then on staff at the Dallas Theological Seminary. Maxwell encouraged him to begin attending their classes, and Hobbs considered himself blessed to be sitting among men studying to become pastors.

Two years later and now living in Amarillo, Billy turned on the television and for the first time saw David Walker, a 27-year-old pastor at the San Jacinto Baptist Church in Amarillo. Hobbs would later say he knew at that moment that Walker was the man who was supposed to baptize him. He turned off the television and drove to Walker's church unannounced.

Hobbs walked up to Walker and said, "You don't know me. My name is Billy Hobbs, and you are to baptize me."[26]

The next summer, Hobbs volunteered at a youth camp hosted by the San Jacinto Baptist Church in Brownwood, Texas. He met and befriended a teenager named Kevin McDonald. Hobbs later said he prayed for the young man to accept Jesus but found him resistant.

Finally, at the end of the week, McDonald approached Hobbs and told him he was ready to accept Jesus into his heart. McDonald became the first of thousands of people Hobbs would lead to the Lord over the next two decades as an ordained minister.

Hobbs and his wife spread the Gospel at stops in Amarillo and San Antonio as well as overseas on mission trips to Kenya, India, and Brazil. His mantra became "Nobody's too tough for Jesus." Along the way, Billy evangelized in prisons and regularly helped feed and clothe the homeless.

Former teammates were both stunned and delighted by his new path in life.

"One of the best linebackers we've ever had," Stegent said of Hobbs. "Billy was a wild man. If you would have told me Billy was going to become an ordained minister, I would have bet against it. And I think everyone else on the team would have, too."[27]

Once, after becoming a pastor, Hobbs traveled to Houston and stayed at Stegent's home. They played golf one day at a local country club.

"He was riding with me, and I wasn't having a good day," Stegent recalled. "And my language wasn't too nice. He said, 'Your language is horrible. It's worse than it's ever been. I'm gonna walk.'

"So he took his clubs off the cart and began walking."[28]

Another member of the foursome traded golf carts with Hobbs so he could ride. Soon after, Stegent again saw Hobbs walking the course and lugging his clubs.

"What's the problem?" Stegent asked his friend.

"He's worse than you," Hobbs replied. "So I'll just walk."[29]

The two old teammates would laugh for years about that day.

Housley loves to tell another story about Hobbs after his baptism. Ironically, the story took place at the Cotton Bowl as the two former Aggies were riding an elevator. A man walked onto the elevator and said, "Oh, wow, Billy Hobbs! Billy, I remember you. You used to charge people for walking across the drill field."[30]

The man soon exited the elevator. Hobbs turned to Housley and asked incredulously, "Wendell, why do they always remember the bad stuff?"[31]

In death, they overwhelmingly remembered the good.

Hobbs died August 21, 2004, when a vehicle struck his Honda scooter at an intersection next to a flea market. A witness to the accident later reached out to Kristi and the rest of Billy's family to share something he saw that day.

"The witness told us he saw a black man in a suit kneel down next to Billy and talk into his ear," Kristi said. "He looked away for a moment and said when he looked up again, the man was suddenly gone. He thought the man was Billy's angel."[32]

A standing-room-only crowd of 2,500 people crammed into the Alamo City Christian Fellowship to memorialize Hobbs. Several people spoke that day, including Stallings.

"Stallings delivered a great talk that day," Kristi remembered. "He said he had been asked many times over the years who was the best player he ever coached. He said he couldn't answer that one. He coached too many great players.

"Then he said, 'But if you ask me who was the toughest player I ever coached, that one's easy—Billy Hobbs. Nobody was tougher than Billy Hobbs.'"[33]

Stallings concluded by pointing out that of all Billy's football glory and accolades, none compared with the thousands of souls he led to the Lord.[34]

Today, Kristi carries on the mission work of her late husband and has gone on to found the JESUS. Hobbs House of Hope in Kenya.

• • •

A number of other Aggies entered the professional ranks.

Tommy Maxwell enjoyed six seasons in the NFL after being drafted by the Baltimore Colts in the second round—the 51st player selected overall. He won a Super Bowl ring with the Colts in his second season, helping defeat the Cowboys 16–13 in Super Bowl V at the Orange Bowl in Miami.

Maxwell also played with the Oakland Raiders (1971–73) and Houston Oilers (1974) before a neck injury forced him into retirement. Later, Maxwell founded Coaches Outreach, a nonprofit Christian organization for high school coaches and their spouses.

Hargett landed with the New Orleans Saints after his days at Texas A&M, where he left as the Aggies' all-time leader in passing with 5,379 yards. The Saints selected him in the 16th round of the 1969 NFL draft. He played four seasons with New Orleans—starting a total of eight games—and then one season with the Oilers before playing in the fledgling World Football League with the Shreveport Steamers.

Hargett, who graduated as an honor student in electrical engineering, later served as general manager of the East Texas Electric Cooperative for 10 years and the Houston County Electric Cooperative in Crockett, Texas, for another 15 years. In November 2017, the Trump administration appointed Hargett as the Texas State Director of Rural Development for the US Department of Agriculture.

Hargett, by the way, remains married to his high school sweetheart, Shirley—a union that has produced three children and eight grandchildren.

Krueger played six seasons in the NFL after being a second-round selection by the St. Louis Cardinals in 1969. Three of those seasons were with the San Francisco 49ers, including two seasons (1972–73) in which he played alongside his elder brother, Charlie. The elder Krueger played an amazing 15 NFL seasons from 1959 to 1973 and was a two-time All-Pro.

Housley, another hero of the 1968 Cotton Bowl, was also selected in the 1969 NFL draft. He was taken by the Minnesota Vikings in the 17th round, but he was nursing a left knee injury at the time. After a workout, the Vikings asked Housley to see a doctor in Oklahoma City. Two surgeries ensued.

"The doctor told me, 'Wendell, to be perfectly honest, you could out there and play for ten years or ten minutes,'" Housley recalled. "He said, 'But if you get hurt again, you'll be crippled for the rest of your life.' And I said, 'Well, you made up my mind.'"[35]

Housley was later diagnosed with Charcot-Marie-Tooth (CMT) disease, an inherited nerve disorder that causes muscles in the feet, legs, and hands to lose muscle over time.

"I'm supposed to be wearing braces," Housley said. "I consider myself blessed. I can still walk and get around with a cane and motivate."[36]

Today, Housley is an inspiration whenever he walks into a room.

Larry Stegent finished his stellar collegiate career in 1969 as a three-time All-Southwest Conference tailback. His stock as a professional prospect earned him a first-round selection—the eighth player taken overall—by the St. Louis Cardinals in the 1970 NFL draft. But his professional career ended almost as soon as it started when he suffered a knee injury in his first and only preseason game.

Stegent played in seven games with the Cardinals, producing one reception for 12 yards.

Life after football proved especially prosperous for Stegent, who built an insurance empire in his hometown of Houston—Stegent Insurance Associates. He has served as the company's CEO for more than four decades.

Bob Long chose to take his talents into professional baseball—his greatest love. The Chicago Bears selected him in the 1969 NFL draft, but he opted to sign instead with the Los Angeles Dodgers. Long completed an outstanding college career by earning All-American status in 1969 as an outfielder.

Long played five seasons in the minor leagues as a third baseman, climbing as high as Class AA in one of the toughest organizations in baseball before calling it quits. The left-handed hitter posted a respectable .266 overall batting average in a combined 444 minor-league games.

"I didn't do too bad," Long said. "My biggest problem was I played behind a guy named Ron Cey."[37]

(Cey, by the way, was one of the cornerstones of the Dodgers' famed infield, which also once featured Steve Garvey at first, Davey Lopes at second, and Bill Russell at shortstop. The quartet played together for nearly nine seasons [1973–81], winning four National League pennants and one World Series.)

Long later opened a photography studio in his hometown of Paris, Texas.

Curley Hallman lived out his dreams. He first attained his lifelong aspiration of playing college football and later climbed to the highest ranks of his profession as a college coach.

Along the way, Hallman continually seized every opportunity with tenacity, thankfulness, and a positive attitude. His first job after graduating from Texas A&M came as an assistant coach to Dexter Bassinger at Stark High School in Orange, Texas. Incredibly, Bassinger's other assistant coach was Wade Phillips—the present defensive coordinator for the Los Angeles Rams and son of legendary football coach Bum Phillips.

Hallman served as an assistant to Bassinger for two seasons when he unexpectedly received a call one day with a job offer. The deep, graveled voice on the other end of the phone was Bear Bryant, who asked the former Aggie if he would like to become his new defensive backs coach.

"Just out of the blue," Hallman recalled. "I still don't know if he just remembered me as ol' Curley Hallman, the Alabama kid from the Cotton Bowl or if someone called on my behalf, perhaps Coach Stallings or Bud Moore. . . . I never did know."[38]

Hallman jumped at the offer immediately, but Bryant cautioned him to slow down.

"We were still in the middle of a semester at Stark, and Coach Bryant said I had better check with my superintendent first," he said. "So I did. My superintendent told me, 'You need to get out of here.'"

So he did.

For the next 16 years, Hallman earned his keep as an assistant coach at Alabama (1973–76), Clemson (1979–81), and Texas A&M (1982–87). On September 27, 1987, he watched a 17-year-old Brett Favre make his first college start for the University of Southern Mississippi in a home game against A&M. Though Favre more than held his own with the Golden Eagles, Hallman coached the Aggie defensive backs in a 27–14 A&M victory.

A week earlier, Favre had unexpectedly taken the field for the first time in the collegiate ranks with 5:49 left in the third quarter, with Southern Mississippi trailing Tulane by 10 points. The then-unknown freshman led Southern Miss to a 31–24 come-from-behind victory.

"We were in the locker room after our game [against Southern Miss], talking about the game," Hallman recalled. "A few coaches kinda shrugged off Favre, saying he was just a big country kid with a pretty good arm, but probably wouldn't amount to much. I said, 'No. I can't pronounce the kid's name, but he's special.'"[39]

As fate would go, Hallman would become Favre's new head coach by the end of the year. In his first season, Hallman—with Favre behind center—led the Golden Eagles to a 1988 Independence Bowl victory over the University of Texas at El Paso (UTEP) and a 10–2 overall record. He compiled a combined record of 23–11 in three seasons as head coach at Southern Miss before being named Louisiana State University's new head coach.

Hallman's tenure at LSU proved rocky and tumultuous. He left Baton Rouge after four seasons and a combined 16–28 record, although one of those victories was a stunning 17–13 triumph over a Stallings-led Alabama squad at Bryant-Denney Stadium in 1993—a victory that snapped the Crimson Tide's 31-game unbeaten streak at home.

Despite the disappointment at LSU, Hallman reflects on all his experiences in a positive light.

"Hey, I've been fortunate enough to live out my dreams," Hallman said. "Sure, I wish things had gone better at LSU, but that's life. You learn from your experiences and move on."[10]

Rick Rickman continued to serve under Stallings as head student manager for his junior and senior years. He graduated in 1970 with a bachelor's degree in finance before being commissioned in the Army Air Defense Artillery as a second lieutenant. He was honorably discharged after a four-year stint as a first lieutenant and continued his education.

In 1977, Rickman graduated from St. Mary's University with a law degree, and he subsequently served as a briefing attorney on the Texas Supreme Court. He rose to become a successful trial lawyer and was a founding member of the law firm Hallett & Perrin in Dallas, Texas.

Rickman earned the distinction of being inducted in the Texas A&M Corps Hall of Honor. During the ceremony, some attendees asked Rickman about serving as a student manager under Stallings.

"I told them what I've told coach face to face," Rickman said. "I told him, 'Coach, after working for you, and working with generals, titans in the business industry and judges, it didn't faze me at all.'

"You had to be on top of your game at all times, and if you were busting your butt, he really appreciated it and rewarded you in very subtle ways. But he expected it, and he'd let you know. And if you couldn't match expectations, you moved out of the way."[41]

Once, during his junior year, Rickman found himself in Stallings's line of fire. A defensive player had hurt his shoulder because he was wearing a poor set of shoulder pads. Stallings fumed and began yelling at his newly appointed head student manager.

"He took me in the dressing room," Rickman recalled. "He said, 'That boy broke his collarbone because you put him in these flimsy shoulder pads.' For some reason, that really irked me."[42]

Rickman instinctively broke his silence.

"I said, 'Coach, I didn't put him in those damn pads,'" he continued. "'Your defensive backfield coach told me to put him in those pads.'"[43]

Stallings stared at Rickman for several seconds. Then the coach turned and walked away.

"Well, I thought I was dead," Rickman said. "But from that moment on, we had a very interesting, frank, close relationship."[44]

One episode during his senior year especially remains with Rickman regarding that relationship.

"Rick, I want you to hold for extra points," Stallings told him one day. "I wanna see how you hold."[45]

Rickman began holding extra points in practice for a nervous kicker.

"I told him, 'Look, ignore Coach Stallings,'" Rickman recalled. "I said, 'He's not gonna kill you. I'll talk you through this.'"[46]

The kicker began to show more confidence, prompting Stallings to order Rickman a uniform—No. 9. Rickman even dressed for a scrimmage, though he never entered the game. But he carried the jersey to each game "just in case" Stallings called upon him in an emergency.

"Now, upon reflection, I think when he was at Junction they gave Troy Summerlin—also a manager—a jersey," Rickman said. "I think that Coach Stallings was sending me a very nice signal because I had fun doing it. I never got in. I was always a manager. . . . I think he was just saying, *Hey, I think a lot of you, Rick*.

"That's a warm memory."[47]

Today, that No. 9 jersey is displayed proudly in a frame.

• • •

Of all the great players Bryant coached—and there are too many to count—none attained more notoriety and celebrity on and off the field than Joe Namath. The young man who once endured a suspension by Bryant went on to become a football icon known simply as "Broadway Joe."

Namath's professional career spanned 13 seasons and led to his induction into the Pro Football Hall of Fame. The defining moment of his career came in 1969, at Super Bowl III in Miami. Namath led the American Football League's New York Jets to a 16–7 upset of a more established NFL franchise, the Baltimore Colts.

Prior to the game, the brash, young quarterback made national headlines after attending the Miami Touchdown Club.

"We're gonna win the game," Namath boldly proclaimed at the event. "I guarantee it."

Namath then famously backed up his mouth.

The victory—and his charming looks—catapulted him into the realm of popular culture, landing him several endorsement deals and roles in movies and television shows.

Kenny "Snake" Stabler is another Bryant quarterback who reached great heights as a professional, leading the Oakland Raiders to a 32–14 victory over the Minnesota Vikings in Super Bowl XI. True to his mischievous reputation, Stabler attended parties at the Playboy Mansion that week at 4 a.m.

The renegade from Foley, Alabama, never surrendered his bad-boy lifestyle.

In the late 1990s, Stabler returned to his home state like the prodigal son to work radio broadcasts for Alabama football games. He was also offered a radio job with the New Orleans Saints at the time, but he opted for the Alabama gig, because it allowed him to bring his daughters.

In February 2015, doctors diagnosed Stabler with colon cancer. Five months later, while on a Fourth of July trip to Mississippi with his daughter Alexa and longtime partner, Kim Bush, Stabler complained of stomach pain. He was taken to Memorial Hospital in Gulfport, Mississippi, where he was placed in intensive care.

All three of his daughters—Alexa, Kendra, and Marissa—were soon at his bedside.

Stabler wanted to die in Alabama, but without that possible, Marissa played Lynyrd Skynyrd's "Sweet Home Alabama" on her iPhone. Her father died at 10:45 p.m. July 8, with his daughters by his side.[48]

Dennis Homan, Stabler's roommate and favorite target, entered the professional ranks after graduation, as expected. The Dallas Cowboys selected the All-American receiver in the first round of the 1968 NFL draft. He was the 20th player taken overall and went on to play a combined total of five seasons with the Cowboys (1968–70) and Kansas City Chiefs (1971–72).

Homan was a member of the Cowboys when they lost to the Baltimore Colts in Super Bowl V (1971) but didn't record a reception. He enjoyed his best season in 1969, when he caught 12 passes for 240 yards. He later played for a season and a half in the World Football League, which folded midway through the 1975 season. At the time, Homan had grabbed 18 receptions for 277 yards.

He then retired.

"I'll tell ya, I've had a good life," Homan said. "I've been very blessed."[49]

Bobby Johns, Alabama's two-time All-American defensive back, carved out a nice career as a football coach after his playing days. He coached from 1972 to

2000 with stops in Florida, Georgia, Tennessee, Kentucky, South Carolina, and Alabama.

His first coaching job came as an assistant at the University of North Alabama.

"I called Coach Bryant to see what he thought," Johns recalled. "And I ended up getting the job. I called him back to thank him for maybe helping me on it and he said, 'Well, Bobby, I don't know what you're talking about.' But I believe he did. . . . Coach Bryant didn't want me to think he had helped me."[50]

Even Stallings found a place in the heart of Johns for a gesture he made in 1992. That year, Johns lost his 16-year-old son, Jody Ray—a child with special needs whom his father described as "a great little kid." Jody suffered a loss of oxygen at birth and struggled to develop as he grew older.

Jody died October 20, 1992.

Johns received a message to call Stallings—then Alabama's head coach—the week of his son's funeral. Johns returned the call on a Friday, realizing Stallings might be too busy to accept the call. Unbeaten Alabama had a home game against Ole Miss the next day.

"He had called me to tell me how sorry he was for the fact that my son had passed away, and he took the call and was super nice," Johns said. "Super nice. Anyway, that's the kind of guys Coach Bryant and Coach Stallings were."[51]

No two sportswriters knew Bryant and Stallings better than Charles H. Land and Mickey Herskowitz.

Land rose from cub reporter at the *Tuscaloosa News* to serve as its managing editor for nearly the last 25 years of his career. He retired July 28, 1995, after 40 years in the business. During that time, he covered more than 100 of Bryant's games and even received a 1961 national championship ring.

In 2004, Land was inducted into the Tuscaloosa County Civic Hall of Fame by the Chamber of Commerce in West Alabama.

Today, he lives in Tuscaloosa and continues to follow his beloved Crimson Tide.

Herskowitz, meanwhile, went on to author more than 50 books, including biographies on Gene Autry, Nolan Ryan, and, of course, Bryant. He has also helped ghostwrite autobiographies for stars such as Dan Rather, Mickey Mantle, Howard Cosell, and Bette Davis.

The retired Houston sportswriter always contended Bryant wasn't racist and related a personal story as evidence. In 1973, he and his wife, Razil, adopted an African American boy named Christopher.

"I remember how proud Coach Bryant was of us," Herskowitz recalled. "On Christopher's third birthday, I got a lovely note from Coach Bryant about Christopher. I don't know how he knew, but he always seemed to know these things."[52]

Herskowitz remembered a funny story about a brief encounter he had with Bryant.

"Years later, we were walking out to a press conference, and I was bragging on Chris," he said. "Chris was a pretty good athlete, and I said something like, 'Yeah, and he can throw with either hand.'

"Coach Bryant, without missing a beat, said, 'He oughta charge double.'"[53]

NOTES

1. Michael Casagrande, "Gene Stallings Talks Heart Attack, Desire to Be in Alabama Two Weeks Later," *AL.com*, October 13, 2017.
2. *Bryan (TX) Daily Eagle*, October 8, 2017.
3. Hargett, interview with author, March 22, 2018.
4. Ibid.
5. Ibid.
6. Long, interview with author, August 23, 2018.
7. Hargett, interview with author, March 22, 2018.
8. *Bryan (TX) Daily Eagle*, November 26, 1971.
9. *New York Times*, December 16, 1982.
10. Ibid.
11. *New York Times*, January 27, 1983.
12. *Bryan (TX) Daily Eagle*, January 29, 1983.
13. Ibid.
14. *Bryan (TX) Daily Eagle*, January 28, 1983.
15. Ibid.
16. *Bryan (TX) Daily Eagle*, January 29, 1983.
17. Ibid.
18. Ibid.
19. Kristi Hobbs, interview with author, February 5, 2019.
20. Ibid.
21. Housley, interview with author, August 28, 2018.
22. Ibid.
23. Ibid.
24. Ibid.
25. Ibid.
26. Ibid.
27. Stegent, interview with author, August 29, 2018.

28. Ibid.

29. Ibid.

30. Housley, interview with author, August 28, 2018.

31. Ibid.

32. Kristi Hobbs, interview with author, February 5, 2019.

33. Ibid.

34. Ibid.

35. Housley, interview with author, August 28, 2018.

36. Ibid.

37. Long, interview with author, August 23, 2018.

38. Hallman, interview with author, February 7, 2019.

39. Ibid.

40. Ibid.

41. Rickman, interview with author, September 5, 2018.

42. Ibid.

43. Ibid.

44. Ibid.

45. Ibid.

46. Ibid.

47. Ibid.

48. Browning, "One Last Smile."

49. Homan, interview with author, September 26, 2018.

50. Johns, interview with author, October 3, 2018.

51. Ibid.

52. Herskowitz, interview with author, August 20, 2018.

53. Ibid. Christopher died of leukemia in 2002, at age 28.

Acknowledgments

By now, one might think nothing would surprise me about the workload required to publish a book. I've published seven books to date, am in the process of writing my eighth, and have already laid the groundwork for yet another. The process of writing a book is neither burdensome nor daunting but rather a passion for me. I'm driven to write nonfiction historical narratives that escort readers—as well as myself—on new journeys through time.

In 2015, I coauthored *Joe: The Slave Who Became an Alamo Legend* with my dear friend Lee Spencer White. The ground-breaking, 325-page book pieced together the life of a slave who survived the 1836 Alamo battle, tracing for the first time his birth in Kentucky and the fates that led him into the entrapped Texas garrison and beyond. Our cradle-to-grave research spanned 11 years—an extraordinary amount of time by any standard. Then again, our subject had been forced to live a life in the shadows.

Most history books generally take anywhere from three to five years to research and write, depending on the scope of the project and, of course, the writer. Yet each time I have finished a manuscript, I stand in awe of the number of people who actually had a hand in its creation. This book is no different.

From librarians who ordered old newspapers through interlibrary loans to those who simply gave me directions during a research trip, the list of those who assisted me over the past four years is incalculable. Nor do I take any of those people for granted, regardless of the size of their contribution. One book can also take a village.

Friends and acquaintances have often asked how I got the idea for this book. I didn't.

Credit for that deed goes to Texas A&M University Press senior editor Thom Lemmons, who was brainstorming one day about a series of new sports books.

Lemmons glanced at his office wall and saw the now-iconic photograph of Alabama coach Paul W. "Bear" Bryant hoisting his former player and then-A&M head coach Gene "Bebes" Stallings in the air after the 1968 Cotton Bowl Classic. Lemmons immediately thought a book about the relationship between Bryant and his loyal protégé would be a worthy subject for the Press. Editor-in-Chief Jay Dew agreed and tossed my name out as a prospective author. I'm glad he did.

Frankly, it's been a pleasure working with Lemmons and Dew throughout this journey. Both are highly knowledgeable, great gentlemen, and a credit to their profession. I'm honored to have worked by their sides as well as with the entire staff at the Press.

Once I accepted the project and had finished my preliminary research, I began to reach out to the book's main subjects in early 2015. My first call was to Coach Stallings. Based on what I had read about Coach Bryant and Coach Stallings and the legend of Junction, I anticipated a gruff, no-nonsense former coach immersed in the old ways. Some might refer to a person of that description as an "old-school" coach (which, in my upbringing, is considered a compliment).

I was right.

My first conversation with Coach Stallings ended after a short introduction with "call me back in a couple weeks, and we'll see what my schedule looks like then." He politely—and bluntly—informed me in his Southern drawl that he had a working ranch and cattle to tend to, and the duties almost entirely fell on him. He was then 80 years old. Completely understandable. I thanked him for his time and promised a return call.

Two weeks later, I again called Coach Stallings. Once more he spoke briefly and plainly, explaining how he didn't have time to devote to an interview given his heavy workload. "Call me back in a couple weeks," he repeated, "and we'll see what my schedule looks like then." I thanked him and then began to wonder if this was perhaps some sort of test—one I was failing.

Did Coach Stallings want some indication as to how serious I was about the book? Or was he actually that busy? Both scenarios seemed entirely plausible.

For the record, I'm not shy. I began interviewing professional athletes as an 18-year-old sportswriter in California in 1985 and had encountered my share of bullish personalities who simply wanted me to go away. Especially then. I was a novice in a shark tank. Although I always conducted myself politely and professionally, I quickly learned to also be bold, prepared, and persistent. Since then,

I've interviewed people from all walks of life including astronauts, governors, a secretary of state, five world heavyweight champions, and countless working-class heroes.

Still, Coach Stallings proved elusive.

Then, two weeks later, I again called Coach Stallings, and once more he began to speak of his heavy workload on the ranch. Finally, I chimed in with my own authoritative voice, "Coach, here's the deal: You and Coach Bryant are the main subjects of this book. Without you, there is no book. I'll tell you what, I'm not afraid of hard work or getting my hands dirty. How about I come down and work by your side on the ranch for a few days, and during breaks, I interview you?"

A moment of silence prevailed.

"Well," Coach Stallings finally replied, "there's no need in that." He told me what day and time to meet him in his hometown of Paris, Texas, and I informed him I would gratefully be present. I also knew not to be late. And I wasn't.

My first impression of Coach Stallings in July 2015 was that of a sturdy, stately man of presence. He carried himself with a natural charisma and a sense of strength but was also instantly disarming with his smile and humor. Over the next several days, I tagged along with him at his beloved ranch and also had the pleasure of visiting with his lovely wife, Ruth Ann. I learned a lot about their life together and his childhood and career. Yet I constantly found myself drawn to his wisdom on life. I soaked in everything he said, realizing he had experienced the greatest of joys and pains in his legendary lifetime.

Some of those words would comfort me two years later during my darkest hours when I lost my firstborn son, Joseph. I remember asking Coach Stallings how he had dealt with the loss of his son, John Mark, during my 2015 visit (John Mark had died August 2, 2008).

"The pain never goes away," Coach replied. "The best you can do is pray for contentment."

These days I, too, pray for contentment. So to Coach Stallings and Ruth Ann, I thank you from the bottom of my heart for your hospitality. I left your home with far more than notes for a book.

My research also carried me to the rich, black soil of Coach Bryant's home turf in Arkansas, a wide spot in the road called Moro Bottom. I made the journey with my friend and former reporter colleague Jay "Sweet Tea" Grelen. Jay is an exceptional writer and an even more exceptional man who, along with his wife,

Sloane, sheltered me for a night at their Little Rock metropolitan home. The next day, Jay and I climbed into his Jeep and made the 70-mile road trip south to Moro Bottom and neighboring Fordyce, where Bryant had earned high school football notoriety and a famous nickname for wrestling a carnival bear.

In Fordyce, I met Col. James Phillips and his wife, Agnes. They were instrumental in the creation of the Dallas County Museum, which pays homage to Bryant and other local legends. The colonel and his wife also introduced me to Buster Garlington, who owns the old Lyric Theatre building where Bryant famously grappled a circus bear. Garlington kindly gave us a tour of the building—a gesture that undoubtedly allowed me to more accurately paint a historic picture of the property as Bryant found it at the time of his noted match.

My journey also took me to the far-flung western reaches of the Texas Hill Country and the Kimble County town of Junction. I wanted to walk where Bear, Stallings and the rest of the Junction Boys walked in the summer of 1954. Back then, Bryant and his team encountered a desolate outpost plagued by an epic drought. When I drove into Junction in April 2017, I saw a quaint town, lush with greenery and hospitality, located at the fork of the rushing North and South Llano rivers.

Robert Stubblefield, the present facility director of the Adjunct, kindly gave me a tour of the sprawling property on a golf cart. Amazingly, most of the historic buildings at the site have remained just as they were 65 years ago, including the old Quonset huts that once housed the Aggie players. By the way, the property today is beautiful and immaculate.

In town, Constance E. Booth—executive director of the local chamber of commerce—warmly greeted me and introduced me to a number of locals with ties to the Junction Boys episode. I was grateful to visit with Rob Roy Spiller, who worked at the local bus station where a number of Aggies made their escape from Bryant's grueling camp in 1954. I also met Wanda Teel, the daughter of Elmer Parrott—the facility manager in 1954. Parrott captured the only known footage of the Junction Boys practicing, and Teel graciously allowed me to watch the historic film. Constance also introduced me to her husband, Bryan, who helped with the 25th anniversary reunion of the Junction Boys in 1979 as a member of the A&M club of Junction. To each I say thank you.

Along the way, I also encountered a number of archivists and librarians from various institutions who provided me with assistance in one way or another. The staffs of the Arkansas State Archives in Little Rock and the University of

Oklahoma were especially helpful, as was library specialist Jennifer Reibenspies at Texas A&M University's Cushing Memorial Library and Archives.

Of course, there is no substitution for the opportunity to interview those who lived the history one is trying to corral. Many of my previous books and magazine articles have featured 19th-century episodes from the American frontier whose subjects are long gone. In those situations, as a historian the best one can do is intensely mine the primary sources and hope to capture as much of the truth as possible through the haze of time.

This book presented me with a refreshingly different path. I was able to reach out to former players, sportswriters, and even a student manager who witnessed—and made—the history told in these pages.

Retired sportswriters Mickey Herskowitz of the *Houston Post* and Charles H. Land of the *Tuscaloosa News* each provided me with great behind-the-scenes stories. Both Herskowitz and Land covered Bryant and Stallings during their illustrious careers, and their remembrances are invaluable.

Equally important are the contributions of former players who generously shared their memories. Aggie legends Edd Hargett, Wendell Housley, Curley Hallman, Bob Long, Larry Stegent, and Rolf Krueger unhesitatingly gave of their time for this book. They, along with former student manager Rick Rickman, took me inside the huddles and the locker rooms during their storied 1967 season—one that culminated with a Cotton Bowl appearance against Bryant's University of Alabama squad. Kristi Hobbs—the widow of the great Aggie linebacker Billy Hobbs—was yet another invaluable resource. She shared a number of the colorful stories told to her by her charismatic, late husband.

Alabama legends Bobby Johns and Dennis Homan also graciously spoke with me, and both provided priceless anecdotes that will be treasured by college football fans for generations to come. Former Auburn University linebacker Gusty Yearout also agreed to an interview, recalling his team's gut-wrenching loss to Alabama in Kenny "Snake" Stabler's fabled "Run in the Mud" game at Legion Field in Birmingham.

In each case, those I interviewed strained to accurately remember the details of events long ago. Some memories were clearly vivid in their minds, as if being recalled only a day later. Other memories were obviously more elusive. I was especially impressed with each person's candid responses to my questions. If there were details they had forgotten or didn't remember clearly, they told me so. They, too, understood and appreciated the importance of obtaining as much historical accuracy as possible.

As far as I'm concerned, this book is as much theirs as mine. Thank you.

Previous historians who chronicled the lives of Bryant and Stallings must also be noted. All historians stand on the shoulders of those who came before them, and I am no different. I only hope I have moved the football farther downfield with this work.

Other members of "Team Jackson" who deserve a hearty thanks include my father, Ron Jackson Sr., who read and edited the first version of my manuscript; Lee Spencer White, my loyal compadre who is always armed with a fresh perspective on all things historical; and my friends back home in Vacaville, California, who have inspired me with their constant support and encouragement through the years.

Lastly, and certainly not least of all, I want to thank my family. My wife, Jeannia; children Joseph, Ashley, Tristan, and Rose; and granddaughter, Emma, all deserve credit for their love and support. Long ago they accepted my passion to be an author and storyteller, and each has sacrificed in one way or another so I can fulfill my dream. Those sacrifices are not always easy. And I love you dearly for what you do for me.

As for my late son, Joseph—he loved the story of this book and frequently prodded me to finish the manuscript. He was an epic reader who often accompanied me to speaking engagements and book signings. Joseph also read and edited my previous manuscripts, and when I typed the final words on this one, I painfully realized he would not be able to do so this time.

So I dedicated this book to him instead. I humbly hope it honors his memory.

Appendix

1967 Season Results

Texas A&M Aggies

(7–4, 6–1 Southwest Conference)

Date of Game	A&M Points	Opposing Team	Opposing Team's Points	A&M's Record
September 16	17	Southern Methodist University	20	(0–1)
September 23	20	Purdue	24	(0–2)
September 30	6	at Louisiana State University	17	(0–3)
October 7	18	Florida State	19	(0–4)
October 12	28	at Texas Tech	24	(1–4)
October 21	20	at Texas Christian University	0	(2–4)
October 28	21	Baylor	3	(3–4)
November 4	33	at Arkansas	21	(4–4)
November 18	18	at Rice	3	(5–4)
November 23	10	Texas	7	(6–4)
*January 1, 1968	20	Alabama	16	(7–4)

*Cotton Bowl Classic in Dallas

Alabama Crimson Tide

(8–2–1, 5–1 Southeastern Conference)

Date of Game	A&M Points	Opposing Team	Opposing Team's Points	A&M's Record
September 23	37	Florida State	37	(0–0–1)
September 30	25	S. Miss	24	(1–0–1)
October 7	21	Ole Miss	7	(2–0–1)
October 14	35	at Vanderbilt	21	(3–0–1)
October 21	13	Tennessee	24	(3–1–1)
October 28	13	at Clemson	10	(4–1–1)
November 4	13	Miss State	0	(5–1–1)
November 11	7	at Louisiana State University	6	(6–1–1)
November 18	17	South Carolina	0	(7–1–1)
December 2	7	Auburn	3	(8–1–1)
*January 1, 1968	16	Alabama	20	(8–2–1)

*Cotton Bowl Classic in Dallas

Bibliography

PRIMARY SOURCES

Archival Collections

Cushing Memorial Library and Archives, University of Texas A&M, College Station, Texas
    Graphic Series Photographs
    1967 Football Season Photographs
    Paul W. Bryant Vertical File
    Curley Hallman Vertical File
    Edd Hargett Vertical File
    Bill Hobbs Vertical File
    Gene Stallings Vertical File
    1967 A&M vs. Texas Tech DVD
    1967 A&M vs. Texas DVD
    1968 Cotton Bowl Classic DVD
Paul W. Bryant Museum
    Paul W. Bryant Vertical Files
University of Alabama Archives, Tuscaloosa, Alabama
    Papers of Frank Rose

Newspapers

Amarillo (TX) Globe-News
American-Statesman (Austin, TX)
Associated Press
Battalion (College Station, TX)
Birmingham (AL) News
Bryan (TX) Daily Eagle

Buffalo (NY) News
Cullman (AL) Times
Daily Oklahoman (Oklahoma City)
Dallas County News
Dallas Morning News
Florence (AL) Times
Fordyce (AR) Weekly News
Fort Worth (TX) Morning Star-Telegram
Gadsden (AL) Times
Gazette Telegraph (Colorado Springs)
Hill Country News (Cedar Park, TX)
Houston Chronicle
Houston Post
Junction (TX) Eagle
Los Angeles Times
Lubbock (TX) Avalanche-Journal
Mobile Register
Montgomery (AL) Advertiser
New Orleans Times-Picayune
New York Times
Ocala (FL) Star-Banner
Park City (AL) Daily News
Rome (AL) News-Tribune
San Antonio Express-News
Spartanburg (MS) Herald-Journal
Thomasville (AL) Times-Enterprise
Times-Tribune (Beaver Falls, PA)
Tulsa (OK) World
Tuscaloosa (AL) News
Washington Post

Books

Browning, Al. *I Remember Paul "Bear" Bryant: Personal Memoirs of College Football's Most Legendary Coach, as Told by the People Who Knew Him.* Nashville, TN: Cumberland House, 2001.

Bryant, Paul W., and John Underwood. *Bear: The Hard Life and Good Times of Alabama's Coach Bryant.* New York: Little, Brown, 1974.

Burson, Rusty. *Texas A&M Where Have You Gone?* New York: Sports Publishing, 2004.

Ford, Tommy. *Bama under Bear: Alabama's Family Tides.* Huntsville, AL: Strode, 1983.

Forney, John, and Steve Townsend. *Talk of the Tide: An Oral History of Alabama Football Since 1920.* Birmingham, AL: Crane Hill, 1993.

Gold, Eli. *Bear's Boys: 36 Men Whose Lives Were Changed by Coach Paul Bryant.* Nashville, TN: Thomas Nelson, 2007.

Herskowitz, Mickey. *The Legend of Bear Bryant.* New York: McGraw-Hill, 1987.

Hicks, Tommy. *Game of My Life: Alabama Crimson Tide; Memorable Stories from Alabama Football.* New York: Sports Publishing, 2006.

McNair, Kirk. *What It Means to Be Crimson Tide: Gene Stallings and Alabama's Greatest Players.* Chicago: Triumph Books, 2005.

Namath, Joe, and Dick Schaap. *I Can't Wait until Tomorrow—'Cause I Get Better Looking Every Day.* New York: Random House, 1969.

Stabler, Kenny, and Berry Stainback. *Snake.* Garden City, NY: Doubleday, 1986.

Stallings, Gene, and Sally Cook. *Another Season: A Coach's Story of Raising an Exceptional Son.* Boston: Little, Brown, 1997.

Williams, Pat, and Tommy Ford. *Bear Bryant on Leadership: Life Lessons from a Six-Time National Championship Coach.* Charleston, SC: Advantage Media Group, 2010.

Zwerneman, Brent. *Game of My Life: 25 Stories of Aggies Football.* New York: Sports Publishing, 2003.

Articles

Barra, Allen. "Bear Bryant's Biggest Score." *American Legacy* (Winter 2006): 58–64.

Blount, Roy, Jr. "Bear Bryant's Stompin' School." *Esquire.* October 1, 1977.

Bryant, Paul, and John Underwood. "I'll Tell You about Football." *Sports Illustrated.* August 14, 1966, 52–64.

Bulletin of the Agricultural and Mechanical College of Texas for the Junction Adjunct, Fifth Series 9, no. 2 (February 1, 1953).

Burnett, John. "When the Sky Ran Dry." *Texas Monthly.* July 2010.

Carter, William T. "Historical Sketch of Fordyce, Arkansas." *Arkansas Family Historian* 48 (March 2010): 47–51.

"The Hilarious Aggies Offer Raucous Doings in the Land of Nothing to Do." *Sports Illustrated.* September 8, 1968, 58.

"If They Charge to the Right, Everything Goes Right." *Sports Illustrated.* September 10, 1967, 63.

Jenkins, Don. "Best and Worst of the Bowls." *Sports Illustrated.* January 9, 1967, 20–21.

Mason, Carolyn. "Life on the Ranch." *Tuscaloosa Magazine.* September 7, 2006.

Nilsson, Jeff. "Why Did the *Post* Lose Its $10 Million Libel Case?" *Saturday Evening Post.* March 23, 2013, 80–83.

Putman, Pat. "Pride in the Red Jersey." *Sports Illustrated.* October 11, 1971, 18–21.

"As the Snake Can Testify, Beware the Wrath of the Bear." *Sports Illustrated.* September 10, 1967, 49.

Sweany, Brian D. "Mean Joe Greene." *Texas Monthly.* January 1998.

Programs

1967 University of Texas A&M Football Press Book
1967 University of Alabama Football Press Book
1968 Cotton Bowl Classic

Interviews

Booth, Bryan. Interview with author. Junction, TX. April 20, 2017.

Garlington, Buster. Interview with author. Fordyce, AK. February 10, 2016.

Hallman, Curley. Telephone interviews with author. September 14, 2018; October 9, 2018; February 7, 2019.

Hargett, Edd. Interview with author. Bryan, TX. March 22, 2018.

Hargett, Edd. Telephone interview with author. October 11, 2018.

Herskowitz, Mickey. Telephone interviews with author. August 20, 2018; September 9, 2018.

Hobbs, Kristi. Telephone interview with author. February 5, 2019.

Homan, Dennis. Telephone interview with author. September 26, 2018.

Housley, Wendell. Telephone interviews with author. August 28, 2018; October 26, 2018.

Johns, Bobby. Telephone interview with author. October 3, 2018.

Krueger, Rolf. Telephone interview with author. September 5, 2018.

Land, Charles H. Telephone interviews with author. January 23, 2016; March 30, 2018.

Long, Bob. Telephone interview with author. August 23, 2018.

Reynolds, J. T. Telephone interview with author. April 10, 2016.

Rhodes, Guy. Telephone interview with author. September 13, 2018.

Rickman, Rick. Telephone interview with author. September 5, 2018.

Spiller, Rob Roy. Interview with author. Junction, TX. April 20, 2017.

Stallings, Gene. Interviews with author. Powderly, TX. July 8, 2015; July 9, 2015.

Stallings, Ruth Ann. Interview with author. Powderly, TX. July 9, 2015.

Stegent, Larry. Telephone interview with author. August 29, 2018.

Teel, Wanda. Interview with author. Junction, TX. April 20, 2017.

Teel, Wanda. Telephone interview with author. June 30, 2018.

Yearout, Gusty. Telephone interview with author. September 14, 2018.

Internet

Browning, William. "One Last Smile with the Snake: Remembering Kenny Stabler." *SBNation.com*, December 9, 2015. https://www.sbnation.com/2015/12/9/9854578/one-last-smile-with-the-snake.

Burnett, John. "How One Drought Changed Texas Agriculture Forever." *NPR*, July 7, 2012. https://www.npr.org/2012/07/07/155995881/how-one-drought-changed-texas-agriculture-forever.

Deas, Tommy. "A Look Back at Bryant's Junction Boys at Texas A&M." *BAMAInsider.com*, September 14, 2013.

Graham, Frank, Jr. "The Story of a College Football Fix." *Saturday Evening Post*, March 23, 1963. https://www.saturdayeveningpost.com/2013/03/curtis-publishing-butts.

Shields, Mitchell J. "Stars Don't Just Fall on Alabama—Bear Bryant Recruits Them to Keep His Crimson Tide Rolling." *People*, October 1, 1979. https://people.com/archive/stars -dont-just-fall-on-alabama-bear-bryant-recruits-them-to-keep-his-crimson-tide-rolling -vol-12-no-14.

SECONDARY SOURCES

Books

Barra, Allen. *The Last Coach: A Life of Paul "Bear" Bryant*. New York: W. W. Norton, 2005.

Briley, John David. *Career in Crisis: Paul Bear Bryant and the 1971 Season of Change*. Macon, GA: Mercer University Press, 2006.

Dent, Jim. *The Junction Boys: How Ten Days in Hell with Bear Bryant Forged a Championship Team*. New York: St. Martin's, 1999.

Dethloff, Henry C. *A Centennial History of Texas A&M University, 1876–1976*. College Station: Texas A&M University Press, 2000.

Dunnavant, Keith. *Coach: The Life of Paul "Bear" Bryant*. New York: St. Martin's, 2005.

Dunnavant, Keith. *The Missing Ring: How Bear Bryant and the 1966 Alabama Crimson Tide Were Denied College Football's Most Elusive Prize*. New York: St. Martin's, 2006.

Gentry, Curt. *J. Edgar Hoover: The Man and the Secrets*. New York: W. W. Norton, 2001.

Keith, Don. *Bear: The Legendary Life of Coach Paul "Bear" Bryant*. Nashville, TN: Cumberland House, 2006.

Kemper, Kurt Edward. *College Football and American Culture in the Cold War Era*. Champaign: University of Illinois Press, 2009.

King, Creed, and Heidi Tyline. *I Ain't Never Been Nothing but a Winner*. Boulder, CO: Taylor Trade, 2000.

Kriegel, Mark. *Namath: A Biography*. New York: Penguin, 2004.

Maisel, Ivan, and Kelly Whiteside. *A War in Dixie: Alabama v. Auburn*. New York: Harpers, 2001.

Moneyhon, Carl H. *Arkansas and the New South, 1874–1929*. Fayetteville: University of Arkansas Press, 1997.

Pate, Steve, and Dan Jenkins. *Heart of a Champion*. Dallas: Masters Press, 1997.

Roberts, Randy, and Ed Krzemienski. *Rising Tide: Bear Bryant, Joe Namath, and Dixie's Last Quarter*. New York: Twelve, 2013.

Stoddard, Tom. *Turnaround: The Untold Story of Bear Bryant's First Years as Head Coach at Alabama*. Montgomery, AL: River City, 2000.

Williamson, Rana. *When Catfish Had Ticks*. Austin: Eakin Press, 1997.

Willis, James F. *Southern Arkansas University: The Mulerider School's Centennial History, 1909–2009*. Magnolia: Southern Arkansas University Foundation, 2009.

Internet

Encyclopedia of Arkansas History and Culture. s.v. "Redbug Field." Accessed February 1, 2016. www.encyclopediaofarkansas.net.

Theses

Balogh, George Walter. "Entrepreneurs, City Builders, and Pine Forest Industries in South Arkansas, 1881–1963." PhD diss., University of Oklahoma, 1992.

Index